SIDELIGHTS ON ELIZABETHAN DRAMA

SIDELIGHTS ON
ELIZABETHAN DRAMA

A series of studies dealing with the authorship of Sixteenth and Seventeenth Century Plays

H. DUGDALE SYKES

LONDON AND NEW YORK

Published by Routledge
2 Park Square, Milton Park,
Abingdon, Oxon, OX14 4RN
and
711 Third Avenue, New York, NY 10017

Routledge is an imprint of the Taylor & Francis Group, an informa business

First issued in paperback 2016

First edition 1924
New impression 1966

Transferred to Digital Printing 2006

Publisher's Note
The publisher has gone to great lengths to ensure the quality of this reprint but points out that some imperfections in the original may be apparent

ISBN: 978-0-714-62085-5 (hbk)
ISBN: 978-1-138-98189-8 (pbk)

For permission to republish all but three of the following articles I have to thank the proprietor of *Notes and Queries,* in which they originally appeared. The paper on *The Taming of a Shrew* and *The Famous Victories of Henry V* was issued as a pamphlet by the Shakespeare Association in 1920, while that on *The Spanish Gipsy* is reprinted from *The Modern Language Review.* To the Council of the Association and the proprietors of the *Review* my thanks are accordingly due for allowing me to include them in the volume. The paper on Webster's *Appius and Virginia* appears here for the first time.

H. DUGDALE SYKES.

Enfield.

1924

CONTENTS

I

THE PROBLEM OF 'TIMON OF ATHENS'

It is generally agreed that *Timon of Athens* was not wholly written by Shakespeare, and that considerable portions of the text as printed in the First Folio are from some inferior hand. But as to the circumstances of its composition there is much difference of opinion, one school of critics holding that Shakespeare worked over an older drama the remains of which are visible in the inferior portions of the play, the other that Shakespeare was the original author, the inferior portions, on this hypothesis, being passages that have been interpolated in Shakespeare's text.

The latter theory was in 1874 so vigorously and plausibly presented by Fleay that of late years scarcely a voice has been raised against it. Among recent critics Deighton has adopted it in his admirable introduction to the 'Arden' edition of *Timon*, and still more recently it has been elaborately restated and developed in a careful and exhaustive monograph by an American scholar, Dr. Ernest Hunter Wright.[1] Both these critics assign to Shakespeare a considerably larger portion of the play than is attributed to him by Fleay, but on the main point, that the nucleus of the play is Shakespeare's and that the text as it stands is distinctly divisible into Shakespearean and non-Shakespearean portions, all three writers concur.

In spite of the apparently convincing arguments that have been adduced in support of this view, a careful study of the text has satisfied me that it is wrong, and that the earlier critics—Delius, Knight, and the Cambridge editors among them—were right in holding that Shakespeare worked over an existing play, or draft of a play. Accordingly

[1] *The Authorship of 'Timon of Athens'*. Columbia University Press, 1910.

my first task will be to demonstrate that there are plain marks of the hand which both Fleay and Wright pronounce to be non-Shakespearean in the parts that they attribute to Shakespeare, and that there is in fact no such cleavage between the Shakespearean and non-Shakespearean portions as they have assumed.

Those who hold that the extant text presents Shakespeare's revision of an earlier play, and those who believe it to be an alteration and expansion of a Shakespearean *Timon*, have alike assumed that Shakespeare's work is associated with that of another dramatist, and of one dramatist alone. I find plain evidence that two authors were concerned in the original play, which Shakespeare revised. It is possible, indeed, that there may have been more than two, but of the presence of two distinct hands other than Shakespeare's I have no doubt whatever. With the evidence of the composite authorship of the original play, and the identification of its authors, I shall shortly deal. But it is necessary that I should emphasize the importance of the hypothesis that the original draft was itself the work of more hands than one, because this affords an explanation of certain peculiarities of the play that have given rise to much discussion and conjecture—the imperfect co-ordination of certain scenes, the confusion in the names of some of the characters, and other puzzling divergences and contradictions presented by the text. All these can readily be explained on the hypothesis that in *Timon of Athens* we have an imperfect recast by Shakespeare of a collaborated play.

That Fleay and those who have followed him in the attempt to separate the Shakespearean from the un-Shakespearean parts of *Timon* are in the main correct there is no reason to doubt. Apart from the fact that much of the verse is of very inferior quality and full of metrical irregularities, there are many passages, both in verse and in prose, feeble in expression and trite in sentiment. Moreover, at the time this play was written Shakespeare had almost discarded rime, and *Timon* contains a great deal of it, the proportion of riming lines in the verse rising as high as 20 per cent. in certain scenes. If we give to Shakespeare all the great poetry the play contains and all the good blank verse, and to the 'unknown author' all the irregular, halting verse, jingling rime, and uninspired prose, it is clear that the division thus made cannot be very far wrong.

But if we are to proceed on Fleay's assumption that Shakespeare's is the prior hand, there is something beside the relative aesthetic merit of the different parts of the play to be taken into account in separating Shakespeare's work from the work that is not his. The portions of the text assigned to Shakespeare must constitute a play complete in itself, or at least the nucleus of a complete play. And it is precisely in reconciling these two considerations, in arriving at a division that will satisfy aesthetic requirements, yet at the same time be compatible with Shakespeare's authorship of the substance of the play, that the difficulty lies—a difficulty so great that it seems strange that this of itself has not convinced those who have attempted the task of the fundamental error of the assumption that the prior hand was Shakespeare's.

One or two illustrations of this difficulty may be noted here. On aesthetic grounds Fleay (rightly, as I shall try to show) rejects the prose dialogue between Timon and Apemantus in the first scene as non-Shakespearean, as well as other prose talk between the same characters that occurs later in the play. But Dr. Wright, noting in the 'Shakespearean' part of this scene, some hundred lines or so before the cynic appears, a reference to 'Apemantus, that few things loves better than to abhor himself' as pointing to the conclusion that Shakespeare was preparing us for his appearance, and further noting that immediately before his entrance (but still in the 'Shakespearean' portion) Timon warns his friends that they will 'be chid' by Apemantus, finds 'every reason to believe' that Shakespeare must have written the ensuing dialogue in which they *are* 'chid'. Accordingly Dr. Wright—logically enough if the substance of the play is Shakespeare's—endeavours to persuade himself and us that this is 'cleverer' and 'more pointed' than the later Timon–Apemantus dialogues, which (notwithstanding the similarity of their style) he is content to dismiss as spurious. Fleay further rejects the dunning scenes (III. i–iv), finding in them 'no vestige of Shakespeare's style'. Here, again, I believe him to be right. But Deighton objects (and, I think, properly objects) that they are essential to the development of the plot—that it is inconceivable that Shakespeare should have shown us Timon turned misanthrope without also showing in detail the process which caused the sudden revulsion. Once more, there is the scene (III. v) in which Alcibiades appears before the Senate, which Fleay also pronounces to be 'wholly by the vamper'.[1] Dr. Wright agrees, and indeed (whether by a 'vamper' or not) it is so poorly written that if any scene is to be discarded as unworthy of Shakespeare it must surely be this. Yet is it possible—on the assumption of Shakespeare's responsibility for the original play—to deny the force of Deighton's emphatic protest against its rejection? Is it not, as he says, 'absolutely necessary, as leading up to the concluding events, as contrasting the two chief characters, and as showing the Senators to be equally ungrateful to both, hard-hearted, unpatriotic, and richly deserving the lofty contempt with which Timon receives their refusal to help him'?

Clearly, if no one *has* 'vamped' or 'interpolated' Shakespeare's play, if on the contrary Shakespeare has revised, and only partly revised, a piece by other hands, these difficulties too will disappear; there will be no reason to be surprised that we are prepared for the entry of Apemantus, even though his speeches are not Shakespeare's, and the

[1] He further omits all the dialogue preceding the mock-banquet, thus rejecting the whole of Act III but twenty lines, and we are taken straight from Timon's interview with his steward in II. ii. to the scene of the banquet itself, opening abruptly with the words 'Uncover, dogs, and lap!' Wright is less drastic, retaining the last two dunning scenes and (doubtfully) the long prose 'grace' of Timon.

dunning scenes and the scene of Alcibiades' appeal to the Senate may be rejected on aesthetic grounds even though they be essential to the development of the plot.

But it is time that we got to the evidence, and first to the evidence that the text is not—as those who hold that the ground-work of the play is Shakespeare's have assumed—capable of division into clear-cut sections of Shakespearean and non-Shakespearean authorship. Both Fleay and Wright have expended much skill and ingenuity in splitting up the text in this way, allotting one scene, or part of a scene, to Shakespeare, another to the unknown reviser, interpolator, or vamper. As already mentioned, they do not entirely agree, Wright claiming for Shakespeare two complete scenes and parts of others (in all about 500 lines) that Fleay rejects. In the main, however, they do agree. But whether they agree, or do not agree, an attentive examination of the text will show that they are wrong. It is obvious that the methods they have applied, their aesthetic tests, metrical tests, or whatever they may be, will not enable them to distinguish between passages wholly written by Shakespeare and those substantially rewritten by him. If Shakespeare's hand predominates in a scene, their tests will give it to Shakespeare. Neither of them has paid any attention to the marks of continuity of authorship that are clearly visible on an examination of the language of the play in detail. Let us assume for a moment that their division is correct and see what conclusions this will involve.

The first scene up to a point ten lines after the entry of Apemantus, i.e. to the point where verse gives way to prose, is, says Fleay, by Shakespeare. After this begins the work of the vamper, or inferior author. Accordingly (if Fleay is right) this bit of dialogue (182–4) [1] is Shakespeare's :

> *Apemantus.* Are they not Athenians ?
> *Timon.* Yes.
> *Apem.* Then I repent not.

[1] The lines are numbered as in the Globe edition.

and this by the 'inferior author':

> *Poet.* Art not one?
> *Apem.* Yes.
> *Poet.* Then I lie not.

Again, when (l. 189) Timon says to Apemantus:

> Thou art proud, Apemantus

and Apemantus replies:

> Of nothing so much as that I am not like Timon.

it is the inferior author who is speaking. But when (IV. iii. 276–7) Apemantus says to Timon:

> Art thou proud yet?

and Timon replies:

> Ay, that I am not thee.

it is Shakespeare. On this reckoning, then, the inferior author has in the first scene interpolated a passage containing a not particularly brilliant repartee borrowed from a later scene of Shakespeare's. It is only fair to say that Wright ascribes all these bits of dialogue to Shakespeare. That he is wrong I shall endeavour to show later. But at any rate it will be admitted that in each case the passages compared are likely to be from the same hand. And here it may be observed that one of the surest marks of a second-rate writer is a tendency to repeat ideas and phrases, and where we find these repetitions (and they are frequent in this play) it will generally be safe to infer not only that they are from the same hand, but that that hand is not Shakespeare's. But let us proceed. In the two instances noted above, Wright differs from Fleay. In the cases that follow, they are in agreement.

Just before the end of Act I, sc. i, the First Lord thus addresses the Second Lord:

> Come, shall we in
> And *taste Lord Timon's bounty?*

This, according to Fleay and Wright, is in Shakespeare's

part of the play. The next scene (I. ii), which contains Cupid's speech beginning with the lines:

> Hail to thee, worthy Timon, and to all
> That *of his bounties taste.*

is assigned to the inferior hand. And when the poet in v. i visits Timon in his cave, we are told that his speech

> Sir,
> Having often *of your open bounty tasted*, &c.,

was written by Shakespeare. Is this probable? Is it not beyond any reasonable doubt that all three passages are due to one and the same author, who had this idea of 'tasting' bounties running in his mind at the time he wrote them? If the expression were one in constant use at this period there might be a reasonable doubt, but it was not.

Though Fleay and Wright differ slightly as to what is Shakespeare's and what is not Shakespeare's in IV. iii, both assign to him these words addressed by Alcibiades to Timon (170–1):

> If I thrive well, I'll visit thee again.

and Timon's reply:

> If I hope well, I'll never see thee more.

yet when Apemantus says to Timon (358–9):

> When I know not what to do, I'll visit thee again.

and Timon answers:

> When there is nothing living but thee, thou shalt be welcome.

they are equally confident that the other author is responsible. The fact is that Fleay and Wright have been so absorbed in the task of extracting and fitting together solid blocks of the text which should be good enough for Shakespeare and yet afford sufficient material for a complete play, that these and other indications of non-Shakespearean work in the material claimed for Shakespeare have entirely escaped them. The difference between Fleay's and Wright's division is simply this: the parts of the text extracted by Fleay include all the passages in which Shakespeare's hand is predominant, but they do not form a complete play; the parts extracted by Wright do constitute a complete play—at least in outline—but only at the cost of the inclusion of passages which bear no mark of Shakespeare's hand. And it matters not what division of the text is adopted; it is impossible to hit upon any arrangement that will fit in with the theory of Shakespeare's origination of *Timon of Athens*.

The proof of the presence of non-Shakespearean work in the portions of the text assumed to belong to the Shakespearean foundation-play of itself affords a strong reason for believing that Shakespeare was not the original author. But lest it be objected that the evidence to which attention has been directed is insufficient to establish this, and that the dramatist who altered the Shakespearean play may have touched up and tampered with the scenes written by Shakespeare besides adding others of his own invention, I shall here notice other features of the text that point even more clearly to the conclusion that Shakespeare's work on the play was that of a reviser merely.

Timon of Athens, even as it stands, is a very short play, shorter even than *Pericles*, and shorter than any tragedy in the Folio, *Macbeth* alone excepted. If we deduct the parts usually rejected as non-Shakespearean, we are left with a 'Shakespearean' play less than 1,700 lines (if Fleay is correct, only 1,200 lines) in length. On the hypothesis of Messrs. Fleay and Wright this play, too brief for the requirements of the stage, has been expanded by some inferior dramatist—padded out by the interpolation of fresh and largely irrelevant matter. This hypothesis is utterly against the evidence of the text, which plainly shows that the non-Shakespearean work cannot have been added to Shakespeare's text, and that the shortness of the play is due to the fact that it has been abbreviated in the process of revision.

The first indication of this abbreviation is in the stage-direction at the very commencement of the play. Immediately following the words 'Actus Primus, Scœna Prima', the folio has:

'Enter Poet, Painter, Jeweller, Merchant, *and Mercer*, at severall doores.'

That the Mercer has been expunged from this stage-direction in all modern editions is not to be wondered at, for he utters not a single word, nor does the text contain any subsequent reference to him. Fleay, though he professes to print the play as Shakespeare wrote it, and (like every other critic) [1] assigns the beginning of this first scene to Shakespeare, ignores him altogether. Wright relegates him to a foot-note, and this is what he says: 'A mercer who enters with the other parasites, according to the stage-direction, but never speaks, has called forth much comment but no explanation. The mention of him has been used as evidence that Shakespeare here revised an old scene in which the mercer had a speaking part . . . and has predisposed some critics to the theory that Shakespeare was revising throughout. *If that theory is shown to be impossible—and little further evidence shall we find for it*—this explanation of the mercer falls. So do all the others. The last author, whichever one he was, does not seem to have added the mercer in the stage-direction, meaning to give him a part, for he gave him none; or to have cut any part that the first author had already given the mercer, for no cut is apparent. Nor is the error very like a printer's. The important fact here is that the mercer—explain him who can—does not testify to any theory of authorship.'

The important fact here—which Dr. Wright is at some pains to disguise—is that this mention of the mercer in the stage-direction testifies to a theory of the authorship of the play directly opposed to his own. Though forced to admit that the mercer cannot have been inserted in this stage-direction by the reviser, he refuses to draw the obvious inference that the reviser has *cut him out of the text*,

[1] I should except Mr. J. M. Robertson, who (*Shakespeare and Chapman*, 1917) surmises the presence of Chapman's hand in the opening scene as well as in other parts of the play.

and that—the first part of this scene being Shakespeare's—it was Shakespeare who cut him out. Dr. Wright admits that on his theory it is impossible to account for the mercer; on the theory that Shakespeare was the reviser it is possible to account for him. The suggestion that the reviser cannot have cut his part out because 'no cut is apparent' is absurd. However hasty his revision, it is not to be expected that he would have done his work so clumsily as to leave a palpable gap in the text. And if Dr. Wright finds 'little further evidence' that Shakespeare was the reviser of the play, it is not because the evidence is lacking; it is because he has not looked for it.

Now let us turn to the scene marked Act II, sc. ii, in the modern editions. The first fifty lines—as far as the entry of Apemantus—are usually ascribed to Shakespeare, and for the present purpose we may assume that they are his. Neither Fleay nor Wright feels any doubt on the matter. 'Clearly', says Wright, 'it was one author who sent the duns off the stage, another who made them turn and stay for sport with Apemantus'—the first being Shakespeare, the other the anonymous 'vamper'. This anonymous author, on Fleay's and Wright's hypothesis, brings a fool and a page on to the stage merely for the purpose of providing additional dialogue to fill out the text, 'finding it needful,' as Dr. Wright says, 'while he holds the play at a halt, to bring on an unknown fool and an unknown page, with letters of unknown purport to Timon and Alcibiades'. Dr. Wright is very severe on this anonymous author for his stupidity, and if he was half as silly as Dr. Wright supposes, he certainly deserves all that critic's contempt. But is it conceivable that this author can have added *two* new characters to the play merely 'to make fun and confusion', when all the 'comic relief' in fact contributed by them might equally well—indeed more naturally and appropriately—have been supplied by Apemantus himself? During the thirty lines of dialogue until the page enters, the fool has only two brief speeches; the page only four altogether. And all that the latter does is to bring letters addressed to Timon and Alcibiades, of which the contents are never divulged and to which no subsequent reference is made. However gross a bungler this supposed interpolator of Shakespeare's play, he cannot have been so utterly inept as this, introducing two characters, neither of whom has the slightest bearing on the course of events, for the sake of one or two witticisms. That the fool and page were introduced by the original author, or one of the original authors, chiefly for the purpose of providing irrelevant dialogue is likely enough. The fact that in the extant text they contribute so little, surely suggests that their parts have been drastically curtailed. And the words with which Caphis greets the entry of Apemantus and his companion, 'here comes *the fool* with Apemantus, let 's ha' some sport with 'em', seem clearly to imply that in the original play the fool was introduced in an earlier scene. This inference is further supported by the words in which he is subsequently hailed by 'All the servants':

Gramercies, good fool! How does your mistress?

The servants already know (what we do not learn until thirty lines later) that the fool belongs to a mistress, and this mistress a courtesan. This courtesan, not mentioned elsewhere,[1] in all probability also figured in an earlier scene of the original draft of the play, and in that original draft it is reasonable to suppose that the letters brought by the page for Timon and Alcibiades *did* have some bearing on the development of the plot.

I shall here notice but one other feature of the text directly contradictory of the theory that Shakespeare's was the prior hand, leaving others for discussion when I come to consider the various scenes in detail.

All the critics agree that the short penultimate scene (v. iii) cannot be Shakespeare's. In this scene a soldier enters, seeking Timon's grave. The inscription on the tomb is in a language the soldier is unable to read, and accordingly he takes an impression of it with wax in order

[1] Unless she is to be identified with Phrynia or Timandra.

that his captain (Alcibiades) may decipher it. These are his words:

> What 's on this tomb
> I cannot read; the character I'll take with wax:
> Our captain hath in every figure skill.

In the final scene (wholly Shakespeare's, if we are to believe Fleay and Wright) the same soldier enters announcing to Alcibiades that 'Timon is dead':

> And on his gravestone this insculpture, which
> With wax I brought away, whose soft impression
> Interprets for my poor ignorance.

In v. iv therefore we have a direct reference to what has already been described in v. iii. How then is it possible to suppose that Shakespeare's work is anterior to that of the inferior author? Only on the assumption—which I venture to describe as preposterous—that the inferior author 'interpolated' the incident referred to in the final scene.

All the evidence—and there is a great deal more than I have yet mentioned—points to the conclusion that *Timon*, like *Pericles*, is a play not originally written by Shakespeare but merely revised by him. But whereas in the case of *Pericles* the play partly rewritten by Shakespeare was the work of one man—George Wilkins—the original draft of *Timon* was written by two. These two authors I shall now endeavour to identify.

The conclusion that Shakespeare cannot have written the whole of *Timon of Athens* is one that must soon be forced upon any attentive student of the play. Apart from its glaring defects of structure and versification, there are long passages both of prose and verse in which the language is utterly unlike Shakespeare's. And of these perhaps the most noticeable of all are the short snappy Timon–Apemantus dialogues. We have a number of Shakespeare's plays written about the time (1607–9) that this play was composed, but in none of these, nor indeed in any play in the Folio, is there anything in the least akin to these battledore and shuttlecock bouts between Timon and Apemantus. Fleay asserts that Tourneur writes this 'Dumas dialogue' as he calls it. This is not so. No doubt Tourneur, like most of the Elizabethan dramatists, has occasional passages of rapid dialogue in brief speeches, but the more closely Tourneur's plays are studied, the more obvious does the difference of his style from that of the Timon–Apemantus scenes appear. There is something highly distinctive in the manner in which this dialogue is written, altogether apart from the brevity of the speeches, and of this I shall have something to say later. Over and over again I returned to these speeches, reading and re-reading them, for I had a feeling that in them would be found the key to the authorship of the spurious parts of the play. Yet, with a fairly comprehensive knowledge of the dramatic work of the first decade of the seventeenth century, I could think of no author who had written anything like them.

I had all but convinced myself that no other specimen of this author's work could have survived, when suddenly and quite unexpectedly—in a play that must have been written within a year or so of *Timon*—I found the man for whom I had been looking. That man was John Day, and the play was *Humour out of Breath*, licensed in April 1608 and printed in the same year. This—and this alone of Day's plays—contains long, continuous passages of prose indistinguishable from that found in the Timon–Apemantus scenes. It is not a question of picking out here and there a passage: the Timon-like dialogue fills three-fifths of the play. Let the reader turn to any of the recurrent passages of arms between Timon and Apemantus, and he will find all of them in the style of the prose of *Humour out of Breath*; in both plays he will find the same brusqueness and brevity of speech, the same continuous fire of questions and answers. The resemblance is so close that the more often one reads these plays the stronger becomes the impression that the prose is from one hand. To what is this impression due? It is due to two peculiarities that become apparent only on a minute comparison of the passages in question.

The first is a grammatical peculiarity—the habitual omission of the pronoun 'thou' after a verb in the second person singular. Of course occasional omissions of this kind may be found in Shakespeare and many other dramatists of the period. But here the omissions are not occasional, they are a regular feature of the author's style, and they are *only* to be found in the Timon–Apemantus scenes :

The first appearance of Apemantus is at line 177 of the first scene. After this point we have :

I. i. 191 (*Timon.*) Whither art going ?
206 (*Timon.*) Wilt dine with me, Apemantus ?
223 (*Poet.*) Art not one ?
226 (*Apem.*) Art not a poet ?
235 (*Timon.*) What wouldst do then, Apemantus ?

After this first scene until the reappearance of Apemantus in Act II, sc. ii, there is not a single instance of this omission. But here we find :

II. ii. 51 (*Varro's Servant.*) How dost, fool ?
52 (*Apem.*) Dost dialogue with thy shadow ?
84 (*Apem.*) Canst not read ?

We now pass over the whole of the long third act, and the first and second scenes of the fourth, in none of which Apemantus figures, and come to IV. iii where he again appears :

IV. iii. 237 (*Timon.*) Dost please thyself in 't ?
291 (*Apem.*) Where liest o' nights, Timon ?
307 (*Apem.*) Dost hate a medlar ?

At line 398 Apemantus vanishes, never to reappear, and after his departure there is but one other of these speeches, this time addressed by Timon to his steward Flavius :

IV. iii. 480 Why dost ask that ?

If we look at *Humour out of Breath* we shall find the prose parts full of these omissions, e. g. :

Mermaid ed.

I. iii, p. 282 Canst get any living out of them ?
284 Which of them dost ask ?
II i, p. 286 Canst describe service ?
287 Dost know the Duke of Venice ?
II. ii, p. 291 Hast any skill in love ?

III. iii, p. 306 Art sure she hates me?
IV. iii, p. 315 Would'st rob him of his wit?

and so on. To quote more of the sixteen examples in this play (ten of which occur in two scenes) is unnecessary.

I come now to the second peculiarity. Any person knowing his *Timon* well, if asked to say what is the distinctive feature of the Timon–Apemantus dialogues, apart from the brevity of the speeches of the interlocutors, will be pretty sure to refer to the abundance of quibbles in these parts of the play.

Verbal quibbles were so dear to the Elizabethans that the mere fact that these dialogues are marked throughout by persistent quibbling would hardly seem worthy of particular notice; certainly if this were all, it would be quite useless as a means of distinguishing them from Shakespeare's, for he is notoriously addicted to quibbling. But Shakespeare's quibbles (and the remark applies to those of most of his contemporaries) usually have *some* point and substance. In *Humour out of Breath* and the Timon–Apemantus passages there is frequently no real *play* upon words at all—scarce anything that one could dignify with the name of pun. The repartees have an air of being witty but nothing else, the fallacious *appearance* of wit being produced by the simple expedient of bandying a word to and fro between two speakers, without regard to whether one speaker uses it in a different sense from the other or not. For instance, towards the end of the first scene of *Timon* we find this:

Enter two Lords.

First Lord. What *time* o' day is 't, Apemantus?
Apem. Time to be honest.
First Lord. That *time* serves still.

One would scarcely notice this trick were it used in moderation, but it is carried to such an excess that it becomes tiresome. Here is another sample from IV. iii (281–4):

Apem. Here; I will *mend* thy feast.
Tim. First *mend* my company, take away thyself.

Apem. So I shall *mend* mine own, by the lack of thine.
Tim. 'Tis not well *mended* so, it is but botch'd.

It often happens that immediately after one word has been hunted to death, another is seized and worried. A few lines after the passage just quoted we come upon this :

Apem. What man did'st thou ever know unthrift that was beloved after his *means* ?
Tim. Who, without those *means* thou talk'st of, did'st thou ever know beloved ?
Apem. Myself.
Tim. I understand thee; thou had'st some *means* to keep a dog.

and then, with only three lines interval :

Tim. What would'st thou do with the world, Apemantus, if it lay in thy power ?
Apem. Give it to the *beasts,* to be rid of the men.
Tim. Would'st thou . . . remain a *beast* with the *beasts* ?
Apem. Ay, Timon.
Tim. A *beastly* ambition, &c.

Now let us turn once more to *Humour out of Breath* and listen to the talk between Florimel and her page in II. i :

Flo. Dost thou know what gentleman it is ?
Page. Gentle madam, no ; but he is a *man.*
Flo. Believe me, boy, he is a proper *man.*
Page. *Man* is a proper name to a *man,* and so he may be a proper *man.*
Flo. I love him, he 's a very proper *man.*

The Elizabethans must have been easy to amuse if they could extract entertainment from this. And directly we have finished with Florimel and her page we have Aspero and his boy :

Boy. Make but a shot of *flattery* at her broadside, and she'll strike sail presently.
Asp. *Flattery* ?
Boy. Ay, *flattery* ; women are like fiddlers ; speak them fair they'll *play* of any instrument.
Asp. Ay, that they can *play* of.
Boy. She 's a botcher that cannot *play* a little of all.
Asp. And too common that will *play* too much of any ; but come, I'll use *means* to get her.
Boy. Nay, you must first have *means* to give her.

There is much more of the same sort of stuff in the third act, where (III. i, p. 297) may be found one rally of speeches with nine repetitions of the word 'fool'.

Day rarely repeats a phrase or allusion. Consequently we must not expect to find much in the way of 'parallel' evidence in support of his claim to a share in *Timon of Athens*. But it has one or two significant verbal connexions with his acknowledged work. In the first Timon–Apemantus dialogue (I. i. 211) Timon answers a gross observation by Apemantus with

> That 's a lascivious apprehension.

and Apemantus replies:

> So thou apprehendest it, *take it for thy labour.*

Florimel uses the same retort in *Humour out of Breath*, III. i. 298.

> *Flo.* . . . when, by your buzzing flattery, you have sucked the smallest favour from [a lady] you presently make wing for another.
> *Asp.* Marry, buzz!
> *Flo.* Double the zard, and *take the whole meaning for your labour.*

In the following passage (*Timon*, II. ii. 103–7) the Fool's 'The reason of this?' is characteristic of Day:

> *Fool.* When men come to borrow of your masters, they approach sadly and go away merry; but they enter my mistress' house merrily and go away sadly. *The reason of this?*

Compare *Humour out of Breath*, II. i. 287:

> *Octavio.* I cut some few of the Mantuans throats.
> *Asp.* And wert not a knave for 't?
> *Oct.* No, I was a Venetian commander, a great man. *The reason of this question?*

and again, III. iii. 306:

> *Boy.* I have been in her bosom, sir; and this day she intends your execution.
> *Asp.* My execution! *the reason of her hate?*

and I. ii. 280:

> *Asp.* One [reason why a lawyer would not take his wife

to the term with him] was because her gown was of the old fashion; the other was 'cause he would not have her by him when he took fees.

Ant. His reason for that?[1]

The style of repartee is the same, e. g.

Page. Will you sell your findings, my Lord?
Hippolito. They are scarce worth giving.
H. O. B., I. iii. 282.

Timon. What dost thou think 'tis worth?
Apem. Not worth my thinking.
Timon, I. i. 218–19.

Florimel. Would'st rob him of his wit?
Page. If I should he could not hang me for 't: 'tis not worth thirteen-pence halfpenny.
H. O. B., IV. ii. 315.

Tim. Whither art going?
Apem. To knock out an honest Athenian's brains.
Tim. That 's a deed thou'lt die for.
Apem. Right, if doing nothing be death by the law.
Timon, I. i. 191–3.

It will be observed that all the links between *Timon of Athens* and *Humour out of Breath* hitherto noted are connected with the Timon-Apemantus parts of the former play, for it is in these parts and in these alone that Day's hand is unmistakable. There are parallels in his plays with passages in other parts of *Timon*, but although some of these are rather striking, I am anxious not to press this evidence too far. But one more passage in Day's *Humour out of Breath* I shall notice here, because it seems directly to refer to Timon of Athens—at least, I can account for it in no other way. In IV. iii Aspero remarks to Hortensio's servant Assistance:

Let none enter upon the stage where Aspero plays the madman, without Hortensio.

Assistance thereupon observes:

Is he mad, my lord?

[1] Compare also *Humour out of Breath*, I. i, p. 275, 'Your thought of both?' and III. iv, p. 307, 'The life of that jest?' *Isle of Gulls*, II. i (Bullen, p. 26) 'Your reason for that', and III. i (p. 64), 'Your reason for that, sir?'

and Aspero replies:

> As the lord that gave all to his followers, and begged more for himself.

Clearly, the reference is to a particular lord, a lord whose identity the audience would recognize. 'The lord that gave all to his followers, and begged more for himself.' Who can this lord be, if not the Lord Timon?

Having found what I regarded—and still regard—as indubitable marks of Day's hand in *Timon of Athens*, it is not surprising that I at first concluded that I had solved the whole problem of the authorship of the play, and that Day was the author of the original play revised by Shakespeare. I had just come to this conclusion when there appeared in *Notes and Queries* a brief but most valuable paper on *Timon of Athens* by Mr. William Wells urging the claim of Middleton to the non-Shakespearean scenes.[1] I was at first disposed to ignore any suggestion of Middleton's concern in the play, notwithstanding the many remarkable parallels with his work that Mr. Wells brought forward, especially as I found that he was driven to confess that the Timon–Apemantus dialogues were more in Shakespeare's manner than Middleton's. It was not until after I discovered that the marks of Day's hand were confined to certain portions of the play, and that I could detect no trace of it in other scenes which I was convinced were not Shakespearean, that I set to work to test Mr. Wells's theory, with the result that I found abundant confirmatory evidence of Middleton's authorship of precisely those scenes which I could find no sufficient reason to connect either with Day or with Shakespeare.

As the key to Day's hand is to be found in the Timon-Apemantus dialogues, so it is in the dunning scenes (which have been left almost untouched by Shakespeare) that Middleton's is most evident. But before I come to these I shall note certain features of the text at large that are typical of Middleton but not characteristic either of

[1] *Notes and Queries*, 12 S. vi (1920), 266.

Shakespeare or of Day. The first is the contraction of 'he has' to 'has'. One cannot rely upon modern editions of *Timon of Athens* to illustrate the use of this, for most modern editors silently alter the text, printing 'he has' in full where the Folio reads 'has'. In the Folio the contraction appears six times,[1] all the instances of its use occurring in parts of Acts III and IV usually considered to be non-Shakespearean. It is, then, the normal usage of one of the authors of this play, occurring six times in four scenes, in which 'he has' appears only three times.[2] Though occasional examples of its occurrence may be met with in Day and in Shakespeare, as in other writers of the time, it is certainly not specially characteristic of either of them. It is safe to say that there is no play of Shakespeare's in which it is repeatedly used. Both this and ''tas' (=it has)—appearing twice in another scene (I. ii) usually regarded as spurious:

I. ii. 50 'Tas been proved.
I. ii. 149 'Tas been done.

—are so frequent in Middleton as to attract the attention of the least observant reader. To take two plays only—*Michaelmas Term* and *Your Five Gallants*—'has' (=he has) will be found five times in the former play, four times in the latter; ''tas' once in the former and four times in the latter. 'Sh'as' (=she has), also a normal contraction with Middleton, would no doubt also be found in *Timon* had any occasion for its use arisen, but *Timon* is almost destitute of female characters.

The reader will recollect that I have attributed to one hand (Day's) the Timon–Apemantus dialogues in three scenes—I. i, II. ii, and IV. iii—all written in the same staccato style. But there is one other scene (I. ii) that contains a good deal of dialogue between the same characters in which the style is quite different. This scene bears (as I shall show

[1] Including one case of *had* (=he had). These are the references: III. ii. 39, III. iii. 13, 23, III. v. 63, IV. iii. 453, 476.

[2] These all in one speech—the Second Senator's speech in III. v. 68–75.

when I discuss the different parts of the play in detail) the strongest marks of Middleton's workmanship. And now I come to a most remarkable piece of evidence confirming my conclusion that two hands were concerned in the original draft of *Timon*, evidence of a purely bibliographical kind which I did not discover until I examined a facsimile of the text of the Folio. It is concerned with the spelling of the name of the 'churlish philosopher'. I am not the first to notice that this is sometimes spelt '*Aper*mantus' in the Folio. Fleay has drawn attention to this, and it is noticed also by Wright, who observes that the spelling 'appears frequently, but not significantly'. But indeed its appearance is highly significant. In I. i, although the stage-direction is 'Enter Apermantus' and Timon greets the cynic as 'gentle Apermantus' immediately after his entry, he becomes 'Apemantus' and remains so all through the dialogue with Timon. Here his name, when written in full, is invariably printed 'Apemantus' and abbreviated to 'Ape.'—ten times the name appears in full, thirty-three times abbreviated, forty-three times in all. Now we come to I. ii. Although the name is still printed 'Apemantus' in the stage-direction, in the text it is *always* 'Apermantus' and *always* abbreviated 'Aper.'—four times in full, fourteen times abbreviated, eighteen times altogether. Not once do we find 'Apermantus' in the first dialogue nor 'Apemantus' in the second—a highly interesting fact and one that points strongly to the conclusion that the manuscript from which the Folio text was printed was the original manuscript—the actual draft upon which Shakespeare worked. In the two other scenes in which the cynic figures we are (if my opinion is correct) to expect the spelling 'Apemantus' only. And what do we find? In II. ii we have 'Apemantus' five times in full and 'Ape.' sixteen times; in IV. iii 'Apemantus' four times and 'Ape.' (once 'Apem') thirty-eight times. In these two scenes there is one solitary 'Apermantus' (II. ii. 76). As it is the sole instance of this spelling as against sixty-three of 'Apemantus' and 'Ape', it is not unreasonable to suggest that for once the compositor failed to follow his copy. The conclusion is, then, that of the authors of the original draft, one, the writer of the snappy Timon–Apemantus dialogue (whom I call Day) used the spelling 'Apemantus', while the other (Middleton) spelt the name 'Apermantus'.

But to return to Middleton. The marks of the technique of the non-Shakespearean hand in this play noted by Dr. Wright (for he, like all the other critics, assumes that only one hand other than Shakespeare's was concerned in it) are these:

1. Abundance of rime.
2. Irregular, unscannable verse lines.
3. Frequent and aimless shifts from verse to prose.

All are characteristic of Middleton at the time this play was written. *Michaelmas Term* and *The Phoenix* are perhaps most closely akin to *Timon* in these respects. In these plays we find the same high proportion of rime, the same irregularities of metre, the same habit of jumbling together verse and prose, rimed verse and unrimed. For the irregular metre and mixing of rimed verse with unrimed, a passage quoted from *Timon* by Dr. Wright as illustrating the peculiarities of the 'inferior author's' verse may profitably be compared with one or two excerpts from Middleton.

The extract from *Timon* is from the Steward's speech in IV. ii (37–50):

Poor honest lord, brought low by his own heart,
Undone by goodness! Strange unusual blood
When man's worst sin is, he does too much good!
Who then dares to be half so kind agen?
For bounty, that makes gods, does still mar men.
My dearest lord, blest to be most accurst,
Rich only to be wretched, thy great fortunes
Are made thy chief afflictions. Alas, kind lord,
He 's flung in rage from this ungrateful seat
Of monstrous friends;
Nor has he with him to supply his life,
Or that which can command it.
I'll follow and inquire him out:
I'll ever serve his mind with my best will;
Whilst I have gold, I'll be his steward still,

with which we may compare this passage from *The Phoenix,* IV. i (Dyce's Middleton, i. 383):

> None can except against him; the man 's mad,
> And privileged by the moon, if he say true:
> Less madness 'tis to speak sin than to do.
> This wretch that lov'd before his food his strife,
> This punishment falls even with his life.
> His pleasure was vexation, all his bliss
> The torment of another;
> Their hurt his health, their starved hopes his store;
> Who so loves law dies either mad or poor;

or this, from *Michaelmas Term,* IV. ii (Dyce, i. 493):

> The happiest good that ever Shortyard felt!
> I want to be express'd, my mirth is such.
> To be struck now e'en when his joys were high!
> Men only kiss their knaveries, and so die;
> I've often mark'd it.
> He was a famous cozener while he liv'd
> And now his son shall reap 't; I'll ha' the lands,
> Let him study law after; 'tis no labour
> To undo him for ever; but, for Easy,
> Only good confidence did make him foolish
> And not the lack of sense; that was not it:
> 'Tis worldly craft beats down a scholar's wit.

It will be admitted that it would be difficult to find passages more alike in style than these, and plenty of verse of this quality is to be found in Middleton's earlier plays. But it is when we turn to the prose dunning scenes, and especially to the first two scenes of Act III, that we find the clearest evidence of Middleton's authorship. It is true, as Deighton says, that 'the details of these scenes have an air of vraisemblance', that 'there is abundance of humour in the nature of the excuses made, and the character of the sycophants is skilfully discriminated'. But this is not sufficient to stamp them as Shakespeare's. The freshness and ease and vigour of the style of Middleton's early comedies have justly been praised by Swinburne; they are full of humour and of life-like touches in the delineation of character, and Middleton is especially happy in his portraits of rogues and hypocrites like Lucius and Lucullus. The best way to convince any student that these two scenes are Middleton's would be to persuade him to read them through carefully three or four times and then to read Middleton's plays of this period, especially *Michaelmas Term*, *The Phoenix*, *Your Five Gallants*, *A Mad World, my Masters*, and *A Trick to Catch the Old One*, where, apart altogether from specific correspondences of phrasing, he will constantly be reminded of these dunning scenes in *Timon*. And although Middleton (who, by the way, dwells much upon duns and debtors) is no more addicted to the repetition of sentiments and phrases of a striking kind than Day, when his plays are examined closely it will be found that he has a very distinct tendency to repeat turns of expression. How frequently his characteristic expressions appear in *Timon of Athens* we shall now see. For many of those noted below I am indebted to Mr. Wells, to whose acuteness the discovery of the Middletonian origin of much of this play is due. I select the first two scenes in Act III because in them the suggestions of Middleton's hand are so numerous and continuous that it is clear that they can scarcely have been touched by Shakespeare.

Act III, sc. i.

Lines 5–7. Lucullus enters to greet Timon's servant Flaminius, observing, aside:

> One of Lord Timon's men! A gift, I warrant! Why, this hits right; I dreamt of a silver bason and ewer to-night.

Mr. Wells has noted that the association of a dream with a gift occurs twice in Middleton's plays, once in *The Widow*, I. i, and again in *Your Five Gallants*, IV. ii:

> I dreamt to-night, Jack, I should have a secret supply.

To this it may be added that 'hits right'[1] is a characteristic expression of Middleton's. It will be found twice in *Blurt, Master-Constable*, again in *A Chaste Maid in Cheapside*, I. i:

> Maudlin, salute this gentlewoman, our daughter
> If things hit right.

[1] Not elsewhere in the Shakespeare Folio.

and *No Wit, no Help, like a Woman's*, III. i (Dyce, v. 82):

> It may hit right, boys.

Lines 7–8, Lucullus proceeds:

> Flaminius, honest Flaminius, *you are very respectively welcome.*[1]

Compare:

> Gentlemen, *you are all most respectively welcome.*
> *Your Five Gallants*, II. i.

Lines 9–11. The servant departs to fetch wine, and Lucullus continues:

> And how does that honourable, complete, free-hearted gentleman of Athens, thy very bountiful good lord and master?

The hand of the author of this speech is clearly recognizable in the next scene (Lucius to Servilius, III. ii. 29–31):

> Commend me to thy honourable, virtuous lord, my very exquisite friend.

These effusively polite speeches are exactly in Middleton's manner. Compare:

> And how does the virtuous matron, that good old gentlewoman, thy mother?
> *A Mad World*, &c., I. ii (ii. 340).

> Pray commend me to the good gentleman, thy husband.
> *Ibid.*, III. ii (ii. 377).

'Free-hearted', which occurs nowhere else in the Shakespeare Folio, is in *Michaelmas Term*, III. ii (i. 472):

> Such a good, *free-hearted*, honest, affable kind of gentleman.

Lines 29–30. Towards the end of Lucullus's speech we find this:

> Every man has his fault, and honesty is his.

Compare Quomodo in *Michaelmas Term*, III. iv (i. 480):

> O what 's a man but his honesty, master Easy? and that 's a fault amongst most of us all.

[1] 'Respectively welcome' occurs in no other play in the Folio.

Lines 37–8 (Lucullus to Flaminius):

> I have observed thee always for a towardly prompt spirit, give thee thy due.

Common as is the expression 'to give a person his due', it is to be met with but once in the whole Shakespeare Folio, apart from this instance in *Timon*, and then in the full form 'I'll give thee thy due'.[1] It occurs frequently in Middleton, and he uses it just in the same way as here:

> he 's a proper gentleman, 'ifaith, give him his due.
> *A Trick*, &c., II. i (ii. 27).
>
> So would I myself, man; give me my due.
> *The Phoenix*, I. ii (i. 320).

I am tempted to notice other passages in this scene, but will now proceed to III. ii. It opens with

> Who? the Lord Timon? he is my very good friend and an honourable gentleman.

—in the style of Middleton's speeches already noted.

The first speech of Lucius after the entry of Servilius—'commend me to thy honourable, virtuous lord', &c.—I have already mentioned. In the next, I note the word 'endear',

> Ha! What has he sent? I am so much *endeared* to that lord,

because it is used in the same way in an earlier scene of this play (I. ii):

> *First Lord.* We are so virtuously bound. . . .
> *Second Lord.* So infinitely *endear'd*,

whereas Shakespeare nowhere has it in the sense of 'obliged' or 'bound' to a person.[2] But it is common in Middleton:

> I would *endear* myself to you for ever.
> *Family of Love*, II. iv (ii. 138).

[1] *1 Henry IV*, I. ii. 59.

[2] Only once, indeed, with the force of 'bound, obliged' at all—*2 Henry IV*, II. iii. 11, 'you broke your word when you were more endear'd to it than now'. Its use, as by these lords in *Timon*, in complimentary speeches was considered affected. See Chapman, *The Gentleman Usher*, III (Pearson, i. 295), where (with 'believe it', 'condole', and others) it is held up to ridicule.

I'm so *endear'd* to thee
For my wife's fruitfulness.
A Chaste Maid, v. iv (iv. 96).

How amply you *endear* us!
A Game at Chess, I. i (iv. 325).

Compare also:

O sir, *endear'd*! *Ibid.*, II. i (iv. 348).
Most of all friends *endear'd*, preciously special!
Ibid., I. i (p. 325).

Lines 39–41. Servilius replies to Lucius:

Has only sent his *present occasion* now, my lord; requesting your lordship to *supply* his instant use with so many talents.

Compare with this the reply of Flaminius to the inquiry of Lucullus ('And what hast thou there under thy cloak, pretty Flaminius?') in the preceding scene:

. . . nothing but an empty box, sir, which in my lord's behalf I come to entreat your honour to *supply*: who having great and *instant occasion* to use fifty talents, hath sent to your lordship to *furnish him*,

and Timon's directions to Servilius and Flaminius in II. ii (199–202), when he sends them on their errands:

Commend me to their loves, and I am proud, say, that my occasions have found time to use 'em toward a *supply* of money, let the request be fifty talents.

Mr. Wells has pointed out that these words, 'occasion' (occurring seven times in Acts II and III of *Timon*), 'supply', and 'furnish', are all used by Middleton's characters in similar situations, e. g.:

Run to Master Gum or Master Profit and carry my *present occasion* of money to 'em.
Michaelmas Term, II. iii.

Let them both rest till another *occasion*, go to Master Quomodo, the draper, and will him to *furnish me* instantly. *Ibid.*, II. i.

Mistress Tiffany commends her to your worship, and has sent you ten pound in gold, and says she cannot *furnish you* of the lawn you desire.
Your Five Gallants, IV. ii.

Take no care, sir, for money to *furnish you.*
A Trick, &c., III. i (ii. 40).

he cannot otherwise choose . . . but *supply* any hasty want that I bring to town with me. *Ibid.*, I. i (ii. 8).

Send a note of all your wants . . . and I'll *supply* you instantly. *Ibid.*, III. i (ii. 41).

In the long prose speech of Lucius, we have (lines 49–50) :

What a wicked beast was I, to disfurnish myself against such a good time.

Compare :

Ah, *what a beast was I* to put out my money t'other day !
A Mad World, II. v (ii. 355).

What a beast was I to utter so much !
A Trick, &c., II. i (ii. 25).

Lines 62–4 :

. . . tell him this from me, I count it one of *my greatest afflictions, say*, that I cannot *pleasure* such an honourable gentleman.

There are three suggestions of Middleton's hand in this brief extract. The close parallel in *Michaelmas Term*, II. iii, Mr. Wells has noted. Here Quomodo excuses himself to Shortyard in the same words :

It is *my greatest affliction* at this instant I am not able to furnish you.

Not less significant is the tell-tale little word ' say '—' It is one of my greatest afflictions, *say* '. We have already had this once in a previous scene (II. ii), where Timon says to his servants :

I am proud, *say*, that my occasions have found time to use 'em, &c.

This parenthetic ' say ' is extremely common in Middleton's plays. A dozen instances of its use might easily be quoted, but these examples will be sufficient :

Tell him the party that sent him a hundred pounds t'other day . . . has likewise sent him . . . this ring, which has that virtue to recover him again, *say* ; name nobody, Winifred. *Michaelmas Term*, IV. ii (i. 494).

I offer him no trash, tell him, but present money, *say*.
Ibid., II. iii (451).

Run swiftly with my commendations to Sir Jasper Topaz, we'll rise and visit him i' th' morning, *say*.
A Mad World, II. i (ii. 348).

Return to him again, sir, tell him his uncle desires his company for an hour; I'll trouble him but an hour, *say*; 'tis for his good, tell him. *A Trick*, &c., II. i (ii. 27).

Finally, for the use of the verb 'to pleasure' (not elsewhere in the Folio in the sense of 'to accommodate' with a loan) we may compare:

I would we could rather *pleasure* you otherwise.
Michaelmas Term, III. iv (i. 482).

Can six pound *pleasure* the gentlewoman?
Your Five Gallants, I. i (ii. 219).

It occurs again in a palpably Middletonian passage in II. i of *The Roaring Girl*, where Laxton says to Mistress Gallipot:

I protest I'm now in extreme want of money; if you can supply me with any means, you do me the greatest pleasure, next to the bounty of your love, as ever poor gentleman tasted,

to which she replies:

What 's the sum will *pleasure* ye, sir?

In this instance I have quoted the context because it affords some ground for the presumption that it is Middleton who is responsible for the expression 'to taste bounties', already noted as occurring three times in *Timon*.

I shall now proceed to examine the text of *Timon of Athens* from beginning to end with a view to determining how much of it is Shakespeare's and how much belongs to the original play which I have attributed to Day and Middleton. Further, I shall attempt to distinguish between the portions of the original draft written by each of these authors. The usual arrangement into acts and scenes (as in all modern editions) I have adopted merely for convenience of reference. It should always be borne in mind that in the Folio (the only authoritative text) the play is printed continuously without either act or scene divisions.

Consequently, assuming the play to be by more than one author, there is no justification for a presumption that the work of one of those authors will in any case be found to be conterminous with an act or scene.

Act I, Scene i

This scene, as far as the entry of Apemantus (1–178), is mainly Shakespeare's, but preserves traces of the original draft. From the entry of Apemantus to the end of the scene (178–293) it is chiefly Day's. I shall take these two parts separately.

A. *To entry of Apemantus* (1–178).

This is usually attributed wholly to Shakespeare. That his work does not extend to line 185, as affirmed by Fleay—at any rate that the first few lines following the entry of Apemantus are from the hand that wrote the rest of the Timon–Apemantus dialogue—I have already shown. Dr. Wright's admission that this first part of the scene, though good enough for Shakespeare, cannot be pronounced distinctively and unmistakably his, lends countenance to the presumption that Shakespeare's work is that of a reviser and adapter only. Attention has already been drawn to the introduction in the stage-direction of a mercer who does not figure in the text as one indication of revision. Note also that the words 'rapt' (19) and 'personate' (69), used by Painter and Poet respectively, recur in v. i, a scene in which (though it is assumed to be chiefly by the 'inferior author') both Painter and Poet again appear. In this scene it is the Poet who uses them. The coincidence is sufficiently remarkable, especially as the word 'personate' occurs only twice elsewhere in the Folio. And in both scenes the Painter refers to his works as 'pieces'. In I. i we have:

> *Poet.* What have you there?
> *Painter.* A picture, sir. When comes your book forth?
> *Poet.* Upon the heels of my presentment, sir.
> Let 's see your *piece.*
> *Painter.* 'Tis a good *piece.*

and in v. i (rejected as non-Shakespearean):

> *Poet.* What have you now to present unto him?
> *Painter.* Nothing at this time but my visitation; only I will promise him an excellent *piece.*

The language of these two characters in the later scene (although in prose) seems to me much in the vein of their verse speeches in I. i. I infer that the Poet and Painter are not of Shakespeare's creation, and that he has rewritten their speeches in the first scene. It is probable that in the original draft these also were in prose, and that they have been rewritten by Shakespeare in verse. No doubt Shakespeare has completely recast the earlier portion of this scene. Yet even here traces of Middleton's hand are not altogether absent. The peculiar elliptic phrasing of lines 110–11,

> 'Tis not enough to help the feeble up
> But to support him after,

has attracted the notice of almost all the annotators. We find it again in Middleton's *More Dissemblers besides Women,* I. i (Dyce, iii. 568):

> 'Tis not enough for tapers to burn bright
> But to be seen, so to lend others light.

B. *From entry of Apemantus to end of scene* (178–293).

I have already given my reasons for attributing the whole of the Timon–Apemantus dialogue to Day. It is assumed that in the fifteen lines between the announcement of the arrival of Alcibiades and Timon's exit (249–64) Shakespeare's hand reappears, and there are here certainly touches pointing to his revision. Note, as an indication of continuity of authorship with the earlier part of the scene, that at line 245 Timon invites the Poet and Painter to dinner in words ('You must needs dine with me') practically identical with those used at line 166 ('We must needs dine together'), and in the latter of these two speeches we again have 'piece' for 'picture': 'Show me this piece.' I find no hint of Middleton, except at line 272:

> He's *opposite to humanity.*

Compare *The Phoenix*, I. ii (Dyce, i. 322):

> Hang thyself!
> How comes it you are *so opposite*
> *To love and kindness?*

Act I, Scene ii

This long scene, admittedly non-Shakespearean, is chiefly, if not wholly, Middleton's. At line 32 we have the word 'apperil':

> Let me stay *at thine apperil*, Timon,

also found in *Michaelmas Term*, I. i:

> A woman that will run upon a man *at her own apperil.*

As this word, though very uncommon, is also used by Jonson and by Heywood, no more can be claimed than that its occurrence here will serve to raise a presumption in Middleton's favour if there are other marks to suggest him. In Apemantus's next speech, lines 41–2,

> It grieves me to see so many dip their meat
> In one lord's blood,

are clearly from the same hand as

> Who can call him
> His friend that dips in the same dish?

in III. ii, a scene which, as I have shown, is full of echoes of phrases in Middleton's acknowledged plays. In the same speech is another passage:

> the fellow that sits next him now, parts bread with him . . . is the readiest man to kill him. . . .

closely akin to one in *No Wit, no Help, like a Woman's*:

> And yet ofttimes, sir, what worse knave to a man than he that eats his meat? I. iii (Dyce, v. 30).

The ''Tas' in the line immediately following (''Tas been proved') has already been noted as characteristic of Middleton, and the whole speech exhibits the same features (irregular metre, and jumbling together of rimed and unrimed lines and prose) as are found in Middleton's plays at this time. When Timon drinks to the health of the Second Lord:

> My lord, in heart, and let the health go round!

the Second Lord replies:

> *Let it flow this way*, my good lord,

like Lethe in *Michaelmas Term*, when his health is drunk by Shortyard:

> *Let it flow this way*; dear Master Blastfield.
>
> III. i (i. 468).

In Timon's long prose speech of welcome to the lords (90–111) we have:

> Friends . . . were the most needless creatures living, should we ne'er have use for 'em, and would most resemble *sweet instruments hung up in cases*, that keep their sounds to themselves.

In *More Dissemblers besides Women*, I. iii:

> I commend
> Thy virtues highly, as I do *an instrument*
> *When the case hangs by the wall*;

a line or two further on, Timon observes:

> O *what a precious comfort 'tis*, to have so many, *like brothers, commanding one another's fortunes.*

In *The Phoenix*, I. vi (Dyce, i. 340), Falso, the Justice of the Peace, says to Furtivo:

> *What a precious joy and comfort 's this* that a justice's brother can die so well . . . to make me full executor;

and in *Michaelmas Term*, II. i (Dyce, i. 449), Shortyard thus replies to Quomodo's suggestion that he shall apply to his friend Master Easy for a loan:

> you might well assure yourself this gentleman had it not, if I wanted it, why *our purses are brothers*: *we desire but equal fortunes.*

At line 207 we are told by the Steward that Timon's land is 'put to the books' of his creditors:

> His promises fly so beyond his state
> That what he speaks is all in debt; he owes for ev'ry word:
> His land's put to their books.

We find Middleton using the same expression (not, I think, a common one) in *Father Hubburd's Tales*. Here he has a story of a young prodigal surrounded by parasites curiously reminiscent of the first scene of our play. Among the parasites, as in the play, are a merchant and a mercer—

> two notable arch-tradesmen who had fitted my young gentleman in clothes, whilst they had clothed themselves in his acres . . . which now he was forced to pass over to them, or else *all his lands should be put to their book*.
> (Dyce, v. 568).

Here it should be observed that, apart from the preponderance of rime in the suspected parts of Timon, a special feature of this rimed verse is the prevalence of antithetical couplets, of which there are three in this scene.[1] It is an important feature, for there are comparatively few of the Elizabethan dramatists in whose work they are of noticeably frequent occurrence. They are much used by Day, but by Middleton only in one or two plays written about this time, particularly in *The Phoenix* (1607), which contains above a score. So far as I have observed, Wilkins and Tourneur—neither of them possible claimants to a share in the authorship of *Timon*—are the only other contemporary playwrights much addicted to the use of such couplets. And, apart from the antitheses, there is a special reason to suspect that Middleton was responsible for the *Timon* couplets. Dyce [2] has noted as a peculiarity of Middleton, that when he introduces a couplet he 'does not always think it necessary that the first line should consist of as many feet as the second', and there are many such irregular couplets in this play, e. g.

> Friendship 's full of dregs,
> Methinks false hearts should never have sound legs.
> I. ii. 239–40.

> That thought is bounty's foe,
> Being free itself, it thinks all others so.
> II. ii. 241–2.

[1] Lines 45–6, 239–40, and 256–7.
[2] Middleton's *Works*, vol. i, p. 424.

Debts wither 'em to nothing; be men like blasted woods,
And may diseases lick up their false bloods!

IV. iii. 538–9.

Act II, Scene i

This short scene is always given to Shakespeare, and is no doubt substantially his. Yet the recurrence of 'beggar's dog' (line 5) in a part of the play (IV. iii. 358) suspected as spurious ('I had rather be a *beggar's dog* than Timon') suggests that even here he may be working over a draft by another hand.

Act II, Scene ii

Shakespeare is here revising Middleton, except in the portion of the scene between the entry and exit of Apemantus, which is substantially Day's.

The first part, to the entry of Apemantus (1–47), is usually supposed to be pure Shakespeare. But the ellipsis of the subject at line 5,

He will not hear till feel,

suggests Middleton. Compare *A Trick to Catch the Old One*, I. i (Dyce, ii. 10):

They seldom meet but fight,

and the 'fie, fie, fie, fie' at the end of this first speech is in his manner. And when Timon is dunned by Isidore's servant (34) he exclaims:

Give me breath!

like Witgood, when dunned by his creditors in *A Trick*, &c.,

Pray, sirs, you'll *give me breath*.

IV. iii (Dyce, ii. 69).

I need say no more of the part of the scene that I attribute to Day, except that the introduction of a page among the dramatis personae, as here, is what we should expect if this dialogue is his. The talkative page is a familiar figure in his plays, appearing in *Humour out of Breath*, *The Isle of Gulls*, and *Law Tricks*.

Immediately after the departure of Apemantus, Shakespeare's presence is unmistakable, though in the speech of the Steward (141–54 and 164–72) I suspect a substratum of Middleton's work. And in the prose bit (196–201) with its 'Commend me to their loves, and I am proud, say, that my occasions have found time to use 'em towards a supply of money', we have pure Middleton, left unversified and untouched by Shakespeare. That the rest of the scene is mainly Shakespeare's there is no reason to disbelieve. But for the two couplets at the close (which may well belong to the original text) there is nothing to suggest the work of an inferior hand.

Act III, Scenes i–iv

For proof that the first two scenes of the third act are Middleton's see pp. 24–9, above. There is perhaps one Shakespearean touch in III. ii:

He ne'er drinks
But Timon's silver treads upon his lip.

The short third scene (Sempronius and Timon's servant) is also Middleton's. Note 'Has much disgrac'd me in 't', at line 13,[1] and in the prose part of the servant's speech (28–9) compare:

> The devil knew not what he did when he made man politic; he cross'd himself by 't,

with

> The devil scarce knew what a portion he gave his children when he allow'd 'em large impudence to live upon . . . surely he gave away the third part of his kingdom. *Your Five Gallants*, IV. v (Dyce, ii. 289).

There is general agreement that Shakespeare can have had nothing to do with the fourth scene. This also is probably Middleton's. The comment of Philotus when Lucius's servant observes that he fears that ''Tis deepest water in Lord Timon's purse',

I am of your fear for that,

[1] Cf. 'sh'as much disgrac'd herself', *The Phoenix*, I. i (Dyce, i. 319); 'You've undone me in 't already', *A Mad World*, II. v (ii. 355).

suggests him. Compare *A Game at Chess*, III. i (Dyce, iv. 358):

I'm of your mind for that, sir.

Note also that the appearance of Flaminius is greeted by Titus in exactly the same words

One of Lord Timon's men!

as those used by Lucullus when his entry is announced in the first scene of this Act (III. i. 5).

The dunning of Timon by his creditors (86–106):

> *Titus.* My lord, here is my bill.
> *Luc. Serv. Here 's mine.*
> *Hor. And mine*, my lord.
> . . . .
>
> [*Re-enter* Timon.]
>
> *Timon.* They have e'en *put my breath from me*, the slaves! Creditors? devils!

is much like the scene in *A Trick to Catch the Old One* (IV. iii) where Witgood is similarly set upon by his creditors:

> *1st Creditor.* ... What say you extempore now to your bill of a hundred pounds?
> *2nd Creditor. Here 's mine*, of forty.
> *3rd Creditor. Here 's mine*, of fifty.
> *Witgood.* Pray, sirs, you'll *give me breath.*
>
> [*Enter* Host.]
>
> I am in hell here, and the *devils* will not let me come to thee.

Further, with Timon's exclamation 'Creditors? devils!' compare Rearage's 'Dice? devils!' at the beginning of II. i of *Michaelmas Term.*

Act III, Scene v

This scene (Alcibiades and the Senators) also seems to be chiefly Middleton's. So far am I from following Dr. Boas [1] and Mr. Deighton [2] in attributing any share in its composi-

[1] *Shakspere and his Predecessors*, 1902, p. 502.
[2] *Timon of Athens*, 'Arden' edition, introd., p. xix.

tion to Shakespeare, that my only reason for hesitating to assign it wholly to Middleton is that I find it below his usual level, the verse being distinctly inferior to that of *Michaelmas Term* or *The Phoenix.* But perhaps the draft of *Timon* is of an earlier date than these plays. At any rate the normal level both of Middleton's verse and Day's is certainly above anything to be found in this scene, and it passes my comprehension that any critic can suppose Shakespeare to have been responsible for such lines as the following:

O my lords,
As you are great, be pitifully good:
Who cannot condemn rashness in cold blood?
To kill, I grant, is sin's extremest gust;
But in defence, by mercy, 'tis most just. 51–5.

If by this crime he owes the law his life,
Why, let the war receive't in valiant gore;
For law is strict, and war is nothing more. 83–5.

'Tis honour with most lands to be at odds;
Soldiers should brook as little wrong as gods.[1] 116–17.

Even allowing some of these lines to be corrupt, no amount of emendation can cure their defects, or conceal the poverty of their author's thoughts. Of the presence of Middleton's hand in this part of the play there can be no doubt, for it is here (lines 90–7) that we find one of the most remarkable of the many parallels between *Timon* and Middleton's acknowledged works:

Alcibiades. Must it be so? It must not be. My lords,
I do beseech you know me.
Sec. Sen. How?
Alcib. Call me to your remembrances.
Third Sen. What!
Alcib. I cannot think but your age has forgot me;
It could not else be I should prove so base,
To sue, and be denied such common grace:
My wounds ache at you.

[1] This couplet repeats a rime used in I. ii. 61–2, and I may note that the locution ''Tis honour '(=it is honourable) is used by Middleton in *The Phoenix*, IV. i:

. . . be mild still:
'Tis honour to forgive those you could kill.

These lines (it is again to Mr. Wells that the discovery of the parallel is due) are from *A Chaste Maid in Cheapside*, v. i:

> *Sir Walter*. Touch me not, villain; *my wound aches at thee*,
> Thou poison to my heart!
> *Allwit*. He raves already;
> His senses are quite gone, he knows me not;
> Look up, an 't like your worship; heave those eyes;
> *Call me to mind; is your remembrance left?*
> Look in my face.

Scarcely less remarkable is the resemblance, in an earlier passage (lines 42–5), of the observation of Alcibiades:

> Why do fond men expose themselves in battle
> And not endure all threats? sleep upon 't,
> And let the foes quietly cut their throats
> Without repugnancy?

to that of Francisco in *The Widow*, III. i (Dyce, iii. 391):

> And what does fond man venture all these ills for,
> That may so sweetly rest in honest peace?

Two other small points may be noted. The expression 'to bring into form' (i.e. into fair semblance) at line 27:

> Your words have took such pains as if they labour'd
> *To bring manslaughter into form*,

occurs in no other play of the Shakespeare Folio, but it is to be found again in *The Phoenix*, IV. i (Dyce, i. 378):

> I'll strive to *bring this act into such form*
> And credit amongst men, they shall suppose . . . the prince
> To be the plotter of his father's murder,

and the use of the term 'sworn rioter' (line 69) also suggests Middleton; the word 'rioter' being, as Mr. Wells has pointed out, constantly used by him about the time this play must have been written,[1] whereas it is not once used by Shakespeare.

[1] In *A Trick to Catch the Old One* Witgood is called 'a common rioter', 'a noted rioter', 'a daily rioter', and we have 'notorious rioters' in *Michaelmas Term*.

Act III, Scene vi

There is no Shakespeare in this (the mock-banquet) scene except in Timon's speech, and possibly the long prose grace that precedes it, though this is rejected by Fleay. That the voice of Shakespeare is heard in Timon's fierce outburst in the banqueting hall is evident enough, but the fact that Timon's words have left so much doubt in the minds of the critics of the actions that accompanied them, give some justification for the supposition that, in rewriting the speech, Shakespeare may have removed lines more clearly indicating how Timon treated his guests—first throwing warm water at them and then stones. The exclamations of the three lords at the end of the scene:

2. Lord Timon 's mad.
3. I feel 't upon my bones.
4. One day he gives us diamonds, next day stones.

plainly show that stones *were* thrown, and explain Timon's words as his guests rise from the table in confusion, and make toward the doors (109–11):

What! dost thou go?
Soft, take thy physic first,—thou too,—and thou—
Stay, I will lend thee money, borrow none.
What? all in motion?

It is true that we have no stage-direction 'Pelts them with stones' to explain this reference to 'money', but the Folio text here contains *no stage-direction whatever*, the directions 'The dishes are uncovered and seen to be full of warm water' at the line 'Uncover, dogs, and lap!' and 'Throwing the water in their faces' after

. . . smoke and luke-warm water
Is your perfection. This is Timon's last;
Who stuck and spangled you with flatteries,
Washes it off and sprinkles in your faces
Your reeking villainy.

both being modern insertions. Nevertheless, in spite of the explicitness of the Fourth Lord's 'One day he gives us diamonds, next day *stones*', most modern editors unwarrantably insert Rowe's stage-direction, 'Throws the dishes at them', after

Soft, take thy physic first,—thou too,—and thou—

while Fleay[1] and Wright[2] profess to believe that nothing was thrown at them but water, which, says Fleay, 'apparently freezes before it reaches them, so that they feel it upon their bones'. He is, of course, still baiting the unfortunate 'vamper', who is assumed to have interpolated the prose speeches of the lords following Timon's speech and borrowed the idea of the stone-throwing from the academic comedy of Timon, usually supposed to have been written about 1600, where stones 'painted like to artichokes' are provided for, and hurled at, the guests.

The portion of the scene from line 115 to the end is certainly spurious in the sense of being un-Shakespearean, but why Deighton (following Fleay) should assert that the reference to stones 'makes it look like an interpolation' I cannot conceive. If Timon's allusions to 'physic' and 'money' are to be taken as referring to the throwing of warm water only, or the dishes in which it was contained, the *interpolation* of the concluding couplet would be absolutely pointless.

There is one strong suggestion of Middleton's hand in the final portion of this scene—the exclamation of the Third Lord:

Push! did you see my cap?

'Push!' as Mr. Wells has observed, is one of Middleton's commonest expletives. It is seldom used by other authors of the time; never by Shakespeare.

Act IV, Scene i

There can be no doubt that this is pure Shakespeare—except, I think, the two couplets at the end:

The gods confound—hear me, you good gods all—
The Athenians both within and out that wall!
And grant, as Timon grows, his hate may grow
To the whole race of mankind, high and low!

[1] *Shakespeare Manual*, p. 192. [2] *Op. cit.*, p. 20.

These come as a sad anticlimax after the tremendous vigour of the preceding lines, and I strongly suspect that they belong to the original draft.

Act IV, Scene ii

It is clear that the first half of this scene to the point where the Steward parts from the servants (1–29) was written, or rewritten, by Shakespeare.[1] The last twenty-two lines I have (with some hesitation, owing to the wretched quality of the verse) attributed to Middleton. In his earlier plays Middleton's verse is sometimes, as I have shown,[2] almost as bad as this.

Act IV, Scene iii

Timon's first speech (1–47) is pure Shakespeare, and indeed throughout the whole of this long scene all the important speeches of Timon are clearly from his pen. From the entry of Alcibiades to that of Apemantus (48–196) is mainly Shakespeare's, with occasional traces of the draft that he revised. The Timon–Apemantus part (196–400), originally Day's, has been rewritten by Shakespeare as far as line 276 (' Thou hadst been a knave and flatterer '), but after this point Day's work has been left practically untouched, only one speech of Timon's (' Rogue, rogue, rogue ! ' &c., 375–93) being Shakespeare's.

From the entry to the departure of the banditti (400–63) only Timon's speeches are Shakespeare's, the original author being probably Middleton. The visit of the Steward (463 to the end of scene) seems also to be Middleton's, with some revision by Shakespeare after the Steward's soliloquy.

More briefly the results of my analysis may be stated as follows :

(A) 1–276. [Timon, Alcibiades, Apemantus.] Shakespeare with slight traces of earlier work.

(B) 276–400. [Timon, Apemantus.] Day. (One speech only rewritten by Shakespeare.)

(C) 400–543. [Banditti, Steward.] Shakespeare revising Middleton.

[1] Fleay, however, rejects the whole scene. [2] Pp. 22–3 *supra*.

The differences between this division and those of Fleay and Wright are considerable; they differ also considerably from one another as to the extent of Shakespeare's share in this scene. Both give 1–291 entire to Shakespeare, together with the end of the Timon–Apemantus dialogue, either from line 361[1] (Fleay) or 376[2] (Wright), to 400. The earlier prose speeches of the Banditti (15 lines) Fleay attributes to the inferior author; Wright thinks all the Banditti part Shakespeare's. Finally Fleay rejects the whole of Timon's interview with the Steward, whereas Wright gives the last thirteen lines of the scene to Shakespeare.

I take the three parts, indicated A, B, and C above, separately:

(A) Shakespeare (1–276).

One indication that Shakespeare is here revising earlier material I find in the dialogue between Timon and the courtesan Phrynia (63–5):

> *Phrynia.* Thy lips rot off!
> *Timon.* I will not kiss thee; then the rot returns
> To thine own lips again.

These lines are surely by the same hand as this Timon–Apemantus bit (369–70) which Fleay and Wright agree to be non-Shakespearean:

> *Timon.* I'll beat thee, but I should infect my hands.
> *Apem.* I would my tongue could rot them off!

The remark of Alcibiades at line 170:

> If I thrive well, I'll visit thee again.

and Timon's retort:

> If I hope well, I'll never see thee more.

are, as I have already noted,[3] exactly in the style of a later passage of arms between Timon and Apemantus, also admittedly non-Shakespearean.

(B) Day (276–400).

According to Fleay and Wright, the non-Shakespearean

[1] 'Thou art the cap of all the fools alive.'

[2] 'I am sick of this false world', &c.

[3] See p. 7, *supra*.

work begins at line 291—'Where liest o' nights, Timon?' 'A child', says Wright, 'would feel the drop at this point from the stateliness of Shakespeare's poetry to the other man's tomfoolery.' I should distrust the child who professed to find 'stately poetry' in the squabbling of Timon and Apemantus immediately following the last lines of Timon's speech (275–6):

> If thou hadst not been born the worst of men,
> Thou hadst been a knave and flatterer.

especially when I found Apemantus leading off with

> Art thou proud yet?

and Timon countering with a retort already used in the Timon–Apemantus bout in the first scene. It is at this point (276), if anywhere, that the 'drop' is apparent. From here onwards the dialogue is full of the verbal repetitions and empty quibbles characteristic of Day's prose in *Humour out of Breath*, until we reach the one clear flash of Shakespeare in Timon's speech following line 376:

> I am sick of this false world, and will love nought
> But even the mere necessities upon 't, &c.

(C) Shakespeare revising Middleton (400–543).

The Banditti (400–63):

I see no reason to suppose that the piece of prose following the entry of the Banditti and that immediately preceding their departure are not by the same author. The 'has' (=he has) in the latter passage:

> Has almost charmed me from my profession,

occurring again in the Steward's speech immediately following

> Has caught me in his eye,

suggests Middleton. Of Shakespeare's hand in the verse, especially in Timon's principal speech (just before the Banditti depart) there can be no doubt.

The Steward [1] (463–543).

The style of the Steward's soliloquy, with its irregular verse, rimes, and antitheses, is clearly that of the author of the Steward's speech at the end of IV. ii. The matter is put beyond a doubt by the Steward's profession of fidelity to his master at the end of both speeches. Here (476–8) we have:

I will present
My honest grief unto him; and, as my lord,
Still serve him with my life,

and, at the end of IV. ii:

I'll ever serve his mind with my best will;
Whilst I have gold, I'll be his steward still.

Not content with this, this author echoes the sentiment of the speech just quoted a few lines later:

I beg of you to know me, good my lord,
T' accept my grief, and *whilst this poor wealth lasts,*
To entertain me as your steward still,

and prefaces it with a line that also shows him to be the author of Alcibiades' appeal to the Senate (III. v):

My lords,
I do beseech you, know me.

That this author was Middleton I feel little doubt. Apart from the style of the verse it is strongly suggested by the opening words of Timon's speech that follows:

Had I a steward
So true, so just, and now *so comfortable?*

[1] I have avoided the name Flavius for the Steward, adopted in all modern texts, because only in one scene (I. ii.) is he called by that name in the Folio; elsewhere he is 'The Steward' simply. It is curious (considering the importance of his part) that he does not appear at all in the list of 'The Actors' Names'.

Compare the courtesan Florida's remark to Antonio's servant in *The Witch*, I. i (Dyce, iii. 253):

> I find thee still *so comfortable*,
> . . . .
> Give me the kindness of the master's man
> In my distress, say I.

Act V, Scene i

This is chiefly Shakespeare's, but there are occasional traces of the earlier draft throughout the scene. Fleay gives the first fifty lines (the conversation between the Poet and Painter) to the inferior author; all after the point where they are joined by Timon to Shakespeare. No doubt Shakespeare's hand is more obvious after Timon's appearance—it is evident all through the play that he has devoted his chief attention to its central figure—but this splitting up of the Poet and Painter dialogue into Shakespearean and non-Shakespearean portions is altogether arbitrary. Assuming (as is probably the case) that this first portion is almost entirely non-Shakespearean, the words 'piece' (= picture) at line 21,

> I will promise him an excellent piece;

and 'personate' (line 36):

> It must be a *personating* of himself,

show that there is also non-Shakespearean work in the first scene. And, unless we are entitled to ignore its connexions with admittedly non-Shakespearean passages in the play, the latter part of this scene cannot be pure Shakespeare.

The only direct clue to Middleton that I have noticed is the word 'whittle' (= knife) at line 182. It is nowhere used by Shakespeare, and seems to be rare. Middleton has it in *The Widow*, I. i: 'here 's the length of one of their *whittles*'.

Act V, Scene ii

This short scene is usually given to Shakespeare. As Dr. Wright says, it 'has not been doubted' to be his. But it is too short to enable one to arrive at a definite conclusion. The style of the Messenger's speech is certainly Shakespearean. But if Shakespeare wrote the final couplet

> In, and prepare:
> Ours is the fall, I fear; our foes the snare,

there seems to be no reason why the final couplet of the following scene:

> Before proud Athens he 's set down by this,
> Whose fall the mark of his ambition is,

should not also be assigned to him.

Act V, Scene iii

These ten lines cannot be Shakespeare's. It seems probable that the first

> By all description this should be the place.

is from the same hand as the Painter's speech at the beginning of v. i:

> As I took note of the place, it cannot be far where he abides.

In spite of what has been said to the contrary, I feel no doubt whatever that the third and fourth lines:

> Timon is dead, who hath outstretch'd his span:
> Some beast read this: there does not live a man.

are not the soldier's own words, and that he is here repeating an inscription that Timon has placed near his tomb. That the soldier himself should sententiously observe that Timon has 'outstretch'd his span' is most unlikely.[1] And I feel convinced that Dr. Johnson has misunderstood the line

> Some beast read this; there does not live a man.

[1] Note that it is Timon's wont to address himself by name. Cf. the couplet at the end of his last speech in v. i:

> Graves only be men's works, and death their gain;
> Sun, hide thy beams! Timon hath done his reign.

when he explains that the soldier, not being able to read the inscription, 'peevishly exclaims "Some beast read this", for it must be read, and in this place it cannot be read by man'.[1] The second line of the couplet surely means nothing more than that the world is inhabited by beasts alone—that all mankind are beasts—a sentiment entirely in accord with Timon's utterances elsewhere.[2]

Wright observes: 'We are rather impatient with a soldier who cannot read in line 6, though he could read in line 4.' But there is no contradiction between the two passages. What the soldier says at line 6 is that he is unable to read *what is on the tomb*:

> What 's on this tomb
> I cannot read; the character I'll take with wax:
> Our captain hath in every figure skill, &c.

He is unable to read what is on the tomb, because, unlike the first inscription, this is not in the language of the country. Otherwise—if the 'character' was one that could be read by anybody—for what reason should the soldier tell us that his captain is 'an aged interpreter, though young in days' and that he 'hath *in every figure* skill'?

Act V, Scene iv

Nothing need be said of this final scene, except that its style is Shakespearean. But the two inconsistent epitaphs (from Plutarch's *Life of Antonius*) I take to be a relic of the original rough draft, and the fact that Shakespeare has allowed both to stand, as evidence of the hasty and perfunctory nature of his revision.

1921.

[1] Dyce interprets the words in the same sense; so also Gollancz (Temple Shakespeare): 'These words are in all probability the reflection of the soldier. . . . The soldier, seeing the tomb, infers that Timon is dead, but cannot read the inscription: 'Some beast read this! there does not live a man *able to do so*.'

[2] In IV. iii, when Alcibiades calls out 'What art thou there? speak', Timon replies—'A beast, as thou art', and in a later part of the same scene he greets the approach of the Banditti with the exclamation 'Moe *things like men*!'

II

THE AUTHORSHIP OF 'THE TAMING OF A SHREW', 'THE FAMOUS VICTORIES OF HENRY V', AND THE ADDITIONS TO MARLOWE'S 'FAUSTUS'.

THE *Famous Victories of Henry V* and *The Taming of a Shrew* were both published anonymously, and there is no record of the names of their authors either in Henslowe's diary or anywhere else. Nor has any effort to determine the authorship of either play on internal grounds proved successful. *The Famous Victories* has been conjecturally assigned to the actor Tarlton, but the conjecture is unsupported by any evidence. *The Taming of a Shrew* has been ascribed to Marlowe, to Greene, to Kyd, and even (wholly or in part) to Shakespeare himself, but there are good reasons for rejecting all these ascriptions.

In the following pages I shall endeavour to throw light upon the authorship of both plays, and incidentally upon the authorship of other anonymous dramatic work of the period. I shall set forth my evidence exactly in the way and in the order in which it presented itself to me, beginning with my first clue and showing how it took me from one play to another until, with the aid of a small piece of external evidence, I was led to connect these plays with a dramatist who has hitherto occupied only a very humble place in the annals of Elizabethan dramatic literature.

On first reading *The Taming of a Shrew*, a year or two since, I was struck by the constant appearance of the exclamation 'souns!' in the prose parts. It occurred to me at the time that this might prove a useful clue; that it should be possible to recognize this writer who found such relief in 'souns', if there were any other work of his extant. I gave no more thought to the matter until, some time afterwards, I made the acquaintance of *The Famous Victories of Henry V*. The style of the prose seemed strangely familiar. Gradually, as my reading progressed, 'souns' once more obtruded itself upon my notice. Its constant recurrence brought back to my mind *The Taming of a Shrew*, and led me to compare the texts of the two plays. My suspicion that the prose scenes of *A Shrew* and *The Famous Victories* were the work of the same hand grew stronger and stronger as the examination proceeded.

First, I noted that, besides the extraordinary frequency with which the exclamation was used in both plays, in neither was it put into the mouth of one character alone, as a distinctive mark of his vocabulary. In *A Shrew* it is used indiscriminately by Sander, Ferando, Valeria (servant to Aurelius), Tom (Ferando's servant), Polidor's boy, and once also by one of the players in the Induction. It is the same with *The Famous Victories*. Here, though it is commonest in the speeches of the clown Dericke, Henry V himself uses it freely and other speakers occasionally.

Next I observed that 'I warrant you' was a favourite expression in both plays. No doubt it was in common use at this period; but in these plays it is unusually common, appearing eight times in the text of *A Shrew* and five times in *The Famous Victories*. Then there is the phrase 'as passeth'—not a rare one at this time, but still sufficiently uncommon to make it noteworthy that it occurs twice in *A Shrew*:[1]

> *Boy*. . . . your master's gone to church to be married already, and there's such cheer *as passeth*. II. ii. 16.
>
> *Sander*. . . . my master has such ado with her *as it passeth*. III. i. 8.

and twice in *The Famous Victories*:

> Faith, my lord, such news *as passeth* A2 recto.
>
> . . . for the space of half an hour there was such a bloody fray *as passeth*. B1 recto.

A favourite exclamation in the prose parts of *A Shrew* is 'O brave!':

[1] References to *A Shrew* are by act, scene, and line of the 'Shakespeare Classics' reprint, edited by Dr. Boas; for *The Famous Victories of Henry V* I have used the 1598 Quarto.

Sander. O brave, Sirrah Tom, we must play before
A foolish Lord. Ind., i. 83.

Sly. A play, Sim: *O brave*, be they my players?
Ind., ii. 49.

Sly. O brave, here 's two fine gentlewomen!
I. i. 331.

Sander. O brave, I would I had eat no meat this week!
II. ii. 17.

and this appears five times in *The Famous Victories*.

The verb 'to course' in the sense of to beat, or thrash, is distinctly rare—in Elizabethan plays at any rate. In *A Shrew* it is to be found three times. At III. iii. 17, Sander says to Kate:

> the garlic . . . will make your breath stink, and then my master will *course* me for letting you eat it.

and, a few lines later:

> Here comes my master: now he'll *course* you.

The word appears once more in the Epilogue, where the Tapster says to Sly:

> your wife will *course* you for dreaming here to-night.

In *The Famous Victories* it is used by Dick during an altercation with John Cobler:

> . . . 'yfaith, you gray-beard knave, I'll *course* you.
> B4 verso.

The expression 'let me (him) alone with'—not a familiar one to me—is also common to these plays. 'Well,' says Prince Henry in *The Famous Victories* (A2 verso) 'if the villains come, *let me alone with* them', and in *A Shrew* (II. ii. 24) Sander, warned by Polidor's boy that his mistress is 'a devil' who will make him forget his eating, she'll 'beat him so', replies '*Let my master alone with her* for that, for he'll make her tame well enough ere long, I warrant thee'—using much the same words as Ferando himself in an earlier scene of the play:

> And when our nuptial rites be once performed,
> *Let me alone* to *tame her well enough.* I. i. 139–40.

Other small points of resemblance might be noted, but there are enough tricks of speech here to show that the same hand has been at work on these dramas. In addition there are two or three curious correspondences of phrasing, the significance of which—trivial though they are—it is impossible to mistake. Sander's 'he'll make her tame well enough, I warrant thee,' is echoed by the Constable of France in *The Famous Victories*. Speaking of Henry V, he says to the Archbishop of Bourges:

> Tush, we will make him as tame as a lamb,
> I warrant you. E1 verso.

When (Induction to *A Shrew*) Sly wakes up to find himself clothed in rich apparel, with servants at hand anxious to gratify his least whim, he exclaims:

> By the mass, I think I am a lord indeed.

In *The Famous Victories* (B4 v) John Cobler affirms that he is Lord Chief Justice of England; Dericke replies:

> Mass, thou saist true, thou art indeed.

In *A Shrew* the Duke says to his son Aurelius:

> I pray you, sir, who am I? IV. ii. 40.

and in *The Famous Victories* the Judge says to Prince Henry:

> Why, I pray you, my Lord, who am I? B3 verso.

and shortly afterwards John puts the same question to Dericke:

> But, I pray you, who am I? B4 verso.

Moreover, it is interesting to observe that when Sly, in *The Taming of a Shrew* (IV. ii. 45–8), roused by the order of the Duke in the play that Phylotus and Valeria are to be sent to prison, exclaims:

> I say we'll have no sending to prison. . . .
> I tell thee, Sim, we'll have no sending to prison, that 's flat! Why, Sim, am not I Don Christo Vary?

he is echoing the sentiments of Prince Henry in *The Famous*

Victories, ' 'Tis enough for me to look into a prison though I come not in myself ', the Prince says to Sir John Oldcastle, ' but here 's such ado nowadays, here 's prisoning, here 's hanging, whipping and the devil and all: but *I tell you, sirs, when I am king we will have no such things.*' (C1 recto.)

The connexions between *The Famous Victories* and *A Shrew* being almost without exception confined to the Induction, interludes, and prose ' taming ' scenes of the latter play, and *The Famous Victories* being obviously the work of one hand, and that a hand one would judge to be incapable of the smooth harmonious lines of the Marlowe-imitating versifier of *A Shrew*, the conclusion that two authors were concerned in *A Shrew* is scarcely to be avoided. For convenience I have spoken of the taming scenes and the induction as prose, though in the old copy they are printed in lines of approximately uniform length to look like verse, just like much of the text of *The Famous Victories*, which one may search from end to end without finding a decently rhythmical passage. Although in *A Shrew* the work of the two authors seems often closely intermingled, the Marlowe-imitating poet having apparently recast lines written by his less skilful coadjutor, an approximate definition of each author's share would not appear to be difficult. It would give the induction and interludes and all the lively boisterous comedy scenes in prose or prosaic blank verse to the author of *The Famous Victories*, leaving the more polished, but more insipid, verse scenes to the imitator of Marlowe. The appearance of the text suggests that the whole play was in the first instance written by the author of *The Famous Victories*, and that the other author revised it, altogether rewriting many scenes, but leaving others practically untouched.

Having thus decided that *A Shrew* was of dual authorship, and that one of its authors was also the author of *The Famous Victories*, I concluded that there was no hope of throwing any further light upon the identity of the creator of Sander and Sly, *The Famous Victories* being itself the work of an unknown dramatist. The discovery I had made

—incomplete though it was—seemed at least so far valuable that it set at rest all conjectures as to the presence of a Shakespearean element in *A Shrew*. But no sooner had I reached the conclusion just stated than my attention was drawn to a feature connected with the text of this play which, though it ultimately led to a further most interesting discovery, at first seemed completely to contradict the view that it was divisible between two authors, one of whom was the author of *The Famous Victories*, and the other the plagiarist from Marlowe. On referring to the list of 'passages from Marlowe's *Tamburlaine* and *Doctor Faustus*' set forth in Dr. Boas's edition of *The Taming of a Shrew*, I was disconcerted to find that one of the *Doctor Faustus* parallels was in the *prose* part of *A Shrew* that I assigned to the author of *The Famous Victories*. Moreover, in this case the phrasing of *A Shrew* corresponds with the altered text of *Dr. Faustus* printed in 1616, and not that of the 1604 Quarto. I quote this passage as it appears in the edition of 1604:

> *Wagner*. Sirrah boy, come hither.
>
> *Clown*. How, boy? swouns, boy, I hope you have seen many boys with such pickadevants as I have. Boy quotha.

In the edition of 1616 it stands thus:

> *Wagner*. Come hither, sirrah boy.
>
> *Clown*. Boy? O disgrace to my person: Zounds, boy in your face, you have seen many boys with beards, I am sure.

The later version is echoed in *A Shrew*, though it will be noticed that the 'pickadevants' of the 1604 text is retained:

> *Boy*. Come hither, sirrah boy.
>
> *Sander*. Boy, O disgrace to my person, souns, boy
> Of your face, you have many boys with such
> Pickadevants, I am sure, souns, would you
> Not have a bloody nose for this? II. ii. 1–4.

That Dr. Boas's presumption that the 1616 additions to *Faustus* date back to a much earlier period is correct, there can be no reasonable doubt. But, obvious as it may seem that the writer of *A Shrew* borrowed this passage from the text of *Dr. Faustus*, there is, in fact, no evidence here that these additions were written prior to the publication of *A Shrew* in 1594. In this instance the correspondence between the two texts is not due to plagiarism. An examination of the prose scenes of the later edition of Marlowe's play soon revealed the real explanation, and it is this: the prose scenes of *A Shrew* and the prose alterations and additions to the text of *Dr. Faustus* are *the work of the same hand*—the hand (as we have seen) of the author of *The Famous Victories*. Of the truth of this assertion there can be no question. Even the very passage we have just been discussing can be shown to be exactly in this author's style. To prove this, here is an extract from the dialogue between Robin and Dericke in *The Famous Victories*:

> *Robin.* Why I see thou art a plain clown.
> *Dericke.* Am I a clown, *souns masters*,
> Do clowns go in silk apparel?
> *I am sure* all we gentlemen clowns in Kent scant go so.
> Well, *souns*, you know clowns very well. A4 recto.

The words are rather different, but it is the same voice. And in the case of *Dr. Faustus* we have evidence of a different and more decisive kind. Those familiar with the 1616 text may remember that in some cases the reviser has altered and much expanded parts of the earlier text; in one instance he has condensed a passage and in others he has added entirely new matter. Bearing in mind what has already been said as to the characteristics of the prose of *A Shrew* and *The Famous Victories*, particular interest attaches to the alterations made by the author of the additions in the phrasing of the 1604 text.[1]

The first alteration made by the reviser is the recasting of the prose dialogue between Wagner and the Clown. It

[1] In Mr. Tucker Brooke's edition of *Doctor Faustus* (*Works of Christopher Marlowe*, Clarendon Press, 1910) the additions are printed in an Appendix (pp. 195–229), apart from the original text. In the citations that follow I have numbered the lines as in his edition.

begins with the passage so closely paralleled in *A Shrew*. Next I note that whereas in the 1604 version, when Wagner promises to teach the Clown to turn himself into 'a dog, or a cat, or a mouse, or a rat, or anything', the Clown replies:

> How? A Christian fellow to a dog or a cat, a mouse or a rat? no, no, sir.

in the 1616 edition he says:

> A dog, or a cat, or a mouse, or a rat? *O brave* Wagner!

A few lines further on in the earlier Quarto, Wagner tells the Clown to keep his eye 'diametarily fixt upon my right heel, with *quasi vestigias nostras insistere*', and the Clown exclaims:

> God forgive me, he speaks Dutch fustian.

but in the 1616 version this is altered to:

> Well, sir, *I warrant you.*

The next alteration consists in the interpolation (after the scene presenting the seven deadly sins) of an entirely new prose dialogue between Robin and Dick. The speakers are introduced by the Clown, who tells Dick to look after the horses for him, adding:

> I have gotten one of Doctor Faustus' conjuring books, and now we'll have such knavery *as 't passes.*

Then a few lines after Dick says to Robin:

> *you had best* leave your foolery, for an my Master come, he'll conjure you 'ifaith.

I note this 'you had best', because it happens to be a characteristic locution of the prose author of *A Shrew*. In the Induction the Tapster says to Sly:

> *you had best* be gone:
> And empty your drunken paunch somewhere else.

and in the Epilogue:

> *you had best* get you home,
> For your wife will course you for dreaming here to-night.

and in another place (III. i. 17) Sander says to the serving-men:

> ... *you had best* get supper against they come, for they be hard at hand.

Robin's reply to Dick (807–9) is:

> I'll tell thee what, an my Master come here, I'll *clap as fair a pair of horns on 's head as e'er thou sawest in thy life.*

In *The Famous Victories* Henry V, speaking of his father, says:

> ... the breath shall be no sooner out of his mouth, but I will *clap the crown on my head.* C1 verso.

In Act II, sc. i, of *A Shrew* Kate warns Valeria:

> And see you come no more into this place,
> Lest that I *clap your fiddle on your face.*

and in the Epilogue of the same play Sly says to the Tapster:

> I have had
> The bravest dream to-night, that *ever thou heardest in all thy life.*

Shortly after the speech last quoted, Robin tells Dick that with the aid of the 'conjuring book' they will be able to get any kind of wine they choose at the tavern, without paying for it. Dick greets this joyful news with:

> *O brave!* prithee let 's to it presently, for I am as dry as a dog. 823–4.

at lines 1000–1 (1604 4to) Mephistophiles says to the Clown:

> Well villains, for your presumption, I transform thee into an ape, and thee into a dog, and so be gone.

in the 1604 edition Robin replies:

> How, into an ape? that 's brave.

but in that of 1616:

> *O brave,* an ape?

In the later Quarto the entry of the Emperor with Faustus is preceded by a long passage not found in the 1604 text. Here Frederick says to Martino:

> Where is Benvolio?

And Martino replies :

> Fast asleep, *I warrant you.*

A little later on Martino tells Benvolio that the Emperor is at hand, and the latter replies :

> *Well,* go you attend the Emperor : *I am content for this once* to thrust my head out of a window.

Compare :

> *Well,* sirrah, your fair words hath something allayed my choler : *I am content for this once* to put it up and be friends with thee. *A Shrew,* II. ii. 50–2.

Moreover, Benvolio concludes his speech with :

> I have a charm in my head, shall control him [the Devil] as well as the conjurer, *I warrant you.*

In the 1604 edition the Knight's indignation at the discovery that he has horns upon his head is manifested in four lines of bombastic verse. Not once does he use the interjection ‘zounds !’ But his counterpart, the Benvolio of the 1616 text, three times breaks out into this exclamation :

> O zounds, my head ! 1140.
> Zounds, doctor, is this your villany ? 1146.
> Hold, hold, zounds, he'll raise up a kennel of divels I think anon. 1158–9.

After the entry of Faustus with ‘a false head’, Benvolio deals him a blow which he imagines has killed him. Martino asks ‘what use shall we put his beard to ?’ and Benvolio replies :

> We'll sell it to a chimney-sweeper ; it will wear out ten birchen brooms, *I warrant you.*

When Faustus rises again, Benvolio exclaims :

> Zounds, the Devil 's alive again ! 1246.

and, in a later passage, when he finds his head has again been decorated with horns :

> *Zouns,* horns again !

None of these speeches occur in the 1604 text.

Next we come to the trick played by Faustus on the horse-courser and the latter's retaliation by pulling off Faustus's leg. In the 1616 version these incidents are treated more briefly than in that of 1604. In both, Faustus, after he has sold the horse, gives the horse-courser a final injunction not to ride it into the water. In the 1604 text the latter replies simply:

> Well, sir, now am I a made man for ever.

and in the revised text this is expanded into:

> *I warrant you*, sir; O joyful day! Now am I a made man for ever.

In the 1616 edition there follows a scene in an inn (not in the 1604 Quarto) with a long dialogue between the Clown, Dick, the Horse-courser, and a Carter. The conversation is continually interrupted by clamours for drink:

> *Dick*. Why, hostess, I say, fetch us some beer. 1212.
>
> *Carter*. Some more drink, hostess. 1253.
>
> *Clown*. What ho, give 's half a dozen of beer here, and be hang'd. 1316.
>
> *Horse-courser*. Zouns, fill us some beer, or we'll break all the barrels in the house. 1520–1.

Here we can clearly recognize the voice of the thirsty Sly:

> Tapster, I say, fill 's a fresh cushion here! Ind., i. 7.
>
> Tapster, gi 's a little small ale. Ind., ii. 10.
>
> Gi 's some more drink here; souns, where 's the Tapster? I. i. 326.
>
> Are they run away, Sim? That 's well; then gi 's some more drink. IV. ii. 52.

In the 1616 version of *Faustus*, as in the earlier version, the horse-courser enters ‘all wet’ after his adventure in the horse-pond. In the 1604 edition he describes what has happened to him in these words:

> I was no sooner in the middle of the pond, but my horse vanish't away, and I sat upon a bottle of hay, *never so near* drowning in my life. 1156–9.

In the 1616 edition this is altered to :

> I, riding my horse into the water, thinking some hidden mystery had been in the horse, I had nothing under me but a little straw, and *had much ado to escape* drowning. 1138–41.

The alteration is particularly interesting, because the author of *The Famous Victories* is much addicted to the use of the word ‘ ado ’. In *The Famous Victories* it occurs no fewer than six times. In four passages we have ‘ such ado ’ or ‘ much ado ’ :

> what mean you to sleep
> And such ado in the streets ? A4 recto.
>
> . . . and at the last with much ado they took them. B1 recto.
>
> . . . and at the last with much ado we stayed them. B2 recto.
>
> here ’s such ado nowadays. C1 recto.

and it appears twice in *A Shrew* :

> My master has such ado with her as it passeth. III. i. 8.
>
> Here ’s more ado than needs. III. v. 43.

In the 1616 version the horse-courser relates at length to his companions at the inn the story of the trick played upon him by Faustus, and all with one voice exclaim :

O brave Doctor !

Having traced the hand of this writer who is so free with his ‘ souns ’, ‘ O brave ’, and ‘ I warrant you ’ in the additions to *Doctor Faustus*, the task of discovering his identity becomes less hopeless than it at first appeared, for now we have a small scrap of external evidence to assist us. On the 22nd of November 1602, Henslowe—so he tells us in his *Diary*—paid the sum of £4 to William Birde and Samuel Rowley for their ‘ adicyones in doctor fostes ’. Of William Birde’s literary performances practically nothing is known, no piece bearing his name having survived. But we do know something about Samuel Rowley. He was the author of a play still extant entitled *When You See Me You Know*

Me, or The Famous Chronicle History of King Henry the Eight. This piece was published in 1605 ' as it was playd by the high and mighty Prince of Wales his servants ', and it bears Rowley's name on its title-page, ' By Samuel Rowley, servant to the Prince '. To one, at least, of the plays we have been discussing it has a most obvious resemblance. In this *Famous Chronicle History of King Henry VIII*, as in *The Famous Victories of Henry V*, it is the Clown rather than the King who is the chief figure in the play.[1] A brief examination of the speeches of Will Summers in the Henry VIII play was sufficient to satisfy me that the hand that created him was that of the augmenter of the clowning scenes of *Doctor Faustus*, the creator of Sander in *A Shrew* and Dericke in *The Famous Victories.* Let us first glance through the text for ' souns ', ' O brave ', and ' I warrant thee '. They are all here :

> I'll be wise and say little *I warrant thee.* 1613 4to, B1 recto.
> No, no, *I warrant thee*, Jane. B1 verso.
> I'll thrust some of you down, *I warrant ye.* B2 verso.
> Up, cousin, fear nothing, the storm 's past, *I warrant thee.* C3 verso.
> *O brave*, O brave, give me it cousin. C4 recto.
> he'll conjure thee, *I warrant thee.* C4 recto.

All these are from the speeches of the clowns, Will Summers and Patch. In the two next it is a Watchman who speaks :

> God ye good night and twenty, sir, *I warrant ye.* D3 recto.
> 'tis an honest quiet soul, *I warrant ye.* D3 verso

The ' souns ' are from ' Black Will ', the Highwayman :

> *Souns*, I am hurt, hold I say ! E1 recto.
> *Souns*, the moon 's a waning harlot. E1 verso.

[1] The affinity between these two pieces has been noted by Sir Sidney Lee. ' In 1605 an obscure dramatist, Samuel Rowley, ventured for the first time to bring Henry VIII on the stage as the hero of a chronicle-play or history-drama. The dramatist worked on crude, old-fashioned lines which recall *The Famous Victories of Henry V* '. *Life of Shakespeare*, 1915, p. 442.

> they shall pay thee well . . . *I warrant thee.* E1 verso.
>
> *I warrant you*, sir. E1 verso.
>
> I'll bail him, *I warrant thee.* E2 recto.
>
> had we not been parted, I had taught ye a little school play, *I warrant ye.* E3 verso.
>
> *Souns*, King Harry ! E3 verso.
>
> *Souns*, I shall to Tyburn presently. E4 recto.
>
> Ye never knew fool a flatterer, *I warrant ye.* F1 verso.
>
> it should ne'er have been brought for Will, *I warrant ye.* F3 recto.
>
> 'Tis not your fool, my lord, *I warrant ye.* F3 verso.
>
> *O brave !* he looks like the mirror of knighthood. G3 recto.
>
> all the horses i' th' town cannot haul him into thy presence, *I warrant thee.* K3 verso.
>
> Wine . . . able to set a colour in any man's face, *I warrant it.* K3 verso.
>
> *I warrant you*, Madam. L3 recto.

Notwithstanding the external evidence that associates Rowley with the additions to *Faustus*, it will hardly do to rely entirely upon words and phrases so commonplace as these for our corroborative evidence. But other internal marks are not lacking. For one, we have 'as passes', already noticed in all the other plays. Here it is twice used by Will Summers :

> but I'll tell thee cousin the rarest trick to be revenged *as 't passes.* Sig. C4 recto.
>
> thou hast made all the court in such a pitiful case *as passes.* C4 verso.

and 'you had best' is here too (Will Summers to the King, Sig. C4 recto) :

> *ye had best* be friends with us I can tell you : we'll scare ye out of your skin else.

and 'let me alone' :

> *let my cousin Patch and I alone*, and he go boxing. C3 verso.

reminding us of Henry V in *The Famous Victories*, with his :

> Well, if the villains come, let me alone with them.

One may also notice ' hard at hand ' :

> His majesty is *hard at hand*, my Lord. L1 recto.

since this occurs twice in *A Shrew* :

> my master 's *hard at hand* and my new mistress and all.
> III. i. 2.
>
> you had best get supper ready against they come, for they be *hard at hand*, I am sure, by this time.
> III. i. 17–19.

as well as in the 1616 additions to *Faustus* :

> The sleepy cardinals are *hard at hand*. 1004.

But to put the matter beyond doubt it will be enough to compare these passages from the additions to *Faustus* :

> an my Master come, he'll conjure you i'faith. 806.
>
> . . . and he follow us, I'll so conjure him as he was never so conjured in his life, I warrant him. 960–1 (p. 208).

with this speech of Will Summers, addressed to Patch, Cardinal Wolsey's fool (*When You See Me*, Sig. C4 recto) :

> . . . an thou wert the devil himself he'll conjure thee I warrant thee, I would not have such a conjuring for twenty crowns.[1]

or his reply to the Countess of Salisbury's threat to thrust him out of the presence-chamber (B2 verso) :

> Thrust me, nay and ye go to thrusting, I'll thrust some of you down, I warrant ye.

The additions to Doctor Faustus are written partly in prose and partly in quite respectable blank verse, altogether superior to that of *The Famous Victories*. The prose passages (for the most part sheer buffoonery) having been traced to Rowley, and Birde having also received payment for the additions made in 1602, it is natural to infer that the more

[1] Cf. Dericke in *The Famous Victories* : ' (Give) A Judge a box on the ear, I'll tell thee, John. . . . I would not have done it for twenty shillings.' (B4 recto.)

decorous verse additions were contributed by Birde. But a division that would allot all the verse to Birde and the prose alone to Rowley would not be correct, for the marks of Rowley's hand are as apparent in the verse as in the prose. One need not look beyond the text of the additions for presumptive evidence of the presence of the same hand in both. I have already drawn attention to the expression 'to clap horns on the head' (ed. Tucker Brooke, p. 196, line 808) in the prose, and shown cause for assigning it to Rowley. It appears again not only in another prose passage (p. 214, line 1171) but also in the verse (p. 203, line 885):

> To beat the beads about the friars' pates
> Or *clap huge horns upon the Cardinals' heads.*

But a comparison of the verse additions with the verse of *When You See Me You Know Me* will remove any doubt on the subject. The expanded passages of the revised text of *Faustus* dealing with the visit of Faustus to the Pope at Rome show the same fiercely anti-papal spirit as is manifested in many of the blank verse scenes of *When You See Me*, and they are couched in the same sort of language. In both plays we find repeated allusions to the Pope's 'triple crown' and to 'St. Peter's Chair'; in both we find lines with dactylic endings such as these:

> The which, in state and high solemnity,
> This day is held through Rome and Italy,
> In honour of the Pope's triumphant victory.
> *Faustus*, 1616, 854–6.
>
> In quittance of their late conspiracy
> Against our state and papal dignity.
> *Ibid.*, 971–2.
>
> False prelates, for this hateful treachery,
> Curst be your souls to hellish misery.
> *Ibid.*, 1055–6.
>
> He sends me thus to greet thy majesty
> With stile and titles of high dignity.
> *When You See Me*, D1 recto.
>
> The villain thinks to smooth his treachery,
> By fawning speeches to our majesty.
> *Ibid.*, I1 recto.

You are accused of high conspiracy
And treason 'gainst his royal majesty.
Ibid., I4 recto.

We get also resemblances of this kind :

Twelve reverend bishops are sent post to Rome.
When You, &c., A2 recto.

. . . our elected Pope
That on a fury's back came post from Rome.
Faustus, 1012–13 (p. 210).

Both which [Cardinals] if Wolsey be made Pope of Rome,
Shall be made famous through all Christendom.
When You, &c., A2 verso.

Thou shalt be famous through all Italy,
And honour'd of the German emperor.
Faustus, 1067–8 (p. 211).

Note also the trick of placing polysyllabic adjectives ending in 'al' after the nouns that they qualify :

. . . his holiness ascends
Saint Peter's chair and *state pontifical.*
Faustus, 891–2 (p. 203).

And by *authority apostolical*
Depose him from his regal government.
Ibid., 945–6 (p. 205).

Make haste again, my good Lord Cardinals,
And take our *blessing apostolical.*
Ibid., 994–5 (p. 206).

We would behold that famous conqueror,
Great Alexander and his paramour,
In their true shapes and *state majestical.*
Ibid., 1083–5 (p. 211).

And compare :

. . . see all our train be set in readiness
That in our *state and pomp pontifical*
We may pass on to grace King Henry's court.
When You, &c., A3 recto.

But we shall cross him for 't, I doubt it not,
And tread upon his *pomp imperial.*
Ibid., F1 recto.

. . . from his sacred lips
I bring a *blessing apostolical.* *Ibid.*, D1 recto.

The which, without your majesty's consent,
Is *treason capital* against the crown.
Ibid., I1 recto.

Birde's share in the *Faustus* alterations is, I think, confined to those made in the closing scenes of the play.[1] The presence of a hand other than Rowley's is suggested by the frequent use of antithesis, e. g.:

. . . now sword strike home,
For horns he gave, I'll have his head anon.
Faustus, 1214–15 (p. 215).

We'll rather die with grief than live with shame.
113 (p. 217).

And so have hope that this my kind rebuke,
Checking thy body, may amend thy soul.
1283–4 (p. 226).

His store of pleasures must be sauc'd with pain.
1364 (p. 227).

Why weep'st thou? 'tis too late, despair, farewell!
Fools that will laugh on earth must weep in hell.
1429–30 (p. 228).

To want in hell that had on earth such store.
1439 (p. 228).

No similar bent for antithesis is traceable in *When You See Me*, and a habit of this kind once acquired is not easily abandoned.[2]

We have now traced the hand of Samuel Rowley in three plays, and with these and his named play to guide us we get a clear idea of the kind of work that he produced. We find him the sole author of two quasi-historical dramas, in both of which, though separated from one another by at least ten years, the clown is the most important figure, or at

[1] His hand first appears after the stage-direction 'Enter Benvolio, Martino, Frederick, and soldiers', p. 214 of Tucker Brooke's edition of Marlowe's works (Act IV, sc. ii, of Robinson's and Cunningham's editions).

[2] Note also that, simultaneously with the appearance of these antitheses, we find rimed couplets interspersed in the blank verse. Rowley employs the terminal couplet in his independent play, but does not mix rime and blank verse lines together.

least is elevated to a position of equal prominence with that of the monarch the events of whose reign the author professes to portray. We find him again in *The Taming of a Shrew* devoting himself chiefly to the sayings and doings of clowns and servants, leaving the serious scenes involving the fortunes of the well-bred ladies and gentlemen of Athens to his assistant. Quite early in his career Rowley must have earned a reputation for his clowns, and it was doubtless for this reason that Henslowe selected him to rewrite and expand the clowning scenes of *Faustus*. That 'tragical history' was evidently too gloomy to please Henslowe and his patrons, and Rowley was the very man to enliven it with such matter as would, to use Heywood's words, 'breed in the less capable mirth and laughter', lest the auditory should be dulled with serious courses which are merely weighty and material'.[1] At any rate, quite three-fourths of Rowley's share in the additions are pure clowning: what he provides is more patter for Tom and Dick, more diverting escapades and mishaps of the carter and horse-courser.

We have good reason for inferring that Rowley was regarded by his contemporaries—by contemporary audiences at least—as the comic dramatist *par excellence* of the last decade of the sixteenth century and the first few years of the seventeenth. We have evidence that he was employed as an improviser of clowning scenes many years before Henslowe set him to work on Marlowe's play. Some time before 1594 he had added to Greene's *Orlando Furioso* in the same way, for his hand is plainly apparent in the earliest extant text published in that year.[2] It is again in

[1] 'It may be objected why, amongst sad and grave histories, I have here and there inserted fabulous tales and jests, savouring of lightness. I answer, I have therein imitated our historical and comical poets that write to the stage; who, lest the auditory should be dulled with serious courses, which are merely weighty and material, in every act present some zany, with his mimic action, to breed in the less capable mirth and laughter: for they that write to all must strive to please all.' Thomas Heywood, *The General Historie of Women*, 1624.

[2] I have to thank Mr. J. Dover Wilson (who read in manuscript

the comic prose passages that it appears. Rowley's additions to this play are not extensive, but it is surprising to find what a number of marks he has left upon them. There are none in the verse, which is presumably entirely Greene's. The two passages of prose dialogue in the first two acts (Orgalio and Sacripant in I. i, Orgalio and Orlando in II. i) doubtless also belong to the original text, since neither bears any definite trace of Rowley. Nor is there any clear suggestion of his hand in the Orgalio and Orlando dialogue with which the third act opens. But immediately after Orgalio's exit [1] we come upon the words 'Enter two clowns' and there follows a prose passage of some twenty lines. This is Rowley's.

The clowns are Tom and Ralph. Tom begins with 'Sirrah Ralph, an thou'lt go with me, I'll let thee see the bravest madman that ever thou sawest'. This reminds us of Sly in the Epilogue of *A Shrew*: 'Oh, lord, sirrah, I have had the bravest dream tonight that ever thou heardest in all thy life.' It is enough at least to raise suspicion. Ralph now tells Tom a story of Orlando coming to his house and stealing the meat roasting before the fire, and Tom observes:

> By my troth, that was brave: but, sirrah, he did so *course* the boys last Sunday; and if ye call him madman he'll . . . tickle your ribs so with his flap of leather that he hath, *as it passeth*.

At this point they spy Orlando, and shout 'madman', for which they are soundly beaten. Orlando tells them that they must be his soldiers and fight against Medor, and Ralph breaks in with:

> Yes, *let me alone with him* for a bloody nose.

Wherever the clowns Tom and Ralph appear we find the marks of Rowley's hand. In the next scene (III. ii) they come in with the mad Orlando armed 'with spits and

my notes on the other plays dealt with in this paper) for calling my attention to these additions to *Orlando Furioso*.

[1] J. C. Collins's edition of Greene, vol. i, p. 247; 'Mermaid' edition, p. 198.

dripping pans’. ‘Back, soldiers,’ cries Orlando, ‘look where the enemy is.’ ‘Captain,’ exclaims Tom, ‘they have a woman amongst them.’ ‘What of that?’ asks Orlando. ‘Why,’ says Tom, ‘strike you down the men, and then *let me alone* to thrust in the woman.’ Tom makes his escape during the fight that ensues, but he re-enters with Orgalio before the close of the scene, disguised as Angelica. Orgalio warns Tom not to laugh. ‘No, *I warrant you*,’ replies Tom, ‘but I think *I had best* go back and shave my beard.’ ‘My lord,’ says Orgalio, introducing him to Orlando, ‘here is Angelica,’ and Orlando answers:

> Mass, thou saist true, ’tis she indeed.

The next scene in which Tom figures is IV. ii. This time he enters as a fiddler. Orlando, in a passage that reminds us of the scene of the music-lesson in *A Shrew*, breaks his fiddle about his head. The dialogue here is just in the vein of the comic dialogue of *A Shrew*, though it is not easy to point to any definite suggestion of Rowley, apart from a solitary ‘Tush, I warrant thee’ from Orgalio. There is also one ‘souns’ from Orlando a little later on, after Melissa's entry:

> Souns, Orgalio, why sufferest thou this old trot to come so nigh me?

The ‘I warrant thee’ and ‘souns’ test is, it must be confessed, of little use here. But when Orlando exclaims:

> What? be all the Trojans fled?
> Then give me some drink,

we again hear the voice of the thirsty tinker of *A Shrew*:

> Are they run away, Sim? That ’s well: then gi ’s some more drink.

Though Rowley may have given a few touches to some of the later speeches, the rest of the text, after the point where Orlando falls asleep, is substantially Greene's.

There is yet another anonymous play in which Rowley was concerned, and that is the comedy *Wily Beguiled*, first printed in 1606, but probably written several years earlier.

Here once more we have a piece almost certainly the work of two authors, scenes of realistic prose being interspersed with passages of incongruously high-flown verse. The prose scenes, in which the chief figures are Gripe, a usurer, Churms, a lawyer, Peter Plod-all, and Will Cricket, constitute Rowley's part of the play. It is curious that his partner, whose verse is much like that of the poet of *The Taming of a Shrew*, borrows from Kyd's tragedies almost as flagrantly as the latter does from Marlowe's.[1] This circumstance long ago suggested to my mind the possibility that the verse parts of these plays might be from the same hand. A further examination of the text of *Wily Beguiled* prompted by the discovery of Rowley's authorship of the prose has yielded unexpected confirmation of the accuracy of this conclusion; the evidence in its support being, indeed, so strong that it is scarcely to be resisted. Apart from the general resemblance in the style of the verse, both plays are full of classical allusions, and of classical allusions whose unsuitability to the context in which they are used immediately strikes the reader. They are as out of place as gold lace on a suit of homespun. But this is not all. Many of the allusions are the same, and some are introduced in the same fashion—in identical, or almost identical, words. Nor are the parallelisms between the plays confined to classical allusions, as will be seen from my quotations:

(1) *Wily Beguiled*, Hazlitt-Dodsley, ix. 248:

Churms. He mews her up as men do mew their hawks;
And so restrains her from her Sophos' sight.

A Shrew, III. i. 47–8:

Ferando. I'll mew her up as men do mew their hawks,
And make her gently come unto the lure.

[1] Compare especially *Wily Beguiled*, 'Hazlitt's Dodsley', vol. ix, p. 235, line 22, and *The Spanish Tragedy* (Kyd's Works, ed. Boas), I. ii. 83; *W. B.*, p. 247, line 9, and *Soliman and Perseda*, III. ii, 27; *W. B.*, p. 278, line 5, and *S. T.*, I. i. 66; *W. B.*, p. 281, 19, *S. T.*, II. iii. 7, and *S. & P.*, I. ii. 2; *W. B.*, p. 282, 18, and *S. & P.*, II, ii, 73–4; *W. B.*, p. 282, 25, and *S. T.*, I. i. 13; *W. B.*, p. 286, 5, and *S. T.*, III. ii. 3; *W. B.*, p. 286, 25–6, and *S. T.*, II. iii. 45; *W. B.*, p. 287, 1–2, and *S. T.*, III. ii. 37–8.

(2) *Wily Beguiled*, p. 298:

Churms. Ere I would wrong my love by one day's absence
I would pass the boiling Hellespont
As once Leander did for Hero's love.

A Shrew, III. vi. 35–8:

Philema. And should my love, as erst Leander did,
Attempt to pass the boiling Hellespont
For Hero's love, no towers of brass should hold,
But I would follow through those raging floods.

(3) *Wily Beguiled*, p. 306:

Sophos. Yet would I pass the burning vaults of Ork [1]
As erst did Hercules to fetch his love.

A Shrew, III. vi. 28–9:

Emelia. And should my love, as erst did Hercules,
Attempt to pass the burning vaults of hell.

(4) *Wily Beguiled*, p. 313:

Fortunatus. Now rests nought but my father's free consent
To knit the knot that time can ne'er untwist.

Ibid., p. 313:

To work his will to knit this Gordian knot.

A Shrew, III. vi. 72–5:

Polidor. And at the church your father and the rest
Do stay to see our marriage rites performed,
And knit in sight of heaven this Gordian knot,
That teeth of fretting time may ne'er untwist.

(5) *Wily Beguiled*, p. 328:

Sophos. The love of Lelia is to me more dear,
Than is the kingdom, or the richest crown
That e'er adorned the temples of a king.

A Shrew, II. i. 130–2:

Ferando. . . . as richly wrought
As was the massy robe that late adorned
The stately legate of the Persian king.

[1] Cf. 'Orcus' burning gulf'. *Tamburlaine*, Pt. II, ii. 3.

These parallels seem to me to be altogether different in character from those between *The Taming of a Shrew* and the dramas of Marlowe, or between *Wily Beguiled* and those of Kyd, which clearly imply plagiarism. And the inference of identity of authorship is borne out by a comparison of the vocabularies of *A Shrew* and *Wily Beguiled*, which reveals the presence of numbers of words and phrases common to the two plays, as in the following lines, the first in each case being from *Wily Beguiled* and the second from *A Shrew*:

(*a*) And sound the depth of all their *plotted drifts*. P. 269.
By whom we must comprise our *plotted drift*. III. ii. 31.
(*b*) *The senseless trees* do grieve at my laments. P. 277.
The senseless trees by music have been moved. II. i. 1.
(*c*) That with shrill notes and high resounding voice
Doth pierce the very *caverns of the earth*. P. 278.
To undermine the *caverns of the earth*. II. i. 78.
(*d*) That thou forgett'st the *lasting league of love*,
Long since was vow'd betwixt thyself and me. P. 281.
We will confirm these *leagues of lasting love*. III. iv. 64.
(*e*) That he may think she *loves him as her life*. P. 286.
She 's willing, sir, and *loves me as her life*. I. i. 161.
(*f*) What *frantic fit* possess'd my foolish brain? P. 323.
. . . vouchsafe
To look on me and leave these *frantic fits*. Ind., ii. 40.
(*g*) Thou *great commander* of the circled orbs. P. 329.
. . . the *great commander* of the world. V. i. 126.

There is one identity of phrase that deserves special notice. Marlowe in Part I of his *Tamburlaine* (III. ii. 19) refers to the moon as 'Phoebe's silver eye':

Eternal heaven sooner be dissolv'd
And all that pierceth Phoebe's silver eye
Before such hap fall to Zenocrate.

The poet of *A Shrew*, substituting the name 'Polidor' for 'Zenocrate', repeats the rest of this passage verbatim, except that Marlowe's 'Phoebe's silver eye' becomes 'Phoebus' silver eye'. This *may* be a mistake either on the part of the plagiarist or of his printer, as Dr. Boas assumes, but there is an excellent reason for believing that it is not, or at any rate that the author of *A Shrew* wrote ' Phoebus' silver eye ' deliberately, assuming that Marlowe was alluding, not to the moon, but to the sun.[1] The poet of *Wily Beguiled*, who, as we have seen, uses so many of the allusions and phrases found in *A Shrew*, twice speaks of ' Phoebus' silver eye ', and—inappropriate as the adjective ' silver ' becomes in its altered application—on neither occasion does he allow us to remain in any doubt that he is referring to the sun. In one passage (p. 265) he has :

I swear by Sol, fair Phoebus' silver eye.

and in another (p. 310) :

Now Phoebus' silver eye is drench'd in western deep,
And Luna 'gins to show her splendent rays.

No doubt the discovery of connexions between the prose parts of *Wily Beguiled* and *A Shrew*, and also between the verse of these plays, seems to favour the conclusion that the complete text of both plays is the work of a single author. I am, however, convinced that when these plays are considered in the light of the evidence of Rowley's authorship of *The Famous Victories* and *When You See Me* such a conclusion is impossible.

So far as Rowley's authorship of the prose scenes of *Wily Beguiled* is concerned, I was first led to suspect this by the constant occurrence of ' I warrant thee and ' I warrant ye '. It is even commoner here than in any of the other plays, occurring altogether twenty times—always in the prose. ' O brave ' is absent, but ' Zounds ' is introduced ten times. During the course of a dialogue between the Nurse and the scholar Sophos (Hazlitt-Dodsley, ix. 284), the former, speaking of her mistress Lelia, says to Sophos, ' she leads such a life for you, *it passes* '. There are links with the prose of *A Shrew* just of the same sort as those already noted in *The Famous Victories*. ' I swear . . . that I could get her as soon as he myself,' says Will Cricket in

[1] Strangely enough, the 1605 edition of Marlowe's play also substitutes ' Phoebus ' for ' Phoebes '.

Wily Beguiled (p. 244), speaking of Peter Plod-all's wooing of Lelia, 'And if I had not a month's mind in another place, *I would have a fling at her*, that 's flat.' In *A Shrew* (II. ii) Sander, speaking of Emelia, says to Polidor's boy, 'If I thought thy master would not have her, *I'd have a fling at her* myself.' 'I'll see soon whether 'twill be a match or no,' Sander continues, 'and it will not, *I'll set the matter hard for myself, I warrant thee*'; and in *Wily Beguiled* Robin Goodfellow advises Peter Plod-all how to get into Lelia's good graces (p. 256): 'Tell her thou hast a good stock, some hundred or two a year, and *that will set her hard, I warrant thee.*'

At another point in the play (p. 270) Mother Midnight enters to find Peg alone with Will Cricket. 'What mak'st thou here in this twatter light?' she says to Peg, 'I think thou'rt in a dream; I think the fool haunts thee.' In a voice whose accents have by this time become familiar, Will Cricket replies:

> Zounds, fool in your face! Fool? O monstrous intitulation! Fool? O disgrace to my person! Zounds, fool not me, for I cannot brook such a cold rasher, I can tell thee.

It can scarcely be necessary to give further proof of Rowley's hand, but it is perhaps worth adding that when Will Cricket acknowledges Mother Midnight's attempt to soothe his injured feelings with

> Well, your good words have something laid my choler,

he uses all but exactly the same words as those with which, in *A Shrew*, Polidor's boy brings his quarrel with Sander to a close (II. ii. 50–1):

> Well, sirrah, your fair words hath something alaid my choler.

How does the attribution of this fresh work to Rowley fit in with what is already known of his career? It dates the commencement of his dramatic authorship back to a period certainly eight, possibly twelve or thirteen, years before we find any mention of him as a playwright. There is no record of him as such in Henslowe's diary until December 1601, when he and Birde were paid £6 for a play called *Judas*, no longer extant, though his name occurs in the diary more than four years before this, on the 3rd of August 1597, as witness of a loan by the playhouse manager to 'John Helle, the clown'. *The Famous Victories*, though not printed before 1598, was entered in the Stationers' Register on the 14th of May 1594, the first performance recorded by Henslowe being on the 28th of November 1595. It was acted by the Admiral's men, the company to which Rowley belonged. It is stated that Tarlton acted the part of Dericke,[1] and Tarlton died in September 1588. *The Taming of a Shrew* was entered in the Register just twelve days before *The Famous Victories*, on the 2nd of May 1594, and performed in the following month by the Admiral's and Chamberlain's men. The play was printed in the same year 'as it was sundry times acted by the Earl of Pembroke his servants', and it is usually assumed that it was from them that the Admiral's and Chamberlain's men acquired it, since it is known that in September 1593 Pembroke's company was in such straits that it was driven to pawn its wardrobe. There is presumptive evidence that *A Shrew* was written in or about 1590, since the author of the verse parts, while borrowing freely from the two parts of Marlowe's *Tamburlaine* (*c.* 1587–8) and from *Doctor Faustus* (*c.* 1589), makes no use of his later works, *The Jew of Malta* and *Edward II*, probably composed in 1590 and 1591 respectively. The earliest extant edition of *Orlando Furioso* is also dated 1594, but though there is no record of any earlier edition, the play was entered in the Register on the 7th of December 1593, and Henslowe records a performance by the combined Admiral's and

[1] The authority for the statement is *Tarlton's Jests* (1611) where ('An excellent jest of Tarlton's suddenly spoken') it is recorded that 'At the Bull at Bishops-gate was a play of Henry the fift, wherein the Judge was to take a box on the eare' and that 'because he was absent that should take the blow, Tarlton himselfe (ever forward to please) tooke upon him to play the same Judge, besides his owne part of the Clowne.'

Strange's companies on the 21st of February 1592. Moreover, in 1592, the author of *The Defence of Conny-Catching* taunted Greene with having sold the play twice over, first to the Queen's players for twenty nobles, and then, when they were in the country, to the Admiral's men for a like sum. It was no doubt for the Admiral's men that Rowley altered it, in or shortly after 1592. *Wily Beguiled* is probably later, for the verse seems to show the influence of Kyd's *Soliman and Perseda* (*c.* 1592). The character both of the prose and of the blank verse suggests a date before the end of the sixteenth century, say 1595 or a year or two earlier.[1] Next comes the first dramatic work of Rowley's mentioned in Henslowe's diary, the non-extant *Judas*, which (as already stated) was written in conjunction with Birde and completed in December 1601. In September 1602 this was followed by another lost play recorded by Henslowe, *Joshua*, for which Rowley received £7. Two months later we have the additions to Marlowe's *Faustus*, in the composition of which Rowley was again assisted by Birde. Finally we come to the sole play published under Rowley's name, *When You See Me You Know Me*, printed, as we have seen, in 1605, and obviously written not long after the *Faustus* additions. The chronological order of Rowley's writings for the stage would therefore appear to be as under, it being understood that the dates are in some instances conjectural only :

The Famous Victories of Henry V	*c.* 1588
The Taming of a Shrew (with an unknown author)	*c.* 1590
Additions to Greene's *Orlando Furioso* . .	1592
Wily Beguiled (with unknown author) . .	*c.* 1595
Judas (with Birde ; not extant)	1601
Joshua (not extant)	1602
Additions to Marlowe's *Faustus* (with Birde) .	1602
When You See Me You Know Me	*c.* 1604

[1] It is not necessary to assume that the Lelia-Sophos dialogue beginning 'In such a night did Paris win his love' (Hazlitt-Dodsley, p. 314) is an imitation of the Lorenzo-Jessica dialogue in *The Merchant of Venice*, v. i. Shakespeare may have been the borrower, or the two passages may derive from a common source.

I do not include in this list *The Noble Soldier* (printed in 1634 as by S. R.) because I doubt the correctness of its attribution to Rowley, a close scrutiny of its text having failed to reveal any suggestion of its author's identity with the author of *When You See Me* or of the work here assigned to Rowley on internal grounds.

The years that elapsed between Rowley's early work on *The Taming of a Shrew* and *The Famous Victories of Henry V* on the one hand, and his additions to *Faustus* and the Henry VIII play on the other, show a great improvement in his literary technique. Nevertheless, Sander in *The Taming of a Shrew* is far his most valuable legacy to the English stage. It was clearly as a creator of clowns that Rowley excelled, but neither Will Cricket nor Will Summers—still less Dericke or the tiresome buffoons that disfigure Marlowe's play—are worthy to rank with Sander. But for Sander we should have had no Grumio. And it is well to remember that it is to the hand that created Sander, almost as much as to Shakespeare's, that we owe *The Taming of the Shrew*. 'All the force and humour alike of character and situation', to quote the words of Swinburne,[1] 'belong to Shakespeare's eclipsed and forlorn precursor; he [Shakespeare] has added nothing; he has tempered and enriched everything', and he continues: 'that the luckless author of the first sketch is like to remain a man as nameless as the deed of the witches in Macbeth, unless some chance or caprice of accident should suddenly flash favouring light on his now impersonal and indiscoverable individuality, seems clear enough when we take into account the double and final disproof of his imaginary identity with Marlowe which Mr. Dyce has put forward. . . . He is a clumsy and coarse-fingered plagiarist from that poet, and his stolen jewels of expression look so grossly out of place in the homely setting of his usual style that they seem transmuted from real to sham. On the other hand he is of all the pre-Shakespeareans known to us incomparably the truest, the richest, the most powerful and original humorist; one

[1] *A Study of Shakespeare*, p. 124.

indeed without a second on that ground for " the rest are nowhere ".'

If I am right, the eclipsed and forlorn precursor of Shakespeare to whom Swinburne has paid so handsome a tribute is Samuel Rowley ; it is he who is the powerful and original humorist, the 'man of real if rough genius for comedy', but he is not the clumsy plagiarist from Marlowe. On reflection it is indeed rather strange that it should have been supposed that qualities so diverse could be united in one person—that the same man should have been at once an original humorist and a servile plagiarist, a writer of rough realistic prose and of polished artificial verse.

1918.

III

PEELE'S 'ALPHONSUS, EMPEROR OF GERMANY'

The *Tragedy of Alphonsus, Emperor of Germany* was published by Humphrey Moseley in 1654 as Chapman's. It was in the same year that the publisher Richard Marriot fraudulently issued Glapthorne's *Revenge for Honour* with the same author's name on the title-page. That both these dramas should ever since the date of their publication continue—even though more or less diffidently—to have been associated with Chapman's name affords a striking illustration of the tendency of critics to cling to the most dubious scrap of external evidence as to the authorship of an Elizabethan play, notwithstanding that the internal evidence is altogether against it. The attribution of a late publisher alone ought never to be accepted in the absence of corroborative internal evidence. And there is particular reason that Moseley's testimony should be regarded with suspicion, for, if not deliberately dishonest, he was at any rate utterly reckless in his attributions. It was he who ascribed Massinger's *Parliament of Love* to Rowley and *The Merry Devil of Edmonton* (to say nothing of the non-extant *History of King Stephen, Duke Humphrey*, and *Iphis and Ianthe*) to Shakespeare.

Now nothing can be more certain, if internal evidence counts for anything at all, than that Chapman could not possibly have been the author of *Alphonsus, Emperor of Germany*. In no respect does the play resemble any authentic work of his. Just as *Revenge for Honour* betrays its late date in the abundance of its feminine endings and its clear traces of the influence of the 'Beaumont and Fletcher' plays, so the end-stopped lines and archaic phrasing and vocabulary of *Alphonsus* clearly show that it belongs to a date within a few years of 1590. The construction 'for to' with the infinitive, which is to be found four times in this play, and the use of the words 'the same' in place of a pronoun—

Julio Lentulus
. . . . Gave me this box of poison,
. . . And what 's the special virtue of the same?
Act I (Pearson's Chapman, vol. iii, p. 204).[1]

Come, Princes, let us bear the body hence,
I'll spend a million to embalm the same.
Act IV (p. 260).

—are sure marks of an early date. Then again we have a sequence of lines ending on the word 'revenge' (Act V, p. 273), as in *The Spanish Tragedy* and *Locrine*, and speeches of which the first line echoes the last of the preceding speaker:

Alphonsus. Thou wilt not scorn my counsel in revenge?
Alexander. My rage admits no counsel but revenge.
Act II, p. 222.

Empress. Doubt not the Princes may be reconcil'd.
Alexander. 'T may be the Princes will be reconcil'd.
Act V, p. 275.

These features are characteristic of the pre-Shakespearean drama of Marlowe, Greene, and Peele, and are deserving of notice inasmuch as those who accept Chapman's authorship of *Alphonsus* invariably assume it to be one of the latest of his works.

Alphonsus is a Machiavellian revenge-play clearly showing the influence both of Marlowe and Kyd. The style is neither that of Marlowe nor of Kyd, but the author is obviously one who followed closely in their steps. All the internal evidence, as has already been indicated, and will presently appear more fully, points to 1590 or thereabouts as the date at which it was originally composed. And as it happens, there actually is external evidence, certainly not less trustworthy than Moseley's, that it was written by a dramatist of this very period. Kirkman (1661), Winstanley (1687), and Wood (1691) all state that its author was Peele. The

[1] All subsequent references to *Alphonsus, Emperor of Germany* are by the pages of this edition.

diversity of opinion amongst the early biographers of the English dramatists with regard to the authorship of this play has not received the attention it deserves. Peele's modern editors do not even trouble to record that it has been ascribed to him. It must be admitted that Kirkman is no more trustworthy than Moseley, but his statement is at least valuable as showing that *Alphonsus* was reputed Peele's although it had been published as Chapman's only seven years previously. When we turn to Winstanley (*Lives of the most famous English Poets*) we find that he mentions *Alphonsus* as one of the 'three plays' that Peele 'contributed to the stage', the two others being *Edward I* and *David and Bethsabe.* Next comes Langbaine (*Account of the English Dramatick Poets*, 1691), who, like Winstanley, only mentions *Edward I* and *David and Bethsabe* of the dramas now assigned to Peele, but adds :

> 'I am not ignorant that another tragedy, to wit, *Alphonsus Emperor of Germany*, is ascribed to him in former Catalogues, which has occasioned Mr Winstanley's mistake, but I can assure my Readers that that Play was writ by Chapman, *for I have it by me with his Name affixt to it.*'

That Langbaine had a copy of the play with Chapman's name affixed to it is no proof that Chapman wrote it. His copy was doubtless one of Moseley's edition of 1654. However, the editors of the *Biographia Dramatica* seem to have considered Langbaine's statement conclusive, for they assert that both Winstanley and Wood were 'misled by former catalogues'. Even supposing the conjecture as to the source of their information to be correct, the former catalogues are, as Mr. Fleay has observed, a better authority than Moseley. But there is no ground for supposing that either Winstanley or Wood was indebted to former catalogues, and so far as Anthony à Wood is concerned, his own words seem to negative any such supposition. As his is the fullest and most accurate of these early biographical notices of Peele, it will be well to see exactly what he says :

'. . . His comedies and tragedies were often acted with

great applause, and did endure reading with due commendation many years after their Author's death. *Those that I have seen are only these following,*

The famous Chronicle of K. *Ed. I* sirnamed *Edw. Longshank.* Life of *Llewellin of Wales.* } Lond. 1593, qu.

The sinking of *Q. Elinor* at *Charing-cross* and of her rising again at *Potters-Hith,* now named *Queen-Hith, Lond.* 1593, qu. . . .

The love of *K. David* and fair *Bathsheba,* with the Tragedy of *Absalom,* &c. *Lond.* 1599, qu.

Alphonsus Emperor of Germany, Trag.

Besides these Plays he hath several Poems extant, as that entit. *The Honour of the Garter,* vide *Ashmolean,* p. 30.

A farewell to Sir *Joh. Norrys* and Sir *Fr. Drake,* Lond. in qu. and some remnants of Pastoral Poetry in a collection entit. *England's Helicon* ; but such I have not seen ; nor his book of *Jests* or *Clinches.* . . .'

Athenae Oxonienses (1721, vol. i, 300).

Here Wood makes the definite statement that *Alphonsus, Emperor of Germany* was one of the tragedies of Peele *that he had seen*—presumably in manuscript with the dramatist's name attached, since he does not (as in the case of the other plays seen by him) specify the place and date of publication, nor is there any reason to believe that a printed edition other than Moseley's edition of 1654 (with Chapman's name on the title-page) existed in Wood's time. All the other works enumerated in his list are properly assigned to Peele, and in the absence of some better evidence to the contrary than that of Moseley (clearly not a disinterested witness) we are not justified in assuming that he was mistaken with regard to *Alphonsus.* That its attribution to Peele was due to mere conjecture on any one's part is most unlikely. Its superficial characteristics are rather those that one would associate with Marlowe or Kyd in preference to Peele. But when its language is examined and compared with Peele's acknowledged works we shall find conclusive evidence —and that of a kind which cannot be supposed to have attracted the attention of any seventeenth-century writer or compiler of catalogues—that it is his.

Fleay accepts Peele's authorship of *Alphonsus, Emperor of*

Germany because it was attributed to him by Wood and Winstanley and is 'palpably' of his period. These circumstances are at least sufficient to warrant us in preferring Peele's title to Chapman's. If, in addition, we find that the author's vocabulary resembles Peele's, and that the text of the play shows numerous connexions of one sort or another with his acknowledged work, there can be no valid reason for doubting his authorship.

Up to the present the only critic who has dealt with the internal indications of Peele's hand in this play is Mr. J. M. Robertson, to whose chapter on 'Peele's Unsigned Work' in *Did Shakespeare write Titus Andronicus?* I here acknowledge my indebtedness for a few of the points noted in the following examination of its text. To take first its vocabulary, Mr. Robertson gives a list of eighteen of Peele's 'favourite or special' words met with in *Alphonsus*. These are: Até, doom, emperess, gratulate, hugy, manly, massacre, policy, progeny, sacred, sacrifice, solemnized, successively, suspect (noun), triúmph and triúmphing, underbear, wreak (noun), and zodiac. Now, without exaggerating the significance of this list, it may without hesitation be stated that it raises a strong presumption of Peele's authorship. It is not that the words are peculiar to Peele. There are a few that are rarely to be met with outside Peele's works—such, for instance, as 'wreak' used as a substantive—and are for that reason important, while others are used fairly frequently by some of his contemporaries. But even these less uncommon words may afford equally valuable evidence either from the frequency with which, or the manner in which, they are used. It is not necessary to deal with this list of Mr. Robertson's in detail, but the word 'sacred' is deserving of particular notice because it occurs no fewer than ten times in *Alphonsus*. In one instance the author—in a fashion, it may be remarked, characteristic of Peele—actually uses it twice in the space of four lines. This is in the speech in which Alphonsus simulates grief at the death of the Bishop of Mentz:

> Over thy tomb shall hang a sacred lamp,
> Which till the day of doom shall ever burn,

Yea after-ages shall speak of thy renown,
And go a pilgrimage to thy sacred tomb.
Act IV, p. 260.

In Peele's acknowledged works 'sacred' appears, according to Mr. Robertson, at least thirty times. At any rate I have found it five times in *The Arraignment of Paris* alone, and ten times in his not very voluminous poems.

Another special word of Peele's found in *Alphonsus* but not mentioned in Mr. Robertson's list, is 'scour' = to pass swiftly over, to overrun in search of a thing or person:

. . . we both with our light horse
Will scour the coasts and quickly bring him in.
Alphonsus, Act V. p. 278.

This occurs twice in *Edward I*:

And scour the marches with your Welshmen's hooks.
ii. 357.[1]
. . . methinks 'twere very good
That some good fellows went and scoured the wood.
x. 92.

and in *The Tale of Troy*, l. 255:

Now merrily sail these gallant Greeks to Troy
And scour the seas, and keep their compass right.

Peele is notably diffuse in his style, often using two or three almost synonymous verbs or adjectives in conjunction, and obviously employing words or phrases merely for the purpose of filling up a line. As an illustration of this we may note the addition of the superfluous words 'in the (this, that) cause' at the end of a line:

Then may I speak my conscience in the cause.
The Battle of Alcazar, II. ii. 22.
Your wisdoms would be silent in that cause.
Edward I, xxv. 61.

Other examples might be quoted from *The Arraignment of Paris*. I cannot find that this trick is characteristic of any

[1] For all Peele's works, except where otherwise indicated, I have used Bullen's edition, the Arabic numerals here referring to the numbers of the lines.

of Peele's contemporaries. But we have two lines of this sort in *Alphonsus*:

> Now speak and speak to purpose in the cause
> Act I, p. 202.
> We do admire your wisdoms in this cause.
> Act II, p. 213.

Such a small point as this may seem hardly worthy of notice, but trifling peculiarities of style are often quite as useful in determining a question of authorship as striking parallelisms of phrase, such as that between the following line of *Alphonsus*:

> And fill'd thy beating veins with stealing joy.
> p. 245.

and *The Arraignment of Paris*, II. i. 176:

> To ravish all thy beating veins with joy.

So obvious a resemblance is as consistent with a supposition of plagiarism as with identity of authorship, and it is necessary therefore to examine the play carefully as a whole with a particular eye to such correspondences of phrase or peculiarities of style as cannot reasonably be supposed to be due to plagiarism.

A phrase several times repeated in *Alphonsus* is 'kill my heart':

> O me, the name of Father kills my heart. p. 212.
> But grief thereof hath almost kill'd my heart. p. 226.
> The sound whereof doth kill his dastard heart. p. 281.

Once the word 'slay' is used,

> My body lives, although my heart be slain, p. 252.

When we find this expression four times in this one play, we should naturally expect it to be used elsewhere by Peele, if the play is his. Nevertheless, we should not be justified in drawing any inference from the circumstance that it nowhere occurred in his acknowledged plays; for though we often find that a dramatist of this period will use some pet phrase in one after another of his plays, it is by no means unusual to find that he will repeat a phrase over and over again in the course of a single play and yet never once use it elsewhere. If *Edward I* had not survived we should not have known that such an expression as 'kill my heart' or 'slay my heart' was ever used by Peele. But twice in this play we have 'slay my heart':

> How this proud humour slays my heart with grief!
> x. 196.
>
> . . . this wonder needs must wound thy breast
> For it hath well-nigh slain my wretched heart.
> xxv. 165–6.

In Act v of *Alphonsus* the Emperor alludes to the Empress as

> That venomous serpent nurst within my breast
> To *suck the vital blood* out of my veins.

'Vital blood' occurs twice in Peele's *David and Bethsabe*:

> And to our swords thy vital blood shall cleave
> ii. 45.
>
> Her beauty, having seiz'd upon my heart,
> . . . .
> Sets now such guard about his vital blood . . .
> iii. 14.

It is important to notice that the words used in *Alphonsus* are 'suck the vital blood', for it is again in *David and Bethsabe* alone of Peele's acknowledged works that the expression 'to suck one's blood' is used, and here it occurs three times:

> To suffer pale and grisly abstinence
> To . . . suck away the blood that cheers his looks
> iii. 6–8.
>
> Thou art the cause these torments suck my blood
> viii. 4.
>
> Now sit thy sorrows sucking of my blood. xv. 192.

A few other less important correspondences may be grouped together:

(1) In Act I of *Alphonsus* the Bishop of Mentz addresses Prince Edward as:

> Brave Earl, wonder of princely patience.

In *The Battle of Alcazar* (II. iv. 93) Stukeley calls King Sebastian:

> Courageous King, the wonder of my thoughts.

(2) In Act II of *Alphonsus* (Palsgrave's final speech) we find:

> . . . the better to dive into the depth
> Of this most devilish murderous complot.

In *Anglorum Feriae*, ii. 275–6:

> . . . nor shall it me become
> To dive into the depth of his device.

(3) *Alphonsus*, Act III (p. 245):

> The king of Bohem . . .
> Hath from my knife's point suck'd his deadly bane.

Edward I, XXV. 112:

> The wanton baits that made me suck my bane.

(4) *Alphonsus*, Act V (p. 268):

> . . . we will perform our oaths
> With just effusion of their guilty bloods.

Edward I, V. 156:

> T'avoid the fusion of our guilty blood.

(5) *Alphonsus*, Act V, p. 278:

> Hath Alexander done this damnèd deed?

Edward I, XXV. 150:

> If once I dream'd upon this damnèd deed.

These parallels are at least valuable as showing that the phraseology of the author of *Alphonsus* is just such as we find in Peele's acknowledged works.

In Act IV of *Alphonsus* there is a line for which a parallel of a different kind may be cited. The Emperor here speaks of the poison which he pretends has been administered to him as a 'mineral not to be digested':

> Which burning eats, and eating burns my heart
> p. 257.

A line of similar structure will be found in *The Battle of Alcazar*, IV. ii. 18:

> We come to fight, and fighting vow to die.

In Act I the Empress Isabella, appealing to the electors to make peace between her husband and her brother, Prince Richard, begs them to excuse her tears:

> Bear with my interrupted speeches, lords,
> Tears stop my voice. p. 207.

In just such a fashion does the Queen-Mother in *Edward I* ask indulgence for her inability to restrain her emotion at the return of Edward and his soldiers from their expedition to the Holy Land:

> Bear with your mother, whose abundant love
> With tears of joy salutes your sweet return.
> Sc. i. 50–1.

In Act III, immediately after the murder of the Palatine, Alphonsus, addressing the electors, exclaims:

> . . . suddenly a griping at my heart
> Forbids my tongue his wonted course of speech.
> p. 248.

We have just noted 'Tears stop my voice' in an earlier part of the play, and later on (p. 260) we have 'Grief stops my voice'. In like manner, in the last scene of *Edward I*, Queen Eleanor exclaims:

> Shame and remorse doth stop my course of speech.
> xxv. 56.

In Act V we find the Emperor saying to Prince Edward:

> Hark, Edward, how they labour all in vain,
> *With loss of many a valiant soldier's life,*
> To rescue them whom Heaven and we have doom'd.
> p. 272.

and here we have a most significant echo of a line in Peele's *Tale of Troy*:

> Lo, now at last the Greeks have home again,
> *With loss of many a Greek and Trojan's life,*
> Their wither'd flower, King Menelaus' wife. ll. 447–9.

I have so far confined myself to the comparison of passages drawn from this play and from the plays and poems of which Peele's authorship is acknowledged. But there are several other plays in which there are strong reasons to suspect that he was concerned, amongst them the three parts of *Henry VI*, *Titus Andronicus*, and *Locrine*. In regard to all these the most probable supposition is that Peele was associated with one or more collaborators, or that his work has been revised by others.

There are, however, two dramatic pieces never yet published among Peele's works of which I am convinced that he was the sole author. These are *The Troublesome Reign of King John*—a chronicle-play in two parts, first printed in 1591, upon which Shakespeare founded his *King John*—and *The Life and Death of Jack Straw* published two years later.

With the evidence of Peele's authorship of *The Troublesome Reign* I have dealt elsewhere,[1] while his claim to *Jack Straw* has been strongly supported, and in my opinion conclusively established, by Mr. J. M. Robertson and the late Mr. H. C. Hart.[2] I propose, therefore, to note certain connexions between these two plays and *Alphonsus*.

At the close of Act I of *Alphonsus*, Alexander de Toledo, the Emperor's page, thus laments the death of his father:

> Dead, ay me dead, ay me my life is dead,
> Strangely this night bereft of breath and sense,
> And I, poor I, am comforted in nothing,
> But that the Emperor laments with me.

Note the 'I, poor I', which we meet with again in Peele's *Arraignment of Paris* (Oenone's lament at the faithlessness of Paris, Act III, sc. i):

> . . . would those eyes of mine had never seen
> His 'ticing curled hair, his front of ivory,
> Then had not I, poor I, been unhappy.

and in *The Troublesome Reign*, Part II:

> Grief upon grief! yet none so great a grief
> To end this life, and thereby rid my grief.
> Was ever any so unfortunate,

[1] See my *Sidelights on Shakespeare*, pp. 99–125.

[2] See Mr. Robertson's *Did Shakespeare write 'Titus Andronicus'?* and Mr. Hart's introduction to the 'Arden' edition of *King Henry VI*, Part II.

The right idea of a cursèd man,
As I, poor I, a triumph for despite?
Sc. vi ('The Shakespeare Classics' edition, pp. 135–6).

It will be observed that the triple repetition of 'grief' in the first line of this passage is paralleled by the triple repetition of 'dead' in that quoted from *Alphonsus.*

Twice the author of *Alphonsus* uses the expression 'half dead':

Thus will I vex their souls with sight of death,
Loudly exclaiming in their half dead ears.
Act v, p. 269.

[lest]
After wound received from fainting hand
Thou fall half dead among thine enemies.
Act v, p. 275.

Its appearance twice in this play at once struck my attention, as I could not recall any instance of its use by Peele, and it is just such an expression as this, apparently insignificant in itself, that often affords a valuable clue to a writer's identity. But although it is not in any signed work of Peele's, it crops up again in *Jack Straw*:

If then at instant of the dying hour
Your grace's honourable pardon come
To men half dead, who lie killed in conceit.
Hazlitt, *Dodsley*, v, p. 208.

and as Peele is usually credited with a share in the First Part of *Henry VI*, it is interesting to note its reappearance here (III. ii. 55):

And twit with cowardice a man half dead.

Note again the explanatory 'I mean', in the following passages:

. . . conspiring all your deaths,
I mean your deaths, that are not dead already.
Alphonsus, III, p. 249.

But ah the sweet remembrance of that night,
That night, I mean, of sweetness and of stealth.
Act IV, p. 261.

Mr. H. C. Hart has drawn attention to this as a

'weak unpoetical trick of Peele's'. It will be found three times in *Jack Straw*:

so good a gentleman
As is that knight, Sir John Morton I mean.
Hazlitt, *Dodsley*, v. 389.
I mean against your manor of Greenwich town.
p. 392.
Excepting namely those his foremost men,
I mean the priest and him they call Wat Tyler.

It occurs also in *King Henry VI*, Part I (v. v. 20):

She is content to be at your command,
Command, I mean, of virtuous chaste intents.

and in *Titus Andronicus* (II. iii. 269), which Mr. Robertson has clearly shown to be mainly Peele's.

Another mark that points to Peele is the use of the words 'short tale to make' (equivalent to the popular modern phrase 'To make a long story short') in Alexander's account of the circumstances surrounding the death of Alphonsus:

Short tale to make, I bound him cunningly,
Told him of his deceit, triumphing over him,
And lastly with my rapier slew him dead.
Act V, p. 281.

which will be found again in Peele's *Tale of Troy*, l. 474:

Short tale to make, when thus the town of Troy, &c.

and twice in Part II of *The Troublesome Reign*:

Short tale to make, the see Apóstolick
Hath offer'd dispensation for the fault.
Sc. iii (p. 117).
Short tale to make, myself, amongst the rest,
Was fain to fly before the eager foe.
Sc. vi (p. 135).

Note that the phrase always takes the same position at the beginning of a line.

Another phrase common in *The Troublesome Reign* and *Alphonsus* is 'heir indubitate'. In *Alphonsus*, Act IV, p. 263:

For good thou hast an heir indubitate,

and in *The Troublesome Reign,* Part I (p. 6):

> If first-born son be heir indubitate.

In Act I of *Alphonsus,* p. 209, we find the line

> But private cause must yield to public good;

and again, a few lines before the close of the play:

> Let private sorrow yield to public fame.

The appearance of two lines so closely akin disposes us to expect something similar elsewhere in Peele, and sure enough in *The Tale of Troy* (l. 219) we find:

> But private cause must common cause obey;

and in *Jack Straw* (p. 392):

> I hope, my lord, this message so will prove
> That public hate will turn to private love.

Mr. H. C. Hart and Mr. J. M. Robertson are both of opinion that the hands of Greene and Peele are to be found at work together not only in *Locrine* but in the kindred tragedy of *Selimus,* which appears to be of a later date and contains a number of identical lines, and certainly a comparison of their texts with the independent works of these dramatists seems to support this conclusion. With regard to *Locrine* the internal indications of Peele's handiwork are so conspicuous that Professor Schelling has been led to declare that his authorship 'has long been accepted'. As, however, it possesses many characteristics pointing almost equally strongly to Greene, we are scarcely warranted in saying more than that the presence of Peele's hand in *Locrine* has been established beyond reasonable doubt. At any rate *Alphonsus, Emperor of Germany* is like all the rest of Peele's works in that we find in it a number of links connecting it with *Locrine.* Considerations of space forbid notice of all these, but there is one too important to be overlooked, connected as it is not only with *Locrine* but with an acknowledged production of Peele's. Dyce long ago noticed that two lines in Act III, sc. ii of *Locrine*:

> To arms, my lord, to honourable arms!
> Take helm and targe in hand.

are paralleled in Peele's *Farewell to Norris and Drake* where (l. 50) we have:

> To arms, to arms, to honourable arms!

and (ll. 10, 11):

> Change love for arms; girt to your blades, my boys!
> Your rests and muskets take, *take helm and targe.*

It is surely something more than a mere coincidence that, at the end of Act IV of *Alphonsus*, we find Alexander exclaiming:

> To arms, great Duke of Saxony, to arms! p. 267.

and at the beginning of the same act (first speech of the Bishop of Mentz):

> Brother of Collen, no more churchman now,
> Instead of mitre, and a crosier staff,
> Have you beta'en you to your *helm and targe*?

The association of Peele with *Selimus* may be held to receive further justification in the occurrence in this play and *Alphonsus* of the same allusion—certainly not a stock allusion with the dramatists of the period—in a precisely similar situation. The first scene of *Alphonsus* introduces us to the Emperor indulging in a 'Machiavellian' soliloquy. To him enters the crafty Lorenzo, his confidant and secretary, who instructs him in certain maxims by which to regulate his conduct in his dealings with his enemies. The first maxim is:

'A prince must be of the nature of the lion and the fox; but not the one without the other.'

Upon this Alphonsus comments:

> The fox is subtle, but he wanteth *force*;
> The lion strong, but scorneth policy;
> *I'll imitate Lysander in this point,*
> *And where the lion's hide is thin and scant,*
> *I'll firmly patch it with the fox's fell.*
> Let it suffice I can be both in one.

Lorenzo's second maxim is:

'A prince above all things must seem devout; but

there is nothing so dangerous to his state, as to regard his promise or his oath.'

and the comment of Alphonsus:

> Tush, fear not me, my promises are sound,
> But he that trusts them shall be sure to fail.

Compare this with *Selimus*. Selimus in a soliloquy reveals his bloodthirsty designs for compassing the crown. To him enters 'Abraham, the Jew' (a poisoner like Lorenzo) who undertakes to dispatch Bajazet. On his departure, Selimus, continuing his meditation, observes:

> . . . nothing is more doubtful to a prince
> Than to be scrupulous and religious.
> *I like Lysander's counsel passing well;*
> *'If that I cannot speed with lion's force*
> *To clothe my complots in a fox's skin.'*
> . . . .
> And one of these shall still maintain my cause,
> Or fox's skin, or lion's rending paws.
>
> *The Tragical Reign of Selimus* ('The Temple Dramatists' ed., ll. 1731–5, 1742–3).

This repetition is of so significant a kind that it can only be explained either on the supposition that one of these plays is indebted to the other or that Peele was concerned in both.[1]

Titus Andronicus and the three parts of *Henry VI* also display many affinities with *Alphonsus*, but as my object is merely to show that *Alphonsus* is Peele's, it will be well in this concluding portion of my paper strictly to confine myself to those works which are universally acknowledged to be his.

[1] The former hypothesis I believe to be correct. I think that here and elsewhere the anonymous author of *Selimus* is imitating Peele. Many lines in *Selimus* are closely paralleled in Greene, others in Marlowe, Kyd, and Peele, but neither the style nor the vocabulary of the piece as a whole points to any of these writers. That Marlowe (Crawford) or Greene (Grosart, J. M. Robertson) can have been responsible for the piece as it stands seems impossible, for it contains passages copied from Kyd's *Cornelia*, written at the end of 1593. Marlowe died in the summer of that year, and Greene in 1592.

I have already shown that the peculiarities of vocabulary and phrasing of the author of this play are such as we find elsewhere in Peele's dramas. The same may be said of its versification, which is indistinguishable from that of *Edward I* and *The Battle of Alcazar.* To illustrate the fundamental resemblance of *Alphonsus* to these plays both in its diction and the movement of its verse, I cannot do better than to place the following extracts from speeches in *Alphonsus* side by side with speeches delivered in similar circumstances by characters in *The Battle of Alcazar* and *Edward I*.

The Bishop of Collen urges the Duke of Saxony to make war upon Alphonsus :

Stir now or never, let the Spanish tyrant,
That hath dishonour'd us, murder'd our friends,
And stain'd this seat with blood of innocents,
At last be chastis'd with the Saxon sword.
Alphonsus, Act I, p. 206.

Muly Mahomet urges King Sebastian to make war upon Abdelmelec, King of Morocco :

Now, now or never, bravely execute
Your resolution sound and honourable,
And end this war together with his life
That doth usurp the crown with tyranny.
The Battle of Alcazar, IV. ii. 59–60.

Alphonsus expresses his grief at the death of the Bishop of Mentz :

Come, princes, let us bear the body hence ;
I'll spend a million to embalm the same.
Let all the bells within the empire ring,
Let mass be said in every church and chapel,
And, that I may perform my latest vow,
I will procure as much by gold or friends,
That my sweet Mentz shall be canonizèd,
And numbered in the bead-roll of the saints.

. . . .

I'll build a church in honour of thy name,
Within the ancient famous city Mentz,
Fairer than any one in Germany,
There shalt thou be interr'd with kingly pomp,

Over thy tomb shall hang a sacred lamp,
Which till the day of doom shall ever burn, &c.
Alphonsus, Act IV, p. 260.

Edward I laments the death of Queen Elinor and Joan of Acon:

You peers of England, see in royal pomp
These breathless bodies be entombèd straight,
With tirèd colours cover'd all with black.
Let Spanish steeds, as swift as fleeting wind,
Convey these princes to their funeral:
Before them let a hundred mourners ride.
In every time of their enforc'd abode
Rear up a cross in token of their worth,
Whereon fair Elinor's picture shall be placed.
Arriv'd at London, near our palace-bounds,
Inter my lovely Elinor, late deceas'd;
And, in remembrance of her royalty,
Erect a rich and stately carvèd cross
Whereon her stature shall with glory shine.
Edward I, xxiv. 234–47.

With Mr. Robertson's suggestion that *Alphonsus*—the English portion of the text—shows traces of other hands than Peele's,[1] I do not agree. There are doubtless one or two words and phrases somewhat suggestive of Greene or Marlowe, but then Peele was an imitative writer. Mr. Robertson says that the opening scene of the play can hardly be Peele's. It is, on the contrary, this very scene that most plainly bears his stamp. In the Emperor's first speech there is a passage, referring to Lorenzo:

. . . I, not muffled in simplicity,
. . . .
Haste to the augur of my happiness,
To *lay the ground* of my ensuing wars,
He learns his wisdom, *not by flight of birds,*
By prying into sacrificèd beasts,
By hares that cross the way, by howling wolves,
By gazing on the starry element,
Or vain imaginary calculations;
But from a settled wisdom in itself
Which teacheth to be void of passion.

[1] i. e. of the hand of any author contemporary with Peele. That it may have undergone some revision at a later date I think very probable.

for which a parallel of the most striking kind is to be found in sc. xv of *David and Bethsabe*:

Thou power,
That now art framing of the future world,
Know'st all to come, not by the course of heaven,
By frail conjectures of inferior signs,
By monstrous floods, *by flights and flocks of birds,*
By bowels of a sacrificèd beast,
Or by the figures of some hidden art;
But by a true and natural presage,
Laying the ground and perfect architect
Of all our actions now before thine eyes.[1]

With this evidence before us it is scarcely necessary to note one of Peele's characteristically repetitive lines in the next long speech of Alphonsus:

They ward, they watch, they cast and they conspire.
p. 202.

with which we may compare *Edward I*, v. 3:

They fear, they fly, they faint, they fight in vain.

or the following lines from the same speech:

Thou knowest how all things stand as well as we,
Who are our enemies, and who our friends,
Who must be threaten'd, and who dallyed with,
Who won by words, and who by force of arms, &c.
p. 202.

which should be compared with another passage from the scene of *David and Bethsabe* from which I have just quoted:

It would content me, father, first to learn
How the Eternal framed the firmament;
Which bodies lend their influence by fire,
And which are fill'd with hoary winter's ice;
What sign is rainy, and what star is fair, &c.[2]
Sc. xv. 74.

The more closely one examines the play, the more palpable do the marks of Peele's hand become, and they are nowhere more evident than in this first scene.

[1] I have recently discovered that in both these passages Peele is imitating Du Bartas (*La Seconde Semaine*, 'Les Artifices', 1 Jour, Liv. IV). The greater part of the final scene of *David and Bethsabe* is a close paraphrase of Du Bartas.

[2] This also is from *La Seconde Semaine*, 1 Jour, Liv. IV.

The German dialogue, however, of which there is a considerable quantity, presents a real difficulty. One of the characters (the Princess Hedewick, daughter of the Duke of Saxony) is made to speak German throughout. There are also many passages that reveal an intimate knowledge of the domestic life and political institutions of Germany. Nowhere else does Peele display the slightest acquaintance with the German language or German customs. The play was revived on 5th of May 1636, at the Blackfriars, 'for the Queen and the Prince Elector'. Doubtless, as Fleay conjectures, it was selected for performance on account of the Teutonic part in it. One is tempted to suggest that some person conversant with the German language may have been commissioned to revise the play for the express purpose of this revival. Perhaps some one familiar with the older German literature may be able to say whether the German portion of the text was written in 1636 or forty or fifty years earlier. If it is contemporaneous with the remainder of the text, it would seem difficult to escape the conclusion that a German writer, or some Englishman who had lived in Germany, assisted Peele in the composition of the play.

1916.

IV

'THE SPANISH MOOR'S TRAGEDY'; OR 'LUST'S DOMINION'

HENSLOWE'S diary records in February 1599–1600 a payment to Thomas Dekker, William Haughton, and John Day in respect of 'a book called *The Spaneshe Mores Tragedie*'. No play of that name has come down to us. There is, however, an extant tragedy of which a Spanish Moor is the central figure, published in 1657 under the title of *Lust's Dominion, or The Lascivious Queen*[1] and attributed on the title-page to 'Christopher Marloe, Gent.' This play is certainly not Marlowe's. Is it *The Spanish Moor's Tragedy* of Dekker, Haughton, and Day, as Collier suggests?

So far there has been no definite evidence either way. Fleay (an untrustworthy guide in these matters) and Swinburne accept Collier's identification; Sir Adolphus Ward and A. H. Bullen, on the other hand, reject it. The two latter are followed by Miss Mary L. Hunt, Dekker's most recent biographer, who in her excellent monograph on the dramatist (*Thomas Dekker*, Columbia University Press, 1911, p. 63) confidently expresses her disbelief in Dekker's collaboration in the extant play.

'It is', she says, 'not only wholly unlike the known work of Dekker, but it is also for the most part unlike that of his collaborators. . . . The Queen and Eleazar were conceived by a more robust mind than that of Dekker, who never drew either a convincing villain or a bad woman of imposing presence, or told in his plays a story of successful lust. Nor can I see any evidence in characterization or in phrasing that he retouched this drama, least of all the opening scene, which Swinburne so positively claims for him.'

Nevertheless Miss Hunt is wrong, and Swinburne is right. Although *Lust's Dominion* is unlike most of Dekker's work,

[1] Reprinted in Hazlitt's *Dodsley*, vol. xiv. References are to this edition.

a comparison of the play with his early ventures in the domain of tragedy, and especially with *Old Fortunatus*, would at once have placed its identity with *The Spanish Moor's Tragedy* beyond a doubt. That of all Dekker's plays it should be *Old Fortunatus* that in style and diction is most closely connected with *Lust's Dominion* is natural, since the latter play (taking it to be *The Spanish Moor's Tragedy*) was written immediately after Dekker had finished working on *Old Fortunatus*. This 'pleasant comedy', as it now stands, is Dekker's recast of an older drama. His revision, begun and completed in November 1599, must have been of the most extensive nature, for he was paid £6 for it, as much as was often paid for a new play; and in the following month he received another £3 for still further alterations and additions.[1] The revised version was entered in the Stationer's Register (as *Old Fortunatus in his newe lyverie*) on the 20th of February 1600, just seven days after the payment to Dekker and his collaborators on account of *The Spanish Moor's Tragedy* recorded by Henslowe.

The first act, clearly written by one hand, is wholly Dekker's. Before I had read a dozen lines of the first scene I became convinced that they were his. I suspect that the passage that convinced me, convinced Swinburne, for it bears the unmistakable stamp of Dekker. It was the Queen-Mother's exhortation to the musicians:

> Chime out your softest strains of harmony,
> And on delicious music's silken wings
> Send ravishing delight to my love's ears,
> That he may be enamour'd of your tunes.

Let the reader compare this passage with these from Dekker's acknowledged works:

> Music talk louder, that thy silver voice
> May reach my sovereign's ears.
>
> *Satiromastix*, II. i.[2]

> Go, let music
> Charm with her excellent voice an awful silence

[1] See Dr. W. W. Greg's edition of *Henslowe's Diary*, Part II, 179.

[2] 'Belles Lettres' edition.

Through all the building, that her sphery soul
May, on the wings of air, in thousand forms
Invisibly fly, yet be enjoy'd.

Westward Hoe, IV. ii.

. . . take instruments
And let the raptures of choice harmony,
Thorough the hollow windings of his ear
Carry their sacred sounds, and wake each sense
To stand amazed at our bright eminence.

Old Fortunatus, I. i.[1]

. . . and secretly
Commanded music with her silver tongue
To *chime soft* lullabies into her soul.

Ibid., III. ii.

Not only had Dekker, as these passages show, a keen appreciation of music, but he had (as we shall see later) a great idea of its power to excite amorous desire, and it is to rouse passion in Eleazar that the Queen-Mother invokes the aid of her musicians. Immediately following the lines above quoted, she begs a kiss from him, but he repels her with impatience :

Eleazar. Away, away !
Queen Mother. No, no, says ay ; and twice away, says stay.

So, in *The Shoemaker's Holiday*, when Jane rejects Hammon's advances with 'I love not you', he replies :

All this, I hope, is but a woman's fray
That means : come to me, when she cries ; away !

In this same scene Eleazar has a speech :

I cannot ride through the Castilian streets
But thousand eyes, through windows and through doors,
Throw killing looks at me, and *every slave*
At Eleazar darts a finger out,
And every hissing tongue cries 'There 's the Moor !'

closely resembling one of Galloway's speeches in Act III, sc. i, of *Old Fortunatus* :

. . . see, from the windows
Of every eye derision thrusts out cheeks,
Wrinkled with idiot laughter ; *every finger*
Is like a dart shot from the hand of scorn.

[1] 'Mermaid' edition.

In Act I, sc. ii, Alvero announces to the Queen that the King is at the point of death:

> *Death's frozen hand* holds royal Philip's heart;

while in *Old Fortunatus* (V. ii) Ampedo with his last breath exclaims:

> *Death's frozen hand*
> Congeals life's little river in my breast.

The next passage to be noted is in the first speech of the dying King Philip in I. iii. The Queen-Mother, thanking heaven that she finds him still alive, expresses the hope that he may yet live

> to see
> Unnumbered years to guide this empery.

The King replies:

> The number of my years ends in one day:
> Ere this sun 's down, all a king's glory sets.

It is interesting to compare the sentiments of the speeches put into the mouths of dying men by contemporary dramatists. The last thoughts of Dekker's characters are not of their physical sensations, nor of their sins, nor of the world to come, but of the transitoriness of life, which in one day or minute is brought to a close. Thus in *Old Fortunatus*, V. ii, Andelocia assures the dying Ampedo that Fortune's 'next morn's eye' shall 'overshine the sun in majesty'.

Ampedo replies:

> But this sad night shall make an end of me.

The sentiment will be found twice again in the same play—in the first scene, where Fortunatus hesitates in his choice between the gifts offered him by Fortune:

> The greatest strength expires in loss of breath,
> The mightiest in one minute stoop to death;

and in II. ii, where death comes to Fortunatus himself, and he exclaims:

> No hand can conquer fate;
> This instant is the last of my life's date.

To return to our play, we see Dekker's hand again a few lines further on:

> When a few dribbling minutes have run out,
> Mine hour is ended.

Compare:

> . . . those short-lived minutes
> That dribble out your life. *Old Fortunatus*, II. ii.

In Act I, sc. iv, we have:

> *Alvero.* . . . awake thy soul,
> And on thy resolution fasten wings
> Whose golden feathers may outstrip their hate.
> *Eleazar.* I'll tie no golden feathers to my wings.

References to the pages of *Old Fortunatus* will show how constantly 'wings' figure in Dekker's metaphor at this time, and in one of the scenes he contributed to *The Roaring Girl* (IV. ii) we get:

> Husband, I plucked,
> When he had tempted me to think well of him,
> Gilt feathers from thy wings, to make him fly
> More lofty.

In Act III, sc. ii, the King (Fernando) endeavours to debauch the chaste Maria. This scene is typical of Dekker. The foiling of a royal or noble profligate's design upon a virtuous woman was at this time his stock tragic *motif*. He uses it again in *Satiromastix* and in *Westward Hoe*. Not only so, but the King in *Satiromastix* and the Earl in *Westward Hoe* employ the same machinations to compass their evil design. In both these plays, as in *Lust's Dominion*, music and a banquet are provided to add to the allurements of speech—absurdly enough in the present play, since Maria has been roused from her bed in the dead of night. Note also that it is by means of a soporific drug that Maria foils the King. This is a favourite device of Dekker's, appearing again not only in the kindred scenes of *Satiromastix* and *Westward Hoe*, but in *Old Fortunatus* (III. ii) and the First Part of *The Honest Whore* (I. iii). In *Lust's Dominion* Maria administers the draught to the King; in *Satiromastix* and *Westward Hoe* it is the woman who takes the 'somniferous potion', the sight of her supposed dead body inspiring the royal or noble lover with shame and remorse. If this scene (excluding the few lines introducing Oberon and the fairies at the close) is carefully compared with *Satiromastix*, v. ii, and *Westward Hoe*, IV. ii, its authorship will at once become apparent.

Two parallels with other works of Dekker are worth noting: Maria's speech—

> . . . here you look on me *with sunset eyes*,
> For by beholding you my glory dies,

and *Old Fortunatus*, III. i:

> Dead is my love, I am buried in her scorn,
> That is *my sunset*.

The drugged King exclaims:

> . . . the cold hand of sleep
> Hath thrust his icy fingers in my breast.

in words echoing those of Shakespeare in *King John*:

> And none of you will bid the winter come
> To thrust his icy fingers in my maw.
>
> Act v, sc. vii.

—a parallel noted by Hazlitt. What is more interesting for our purpose is that Dekker uses the same metaphor again in *The Gull's Horn-book*, chap. iii:

> If the morning . . . waxing cold, thrust his frosty fingers into thy bosom

and *The Seven Deadly Sins of London* (Camb. Univ. Press reprint, p. 81):

> . . . he into whose bosom threescore winters have thrust their frozen fingers.

When we come to the next scene (III. iii) the unmistakable rhythm of Dekker may be detected in Maria's dying utterance:

> Heaven, ope your windows, that my spotless soul,
> Riding upon the wings of innocence,
> May enter Paradise.

This should be compared with the invocations of music already quoted, and with the dying Susan's speech in *The Witch of Edmonton*, III. iii:

> . . . my soul's purity
> Shall with bold wings ascend the doors of Mercy.

and also with the lines in Act I, sc. i, of *Old Fortunatus*:

> Thy Heaven-inspired soul, on Wisdom's wings,
> Shall fly up to the Parliament of Jove.

When the King wakes and discovers that Maria is dead, he exclaims:

> O my dear love!
> Yet heavens can witness thou wert never mine,

in words that recall the opening lines of Hammon's speech (*The Shoemaker's Holiday*, IV. i) as he watches Jane at work:

> . . . there my fair love sits;
> She 's fair and lovely, but she is not mine.

In Act V, sc. v, the reference to ratsbane:

> . . . these dignities
> Like poison, make men swell; this ratsbane honour,
> O, 'tis so sweet! they'll lick it till all burst.

is Dekker's. Compare *The Whore of Babylon* (Pearson, ii. 210):

> If the sweet bane
> I lay be swallowed, oh! a kingdom bursts.

Finally in Eleazar's last speech in the play (v. vi) we have one of Dekker's numerous metaphorical allusions to the raising of spirits within a magic circle, from which they cannot stray:

> May'st thou, lascivious queen, whose damnèd charms
> Bewitch'd me to the circle of thy arms,
> Unpitied die;

with which we may compare *Old Fortunatus*, III. i:

> If by the sovereign magic of thine eye,
> Thou canst enchant his looks to keep the circles
> Of thy fair cheeks, be bold to try thy charms.

Apart from these passages, Dekker's hand is evidenced by certain peculiarities of style and the use of some of his favourite words and expressions. One of his most noticeable mannerisms is his habit of iterating words and phrases, often three or four times over. He indulges in this trick to a far greater extent than any of his contemporaries, who, as a rule, affect triple or fourfold repetitions only as a conventional means of indicating mental distraction or madness. There are many of these characteristic expressions in this play, e.g. 'away, away!' 'begone, begone!' 'O he 's dead, he 's dead' (I. i); 'But that he has an eye, an eye, an eye' (II. ii); 'So, gone, gone, gone' (II. iv); 'Heart, heart, heart, heart!' (IV. v); 'see, see, see, see!' 'play that amain, amain, amain' (V. v).

'Hellhound' is one of his most frequently used, and most distinctive, terms of abuse. We find it twice in this play:

> I'll fight thee, damned hellhound. V. i.
> Hear me then, hellhound. V. V.

Another is 'damnation', here twice applied to Eleazar:

> Damnation, vanish from me! V. iii.
> Worse than damnation! fiend, monster of men!
> V. V.

For this last exclamation compare Part II of *The Honest Whore*, III. i:

> Worse than damnation! a wild kerne, a frog,
> A dog whom I'll scarce spurn.

It does not follow that all the scenes showing traces of Dekker's work are entirely his. It is clear that many of them are not. The part of the play written by Dekker alone is the whole of Act I, Act II. i, ii, v (from 'exeunt Friars') and vi, Act III. ii (to the entry of the fairies), iii, iv, and vi, Act V. v and vi. The brief vision of Oberon and the fairies at the end of III. ii is certainly Day's. Even the critics who doubt or deny Dekker's collaboration admit that it may be Day's, and it is in the same riming lines of four measures as the Oberon scenes at the end of *The Parliament of Bees*. The differentiation of Day's and Haughton's work in the remaining scenes is a more speculative matter.

A comparison of the riming octosyllabic lines in the Crab and Cole scenes (II. iii and iv) with Shorthose's similar riming speeches in *Grim, the Collier of Croydon,* and of the prose in III. v with the prose of the same play, seems to justify the attribution of these scenes to Haughton. Dekker's was evidently the controlling hand throughout, for there are many touches suggestive of his revision of his collaborators' work. Subject to this reservation, I would allot Act II. iii, iv, and v (to 'exeunt Friars') and III. v to Haughton; Act III. i, end of ii, and Act IV to Day. Act V. i–iv contains, I think, mixed work of Day and Dekker.[1]

It cannot be said that Dekker's literary reputation is likely to gain anything by the establishment of his substantial responsibility for *Lust's Dominion.* But the proof of its identity with *The Spanish Moor's Tragedy* is interesting as revealing his only extant contribution to the full-blooded Marlovian type of tragedy.

1915.

[1] This differs slightly from the division given in my paper in *Notes and Queries* (12th Series, i. 84) in which I included II. v and vi and III. vi in Haughton's share.

V

WEBSTER'S 'APPIUS AND VIRGINIA' A VINDICATION

EVERY critic of Webster's plays has been struck by the marked difference between *Appius and Virginia* and his other dramatic pieces. Firmly constructed, lucid in style, and with a simple, coherent plot, it is utterly unlike *The White Devil* and *The Duchess of Malfy*, those profounder and more poetic Italian tragedies of passion and intrigue. Its simpler structure and more regular versification have usually been held to be sufficiently accounted for by its classical theme and by the supposition that it is a work of Webster's later years. Recently, however, Webster's authorship has been altogether denied. In an article contributed to *The Modern Language Review* [1] by the late Rupert Brooke it is contended that the play has been wrongly assigned to him. The hypothesis here submitted is that it is substantially the work of Thomas Heywood, and that if Webster had a hand in it at all, the possibility of which is grudgingly admitted, his share is confined to a slight revision of two scenes—Act I, sc. i, and Act IV, sc. i.

The occurrence in *Appius and Virginia* of a number of unusual words,[2] mostly of Latin derivation, distinctive of Thomas Heywood's vocabulary in that outside this play they are rarely or never to be met with except in Heywood's writings, is one of the main grounds upon which Brooke's attribution is based. This feature I had myself noted independently, making use of it as a means of fixing the date of the play. The view I put forward,[3] based upon Webster's

[1] Vol. viii, No. 4, October 1913. Reprinted in *John Webster and the Elizabethan Drama*, Sidgwick & Jackson, 1916.

[2] *Confine* (= banish, expel), *obdure*, *novel* (n.), *palpèd*, *thrill* (= hurl), *infallid*, *lust-burnt*, *strage*, &c.

[3] *Notes and Queries*, 11 Series vii. 401, 402 (May 1913); 11 Series viii. 63 (July 1913).

well-known imitative tendencies, as shown by his wholesale borrowings from his predecessors and contemporaries, was that Webster borrowed these words from Heywood, though incidentally I referred to the possibility that their appearance might be susceptible of the explanation that Heywood himself had a hand in the play. If we are to believe Brooke, there is no doubt on the matter at all. 'There is', he says, 'very little evidence of the play being Webster's, rather more for his having had a finger in it, but much stronger evidence still that he had practically nothing to do with it.' The evidence of Webster's authorship, he suggests, consists only in 'the attribution of a late publisher, which is evidence of a notoriously untrustworthy character, and three or four passages of repetition and resemblance'. 'In any case,' he concludes, '*Appius and Virginia* must be counted among Heywood's plays . . . it is a typical example of him in his finer moments, written rather more carefully than is usual with that happy man.' Further, he favours the supposition that it was written after the appearance of *The White Devil* and before that of *The Duchess of Malfy*, i. e. about 1612–13.

It must be admitted that the external evidence of Webster's authorship cannot be taken as conclusive. The play was printed and published as his in 1654, without any publisher's imprint on the title-page. In 1659 the same edition was issued with a new title-page: 'Printed for Humphrey Moseley.' Moseley's attribution alone would not justify us in accepting the play as Webster's. As Brooke has pointed out, he ascribed *The Merry Devil of Edmonton, The History of King Stephen, Duke Humphrey*, and *Iphis and Ianthe* to Shakespeare, *The Parliament of Love* to Rowley, and was responsible for many other erroneous attributions. If, therefore, we are to accept *Appius and Virginia* as an authentic Websterian play, it is clearly necessary to show that it bears conclusive internal evidence of its authorship. That it does show such evidence I submit that there is no doubt whatever. I differ entirely from Brooke's conclusions both as to the date and the authorship of the play, and I propose to give reasons—based, like his, upon a detailed examination of the text—for believing that it is of a late date—later than *The Duchess of Malfy*, than *The Devil's Law Case*, and even than *A Cure for a Cuckold*—and that the publisher's attribution to Webster is at least substantially correct.

The question of the date can be briefly dealt with. Whether my assumption that its Heywoodian words and phrases are borrowed from Heywood is correct or not, my conclusion that the existing text of the play is not earlier than 1630 or thereabouts remains unaffected. Even if they are Heywood's own words, the fact remains that for the use of at least three of them—words noted independently by Brooke and myself—no authority earlier than 1630 has yet been found. These words are *thrill* (meaning 'hurl'), *strage*, and *infallid*. The correspondence in the use of the first two by Heywood and the author of *Appius and Virginia* is so close that the passages in which they occur deserve particular notice.

Thrill = hurl.

. . . methought I saw thee . . .
Round girt with squadrons of thine enemies
All which their javelins thrill'd against thy breast.
The Iron Age (1632), Part I, Act IV (Heywood's *Dramatic Works*, 1874, iii. 316).

Let him come thrill his partisan
Against this breast. *A. & V.*, IV. ii.

There is no earlier record of 'thrill' in this sense. Heywood has it again in *The Iron Age*, Part I, and in *Pelopœa and Alope* (1637); see *Dramatic Works*, 1874, iii. 299, and vi. 301.

Strage.

Boasting of nought save shipwreck, spoil and *strage.*
Londons Ius Honorarium, 1631 (*Dramatic Works*, iv. 271).

I have not dreaded famine, fire nor *strage.*
A. & V., V. iii.

I have been unable to find any earlier example of *strage* than this of Heywood's. He seems to have introduced the word, and uses it several times in his later writings.

Infallid (*A. & V.*, II. iii) is, as Brooke notes, also in Heywood's *Hierarchie of the Blessed Angels* (1635), p. 308: 'infallid evidence' in the former case, 'infallid testimonies' in the latter. I do not suggest that Webster borrowed it from *The Hierarchie*, for the reference to Webster in this very work seems to imply that he was no longer alive when it was written.[1] We must not forget the 220 plays in which Heywood had 'either an entire hand, or at least a main finger'.

It is noteworthy that one of the points of resemblance between *Appius and Virginia* and Heywood is connected with *The English Traveller*, printed in 1633, and not likely to be of an earlier date than *c.* 1627.

> I know not how the day goes with you, but my stomach hath struck twelve, I can assure you that. *E. T.*, I. i.

> How goes the day? . . . My stomach hath struck twelve. *A. & V.*, IV. ii.

Heywood has this joke again, with a slight variation, in *The Late Lancashire Witches*. It is possible, of course, that he would repeat it three times, but its introduction in the text of *Appius and Virginia* is much more abrupt than in *The English Traveller*, and so seems to point to borrowing on the part of the author of the former play. There are numerous instances of this 'lifting' of jokes from the writings of his contemporaries in Webster's other plays.

[1] In the list of the poets of his day whose names were habitually 'curtail'd' by their contemporaries (*Hierarchie*, 1635, Bk. IV, 206) it is known that all the writers other than Webster to whom Heywood refers in the past tense were no longer living when his lines were written. Three bore the Christian name John—Fletcher, Webster, and Ford. 'Famous Iohnson' (living) is, says Heywood, 'still but Ben', and he continues:

> Fletcher and Webster, of that learned packe
> None of the mean'st, yet neither *was* but Iacke
> . . . .
> And *hee's now* but Iacke Foord that once were Iohn.

Ford was alive, Fletcher had died in 1625. The inference is that Webster, whose name is coupled with Fletcher's, was also dead.

In two other cases it is *The Royall King and Loyall Subject* that affords a parallel. These are of less significance in this connexion, for, although it is true that this play was not published until 1633, it seems probable that it was acted many years previously. Still, it may be as well, for the sake of completeness, to set them forth here:

> . . . to you, my Liege
> A virgin's love I prostrate . . . with the duty
> Of a true subject. *R. K & L. S.*, II. ii.
> Your daughter, noble brother . . . most humbly
> Prostrates her filial duty. *A. & V.*, I. iv.

This parallel has also been noted by Brooke; I quote a little more fully from Heywood's play in order to exhibit the close correspondence of phrase, apart from the metaphorical use of *prostrate*, of which Heywood's works afford a number of other instances.

> We want, Madam? you are deceiv'd, we have store, of rags; plenty, of tatters, &c. *R. K. & L. S.*, III. i.
> The camp wants money; we have store of knocks,
> And wounds God's plenty, but we have no pay.
> *A. & V.*, I. iv.

At any rate these are indisputable facts, that the text of *Appius and Virginia*, as we have it, contains several words not found elsewhere earlier than 1630, and that it exhibits certain fairly close correspondences of phrase with *The English Traveller* and *The Iron Age*, both plays printed after 1630 and probably written within a few years of that date.

Now in regard to the appearance in *Appius and Virginia* of words from Heywood's peculiar vocabulary, a very important fact remains to be noted. Brooke remarks upon their sudden appearance in this play, assuming that Heywood had never previously influenced Webster's vocabulary in the slightest degree, and asks whether we are to suppose that 'suddenly in a transport of "senile" affection he [Webster] hurled aside his own personality, and became mere Tom'. The statement is, of course, in any case an exaggeration. The adoption of a dozen or more of Heywood's words or phrases need scarcely imply any change of personality, and it is quite what we should expect of such an inveterate borrower as Webster. Were there any remarkable resemblance between the style of *Appius and Virginia* and that of Heywood's plays, it would be a different matter. That there is no striking resemblance is surely pretty clear from the fact that no previous critic, from Dyce onwards, has noticed it; such resemblances as do exist would much more reasonably be accounted for by the influence upon the susceptible Webster of a friend and fellow dramatist with whom he seems to have been on terms of close intimacy. However, it is not with the style of the play—of this I shall have something to say later—but with the vocabulary that I am now dealing.

If, as Brooke suggests, there were not the slightest trace of the influence of Heywood's vocabulary in any other of Webster's plays, this would certainly carry a good deal of weight as an argument against the latter's authorship of *Appius and Virginia*. But this is not the case. One of Webster's plays *does* contain several of Heywood's words. What is still more significant is that this play is the one which, according to the consensus of critical opinion, immediately preceded *Appius and Virginia*—*A Cure for a Cuckold*, which probably derives the main feature of its plot from Massinger's *Parliament of Love*, licensed in 1624. That *A Cure for a Cuckold* is substantially Webster's play there can, I think, be no doubt whatever, and Brooke seems to be of the same opinion. No one has yet suggested that any other dramatist but Rowley had a hand in it, and his share is almost, if not entirely, confined to the underplot. This play contains at least five words of Heywood's—'apology' (as a verb), 'asperse', 'ecstasied', 'mediate', and 'unite'—the last as an adjective in the phrase 'unite consent'. I take them in alphabetical order:

asperse, v. *apology*, v.:

I presume
No jealousy can be *aspersed* on him
For which he cannot well *apology*.
C. C., v. i (Hazlitt, iv. 82).

Asperse was at this time very rarely used in other than

its primary sense. It is not in Shakespeare. Heywood has it two or three times, e. g. in *England's Elizabeth* (1632), p. 6:

> . . . neither sterility and [*sic*] barrennesse could be *aspersed* upon her.

and in *The English Traveller*, III. i:

> you may . . . *asperse* the honour of a noble friend.
> *Works*, 1874, iv. 48.

So far as I am aware, the only instance of the form 'apology' for 'apologize', apart from *A Cure for a Cuckold*, is in the same act and scene of *The English Traveller*:

> Thus much let me for him *apology*. *Ibid.*, 55.

At any rate the *Oxford Dictionary* has no other example of its use as a verb.

ecstasied = enraptured, transported with delight:

> I'll give thee reason
> I have to be thus *ecstasied* with joy.
> *C. C.*, IV. ii (Hazlitt, iv. 70).

This is a very special word of Heywood's. It occurs in *The Captives, or The Lost Recovered*, V. i:

> Thou with these words hast *ecstasied* my soul.
> Bullen's *Old Plays*, vol. iv.

in *The Fair Maid of the West*, I. iv:

> Before I doted
> But now you strive to have me *ecstasied*.
> *Works*, 1874, ii. 273.

and again in the same play, II. ii:

> I cannot but wonder why any fortune should make a man *ecstasied*. *Works*, ii. 281.

This last passage is cited in the *O. E. D.*, the only example of the word in this sense earlier than 1660.

mediate = to beg, intercede for.

> . . . nothing now
> Was talk'd of but to yield up ship and goods
> And *mediate* for our peace.
> *C. C.*, III. iii (Hazlitt, iv. 57).

Again in *Appius and Virginia*, II. i:

> You *mediate* excuse for courtesies.

The verb occurs repeatedly in Heywood in a similar sense; the closest parallel to its use in the text is in *The English Traveller*, Act IV:

> And will you leave me to the whip and stocks,
> Not *mediate* my peace? *Works*, 1874, iv. 84.

Outside Heywood's works it is very rare.

We have a still clearer case in the use of the phrase 'unite consent', which is twice to be met with in this play:

> By *unite consent*
> Then the command was his.
> *C. C.*, III. iii (Hazlitt, iv. 57).
> Since from the lord
> To the lowest groom, all with *unite consent*
> Speak him so largely. *C. C.*, v. i (iv. 83).

I felt confident that this very unusual phrase was not coined by Webster. For a long time I sought it in Heywood without success. At last I found it in *The Silver Age* (1613), Act III (Pearson, iii. 124):

> What edge of steel or adamantine chain
> Hath forc'd in two the virtue of my charm?
> Which Gods and devils gave *unite consent*
> To be infract?

The traces of Heywood's vocabulary in *A Cure for a Cuckold* are doubtless less apparent than in *Appius and Virginia*, but this is precisely what one would expect if the former is the earlier play. There are even suggestions of Heywood's influence in Webster's earlier vocabulary—'confine' (= banish, expel) is in *A Monumental Column*, l. 254, and 'ecstasied' (= enraptured) in *The Devil's Law Case*, iv. 1. The presence of these Heywoodian words alone is, then, no justification for discrediting Webster's authorship of *Appius and Virginia*.

There is another important fact to be noted in connexion with the use of these rare words in *Appius and Virginia*. They are 'clapt in clusters', to borrow a phrase of Lyly's, occurring abundantly but in patches. All the conspicuous examples will be found in three scenes—I. iv, IV. ii, and V. iii. In IV. ii 'novel' (as a substantive), 'thrill', 'enthronis'd', 'obdure', all occur within the space of a few lines; in v. iii 'concionate' is followed in the next line by 'oratorize'; and 'operant', 'confine', and 'strage' come close on the top of one another. No similar phenomenon is presented by any play of Heywood's. It suggests the unfamiliar hand—a delight in the practice of a new trick—it suggests, in short, the hand of an imitator.

But the most important evidence as to the authorship of this play is that afforded by a comparison of its language and sentiments with those of Webster's other plays. To what extent (if at all) does it contain repetitions of or parallels with these plays? Brooke makes the amazing assertion that *The Thracian Wonder* is as Websterian as *Appius and Virginia.* And immediately afterwards he provides a list of passages from *Appius and Virginia*—nine in number—for which parallels can be found in Webster's other plays, some of them so close that even he finds a great difficulty in giving any reasonable explanation for their appearance, or concealing their significance as indications of Webster's authorship. For convenience of reference I repeat this list here: [1]

(*a*) *A. & V.*, I. i (Hazlitt, iii. 130):

I have seen children oft eat sweetmeats thus,
As fearful to devour them.

Duchess of Malfy, I. ii (ii. 176):

I have seen children oft eat sweetmeats thus
As fearful to devour them too soon.

(*b*) *A. & V.*, I. ii (iii. 135):

one whose mind
Appears more like a ceremonious chapel
Full of sweet music, than a thronging presence.

Duchess of Malfy, III. ii (ii. 215):

His breast was filled with all perfection,
And yet it seemed a private whispering-room,
It made so little noise of 't.

[1] The figures within parentheses refer to volume and page of Hazlitt's edition of Webster's *Works*, 1897.

Monumental Column, lines 78, 79:

Who had his breast instated with the choice
Of virtues, though they made no ambitious noise.

(*c*) *A. & V.*, III. ii (iii. 172):

Virginia. But she hath a matchless eye, sir.
Clown. True, her eyes are not right matches.

White Devil, IV. ii (ii. 86):

Brachiano. Are not those matchless eyes mine?
Vittoria. I had rather
They were not matches.

(*d*) *A. & V.*, III. ii (179):

I only give you my opinion,
I ask no fee for 't.

Westward Hoe! V. iii (i. 160):

Take my counsel: I'll ask no fee for 't.

White Devil, I. ii (ii. 18):

This is my counsel and I ask no fee for 't.

(*e*) *A. & V.*, III. iii (186):

As aconitum, a strong poison, brings
A present cure against all serpents' stings.

White Devil, III. ii (ii. 71):

Physicians, that cure poisons, still do work
With counter-poisons.

(*f*) *A. & V.*, IV. i (194):

I vow this is a practised dialogue,
Comes it not rarely off?

Duchess of Malfy, I. ii (ii. 171):

I think this speech between you both was studied,
It came so roundly off.

(*g*) *A. & V.*, IV. i (199):

for, we wot,
The office of a justice is perverted quite
When one thief hangs another.

Duchess of Malfy, IV. ii (ii. 249):

The office of justice is perverted quite
When one thief hangs another.

(*h*) *A. & V.*, IV. i (201):

I have sung
With an unskilful, yet a willing voice,
To bring my girl asleep.

White Devil, V. i (ii. 126):

I'll tie a garland here about his head;
'Twill keep my boy from lightning.[1]

(*i*) *A. & V.*, V. iii (222):

Death is terrible
Unto a conscience that 's oppressed with guilt!

Duchess of Malfy, V. v (ii. 276):

How tedious is a guilty conscience!

Now parallels from his own works are of very great significance in Webster's case because he was much addicted to self-repetition. No doubt many other dramatists repeat themselves more or less, but a particularly 'Websterian' characteristic is the word for word repetition of phrases. It is this that gives to the two instances of this kind of repetition in *Appius and Virginia* and *The Duchess of Malfy* ((*a*) and (*g*)) so much weight as evidence in favour of Webster's authorship. To these Brooke himself has added a parallel of his own discovery (*f*) almost equally significant, and his list contains six other parallels of varying degrees of closeness, of less value individually it is true, but collectively of great weight. If it were possible to cite three equally striking parallels and six minor resemblances of phrase or sentiment from *A Thracian Wonder*, I for one should feel strongly inclined to believe that Webster had some share even in that worthless production. But I shall be able to show that Brooke's list by no means exhausts the resemblances between *Appius and Virginia* and Webster's other plays.

Of the nine points of resemblance noticed by Brooke it happens that the three most striking are connected with *The Duchess of Malfy*. In order, therefore, to give plausibility to his theory that *Appius and Virginia* was written by Heywood, Brooke dismisses the others as of no

[1] Cited for 'the same effect of tenderness got by the word "my"'.

importance—as ' common jokes ', ' common ideas ', ' catch-phrases ', and the like—and seeks to account for the three parallels that cannot possibly be disregarded by the suggestion that Webster wrote *The Duchess of Malfy* shortly after the appearance of *Appius and Virginia* and borrowed the passages in question from his friend's play. If we are to remove *Appius and Virginia* from the list of Webster's plays, we shall have to ignore a great deal more evidence than that afforded by the parallels cited by Brooke. A careful examination of the play affords numbers of other correspondences, not only with *The Duchess of Malfy*, but with *The White Devil, The Devil's Law Case, A Cure for a Cuckold,* and even the early partnership play *Westward Hoe.* And so far as Brooke's conjecture as to the date of the play is concerned, it is not *The Duchess of Malfy* but *The Devil's Law Case* that has most in common with it, and *A Cure for a Cuckold* that presents one of the most distinctive parallels. With these points of resemblance to Webster's other plays that have escaped Brooke, I propose now to deal.

The most striking and successful feature of Webster's first independent dramatic work, *The White Devil,* is the trial scene, ' The Arraignment of Vittoria.' It is regarded by modern critics, and was doubtless regarded by the audiences of Webster's own day, as one of the greatest of his achievements as a playwright. Nothing is more evident to the student of his plays than that he was a writer of limited range. The trial scene of his first play had won the suffrages of the public, and accordingly we find him again presenting a trial scene as a conspicuous feature in *The Devil's Law Case.* A trial scene is also a conspicuous feature of *Appius and Virginia,* and it is here, if anywhere, that we should expect to find traces of Webster's hand, if the play be his. Brooke finds in this scene a few phrases, words, and lines ' faintly reminiscent ' of Webster, and admits the possibility that he may have revised it. Let us examine the text of this portion of the play and see whether its resemblances to Webster's other plays are such as can reasonably be accounted for by a hypothesis of his 'revision' of another man's work. I propose to confine this examination to the actual scene that passes in open court, comparing it more particularly with the kindred scene in *The Devil's Law Case.*

On the appearance to the proceedings of Virginius, who is in the position of defendant to the suit in which Marcus claims Virginia as his slave, Appius asks him who is acting as his advocate, and Virginius proudly replies:

I have none, my lord;
Truth needs no advocate; the unjust cause
Buys up the tongues that travel with applause
In these your thronged courts.

Similarly in *The Devil's Law Case* Crispiano advises Romelio to secure professional assistance, but Romelio protests that he is 'so strengthen'd in his innocence' that he desires no adjournment of the trial for this purpose. For the substance of the sentiment conveyed in Virginius's speech *A Cure for a Cuckold* affords us a parallel:

Fight, as lawyers plead,
Who gain the best of reputation
When they can fetch a bad cause smoothly off.
Act III, sc. i.

Note that in all three plays, *The White Devil, The Devil's Law Case,* and *Appius and Virginia,* the defendant appears in person against a professional advocate.

Immediately following Virginius's speech come the opening words of the advocate's address:

May it please your reverend lordships—

interrupted by a question from Appius and by Virginius's impassioned appeal for justice, concluding with an abrupt 'Now, Sir, I stand you,' addressed to the advocate. 'Then have at you, Sir,' replies the lawyer, and resumes his interrupted address:

May it please your lordships, here is such a case,
So full of subtlety, and, as it were,
So far benighted in an ignorant mist,

> That though my reading be sufficient,
> My practice more, I never was entangled
> In the like pursenet. Here is one that claims
> This woman for his daughter, &c.

To embark upon a speech with the words 'have at you!' can surely scarcely have been a common forensic habit of the period. Yet the advocate in *The White Devil* opens his attack upon Vittoria in precisely the same way: 'Well then, have at you,' to which Vittoria retorts, 'I am at the mark, sir; I'll give aim to you And tell you how near you shoot.' With the speech itself compare the corresponding speech of Contilupo, *The Devil's Law Case* advocate:

> May it please your lordship and the reverend Court
> To give me leave to open to you a case,
> So rare, so altogether void of precedent,
> That I do challenge all the spacious volumes
> Of the whole civil law to show the like . . .
> . . . There stands one,
> Romelio the merchant, &c.

The advocate of *Appius and Virginia* concludes the preamble of his address with these words:

> . . . now the question
> (With favour of the Bench) I shall make plain
> In two words only, without circumstance.

So, in *The Devil's Law Case*, Contilupo, reproved by the Judge for his 'stale declaiming 'gainst the person', replies:

> Good my lord, be assur'd
> I will leave all circumstance, and come to th' purpose.

'Fall to your proofs,' says Appius. So the Judge in *The Devil's Law Case*: 'Fall to your plea,' and again, a little later, 'Well then, *to your proofs*, and be not tedious.' 'Tedious' is a typical word of Webster's, and it occurs in the very passage in *Appius and Virginia* with which we are now dealing. The advocate asks for his papers. 'Here, sir,' says Marcus. 'Where, sir?' retorts the advocate, 'I vow y'are the most *tedious* client.' A moment afterwards the untimely prompting of Marcus causes the advocate to turn sharply upon him with 'Hold your prating!' Exactly the same thing occurs in *The Devil's Law Case.* Sanitonella interrupts Contilupo and is met with the same angry retort, 'Prithee, hold thy prating.' The advocate of *Appius and Virginia* proceeds with a detailed statement of the alleged facts upon which the plaintiff's claim is based :

> That honourable Lord Virginius,
> *Having been married about fifteen year,*
> And issueless, *this virgin's politic mother,* &c.,

exactly in the style of Contilupo's similar statement in *The Devil's Law Case* :

> Some nine and thirty years since, which was the time
> This woman was married, Francisco Romelio,
> *This gentleman's putative father,* and her husband,
> *Being not married to her past a fortnight,* &c.

During the progress of his speech the Roman advocate notes that Numitorius is not giving him his attention, and begs him particularly to notice that Virginius received a message from his wife, containing the news of the approaching birth of a child, when he was abroad on active service :

> observe it, I beseech you,
> And note the trick of a deceitful woman.

So in *The Devil's Law Case* Contilupo particularly desires the judge to bear in mind that Leonora's husband went abroad a fortnight after the marriage :

> Take special note o' th' time, I beseech your lordship.

But it is only by comparing the two speeches together in their entirety that their striking similarity, both in substance and manner of treatment, can be fully appreciated. The alleged imposture practised upon the husband is in the one case the palming off of a strange child, in the other of an illegitimate child, as a child of the marriage, and the methods alleged to have been adopted to support the imposture are similar.

The oratory of the advocate of *Appius and Virginia* is interrupted by the indignant protest of Virginia's nurse that 'the fellow i' th' nightcap' has not spoken one true word. It is strange that the significance of this word 'night-cap' as a mark of Webster's authorship should have escaped Brooke. Applied, as here, to the barrister's cap or coif, it is scarcely to be found anywhere but in Webster, who has it again in the same sense (*D. L. C.*, IV. i) and twice also in a transferred sense, as a contemptuous name for a barrister (*D. M.*, II. i, and *D. L. C.*, II. i). The nurse also, be it observed, is silenced with a 'hold you your prating' from Appius.

Next follows an interchange of questions and answers between judge and advocate, Appius feigning a desire to be satisfied with strict proof of the plaintiff's case, and it is here that Icilius breaks in with the exclamation:

> I vow this is a practised dialogue,
> Comes it not rarely off!

for which Brooke has discovered so close a parallel in *The Duchess of Malfy*.

The advocate produces depositions and adduces arguments with which Appius pretends to be impressed, and Virginius cries out:

> My lords, believe not this spruce orator:
> Had I but fee'd him first, he would have told
> As smooth a tale on our side.

In like manner when Crispiano intimates to the advocate in *The Devil's Law Case* that he has heard enough, Ariosto sarcastically observes:

> Pray my lord, give him way, you spoil his oratory else:
> Thus would they jest, were they fee'd to open
> Their sisters' cases.

Later on, the Roman advocate suggests that Virginia's relatives have brought her to the Court dressed as a slave purposely to defraud Marcus of the clothes and jewels she was accustomed to wear:

> . . . see they bring the maid
> In her most proper habit, bond-slave like,
> And they will *save by th' hand* too.

This expression 'by the hand' seems to be very rare

I have met with it only twice outside Webster's plays.[1] The *Oxford English Dictionary*, which gives 'expeditiously' as the meaning, quotes a single example from Gurnall's *Christian in complete Armour*: 'They shall grow rich by the hand.' It seems rather to mean 'by the deal; by the transaction'. Webster has 'lose by th' hand' in *The Devil's Law Case*, IV. ii:

> I will sell him [Romelio] to any man
> For an hundred zecchins, and he that buys him of me
> Shall *lose by th' hand* too.

Numitorius and Virginius point out the improbability of the plaintiff's story:

> *Num.* How is 't probable
> That our wife, being present at the childbirth,
> Whom this did nearest concern, *should ne'er reveal it*?
> *Virginius.* Or, if ours dealt thus cunningly, *how haps it*
> Her policy, as you term it, did not rather
> Provide an issue male? &c.

So also in *The Devil's Law Case* Crispiano interrogates Leonora:

> *How hapt*, gentlewoman, you *revealed this no sooner*?

Appius tells the advocate that he need not trouble to reply; he is already satisfied with the evidence. As a last resource, Virginius proclaims Appius's corrupt motive, and Icilius produces the letters written by him to Virginia, which the senators refuse even to look at. It is in the speech of Icilius at this point that there occurs one of the two verbatim parallels with *The Duchess of Malfy*:

> The office of [a] justice is perverted quite
> When one thief hangs another.

The importance of this exact verbal repetition is obvious, but even more significant is another parallel that follows close upon it. Appius meets an indignant speech from Virginius with the smooth answer:

> Your madness wrongs you; by my soul, I love you.

[1] In Middleton's *Your Five Gallants*, II, i, and in *The Faithful Friends* (ascribed to Beaumont and Fletcher), I. ii.

and Virginius scornfully replies:

> Love me! Thou lov'st me, Appius, as the earth loves
> rain;
> Thou fain wouldst swallow me.

Compare *The Duchess of Malfy*, III. v:

> *Bosola*. Your brothers mean you safety and pity.
> *Duchess*. Pity! With such a pity, men preserve alive
> Pheasants and quails when they are not fat enough
> To be eaten.

The likeness here is a likeness of manner and spirit, more eloquent of Webster's authorship than the most exact verbal parallel. The occurrence of the same phrase in the two plays might possibly be accounted for by plagiarism, but not a resemblance of this kind.

In the course of the last fifty lines of this scene there are several other indications of Webster's hand of a less conspicuous sort—one of which has been noticed by Brooke—but with this extraordinary array of evidence before us it is scarcely necessary to trouble about 'faintly reminiscent' words and phrases. It is not for the scarcity, but for the abundance, of internal evidence of Webster's authorship that this scene is remarkable. I much doubt, indeed, whether in any other of his plays there can be found a single scene containing a like number of distinctive phrases or turns of expression of which he has made use elsewhere. That elsewhere in the play phraseological resemblances and repetitions are less abundant is natural, since no other portion of it presents a situation for which an exact parallel is to be found in one of the other plays. But there are nevertheless a very considerable number besides those mentioned by Brooke.

It is in the first scene of the play that perhaps the most decisive proof of Webster's authorship is to be found, a proof even more conclusive than the repetition of two lines from *The Duchess of Malfy*. One of Webster's most marked characteristics is his fondness for what Dr. Stoll[1] calls 'cheap, deceptive tricks with words', for putting into the

[1] *John Webster*, 1905, p. 40.

mouths of his characters utterances intended to puzzle or deceive the persons to whom they are addressed by the use of words in a sense different from that which they would naturally convey. All Webster's plays from *A White Devil* onwards exhibit this sort of verbal trickery, and so also does this play, where a conspicuous instance is afforded by Appius's speech in reply to the message received from the Senate informing him that he has been elected one of the Decemviri. It should be explained that his refusal to accept the office will entail his banishment from Rome :

> *Appius.* . . . noble friends,
> We now must part ; necessity of state
> Compels it so ;
> I must inhabit now a place unknown ;
> You see 't compels me leave you. Fare you well.
> *First Cousin.* To banishment, my lord ?
> *Appius.* I am given up
> To a long travel full of fear and danger ;
> . . . .
> Banish'd from all my kindred and my friends ;
> Yea, banish'd from myself ; for I accept
> This honourable calling.
> *Second Cousin.* We are made for ever ; noble kinsman,
> 'Twas but to fright us.
> *Appius.* But, my loving kinsmen,
> Mistake me not ; for what I spake was true.
> . . . *I told you first*
> I was to inhabit in a place unknown :
> 'Tis very certain, for this reverend seat
> Receives me as a pupil ; . . .
> . . . *I show'd you next*
> I am to travel ; 'tis a certain truth ;
> Look ! by how much the labour of the mind
> Exceeds the body's, so far am I bound
> With pain and industry, beyond the toil
> Of those that sweat in war. . . .
> *I told you I must leave you ; 'tis most true :*
> Henceforth the face of a barbarian
> And yours shall be all one, &c.

Compare with this the following passage from the dialogue

between Woodroff and Lessingham in Act v, sc. i, of *A Cure for a Cuckold*:

> *Woodroff*. Where 's your friend? . . .
> . . . .
> *Lessingham*. . . . truth is, he 's dangerously wounded.
> *Woodroff*. But he 's not dead, I hope?
> *Lessingham*. No, sir, not dead;
> Yet sure your daughter may take liberty
> To choose another.
> *Woodroff*. Why, that gives him dead.
> *Lessingham*. Upon my life, sir, no:
> . . . .
> *I told you he was wounded, and 'tis true;*
> He is wounded in his reputation;
> *I told you likewise,* which I am loth to repeat,
> That your fair daughter might take liberty
> To embrace another, &c. v. i (iv. 87).

Here we have the same sort of equivocation—the same trifling with words and laborious explanations, added to which there are also close resemblances of phraseology.

In these two scenes alone (Act I, sc. i, and Act IV, sc. i) there are more lines and phrases that can be paralleled from Webster's other plays than Brooke has been able to find in the whole play, and most of these are connected with the plays written after *The Duchess of Malfy*. As, however, these two scenes are those that Brooke suggests that Webster may have revised, I will add a few from other parts of the play:

(1) *A. & V.*, I. iv (Hazlitt, iii. 141):

> What we will, we will.

Duchess of Malfy, v. ii (ii. 257):

> What I have done, I have done.

Cure for a Cuckold, v. i (iv. 85):

> What I have said, I have said.

(2) *A. & V.*, II. ii (iii. 151):

> Shall I tell you truth?
> You account the expense of engines, and of swords,
> Of horses and of armour, dearer far
> Than soldiers' lives.

White Devil, v. i (ii. 113–14):

Francisco. What didst thou think of him? faith, speak freely.

Flamineo. He was a kind of statesman, that would sooner have reckoned how many cannon-bullets he had discharged against a town, to count his expenses that way, than how many of his valiant and deserving subjects he lost before it.

(3) *A. & V.*, II. ii (iii. 153):

Go beg,
Go beg, you mutinous rogues! brag of the service
You ne'er durst look on.

White Devil, IV. ii (ii. 86):

Go, go brag
How many ladies you have undone like me.

Duchess of Malfy, I. ii (ii. 176):

Go, go brag
You have left me heartless.

(4) *A. & V.*, II. iii (iii. 164):

. . . to right our wrongs,
We must not menace with a public hand;
. . . .
We should smile smoothest where our hate 's most deep
And when our spleen 's broad waking, seem to sleep.
Let the young man play still upon the bit,
Till we have brought and train'd him to our lure:
Great men should strike but once, and then strike sure.

White Devil, III. ii (ii. 75):

We see that undermining more prevails
Than doth the cannon. Bear your wrongs conceal'd
And, patient as the tortoise, let this camel
Stalk o'er your back unbruis'd: sleep with the lion,
And let this brood of secure foolish mice
Play with your nostrils, till the time be ripe
For th' bloody audit, and the fatal gripe.

(5) *A. & V.*, II. iii (iii. 164):

We stand in the world's eye.

Sir Thomas Wyat (i. 6):

We stand high
In man's opinion and the world's broad eye.

Devil's Law Case, II. i (iii. 37):

We . . . have long
To th' world's eye shewn like friends.

Ibid., III. iii (iii. 63):

this was merely
To blind the eye o' th' world.

(6) *A. & V.*, III. i (iii. 166):

Lord Appius doth intend me wrong;
And under his smooth calmness cloaks a tempest.

Duchess of Malfy, III. v (ii 225):

. . . like to calm weather
At sea before a tempest, false hearts speak fair
To those they intend most mischief.

(7) *A. & V.*, III. ii (iii. 171):

First Lictor. I know no man more valiant than we are, for we back knights and gentlemen daily.

Second Lictor. Right, we have them by the back hourly.

Westward Hoe, III. ii (i. 113):

Monopoly. . . . thou art a tall man too, it seems; thou hast backed many a man in thy time, I warrant.

Ambush (sheriff's officer). I have had many a man by the back, sir.

(8) *A. & V.*, III. ii (iii. 174):

Uncivil sir,
What makes you thus familiar and thus bold?

and again, in the same scene (iii. 177):

Why, *uncivil sir*,
Have I not begged forbearance, &c.

White Devil, II. i (ii. 32):

Uncivil sir, there 's hemlock in thy breath.

(9) *A. & V.*, III. ii (iii. 180):

. . . we that have such servants,
Are like to cuckolds that have riotous wives;
We are the last that know it.

Cure for a Cuckold, v. i (iv. 87):

(Lessingham tells Woodroff that Annabel is unfaithful to her husband. Woodroff (Annabel's father) replies :)

> Why, then, of all men living do you address
> This report to me, that ought, of all men breathing,
> To have been the last o' th' roll, except the husband,
> That should have heard of't ?

(10) *A. & V.*, III. ii (iii. 183) :

> I am more free to serve the gods, I hope,
> Now I have lost your service.

Devil's Law Case, IV. ii (iii. 97) :

> This law-business
> Will leave me so small leisure to serve God,
> I shall serve the king the worse.

Of these ten additional passages, some of them containing resemblances of phrase, others of sentiment, all but one may be left to speak for themselves. With regard to (7) the lictor's (or sheriff's officer's) joke, common to this play and to *Westward Hoe*, it is worth noticing that it occurs in the same scene as the 'matchless eye' joke, repeated from *The White Devil*. Brooke says that the latter is a 'common joke', but what evidence is there of this ? No doubt it is not of Webster's own creation ; it seems doubtful, indeed, whether Webster was capable of inventing even the smallest joke. I have traced four of those in *The Devil's Law Case*—where jokes are neither numerous nor of striking quality—to the *New and Choise Characters of severall Authors* published with Sir Thomas Overbury's poem *A Wife* in 1615. This particular 'matchless' joke is found in Chapman, and nothing is more likely than that Webster borrowed it from him. So far as Webster's claim to *Appius and Virginia* is concerned, the significant fact about both these witticisms is that they are also to be found in an early Websterian play.

Another indication of Webster's hand is the equivocal observation made by Appius (Act III, sc. ii) when he offers to take Virginia into his charge and to make himself responsible for her appearance at the trial—'I'll use her in all kindness as my wife.' Not only is there here the general resemblance to the equivocal speeches already referred to, there is also a particular resemblance to a passage occurring in the dialogue between Romelio and the Waiting Woman in *The Devil's Law Case* where Romelio pretends to misunderstand the meaning of the Waiting Woman's remark 'You may use me at your pleasure'.

Webster, as is well known, introduced into *The White Devil* and *The Duchess of Malfy* numbers of passages from Florio's *Montaigne*. At the time of writing *The White Devil* he was apparently unacquainted with Sidney's *Arcadia*. After he had written the first two acts of *The Duchess of Malfy* a copy of that work seems to have come into his hands. Perhaps the 1613 edition of the *Arcadia* had just made its appearance. At any rate it is not until the third act of the play that we begin to find traces of Sidney's influence, while from that act onwards the borrowings from the *Arcadia* are even more abundant than those from Montaigne. These borrowings (first discovered by Mr. Crawford) are equally numerous in Webster's poem *A Monumental Column*. In his later plays they are less common, though in *The Devil's Law Case* there are still a considerable number, especially from the *Arcadia*. Heywood, so far as I am aware, made no use either of Sidney's romance or of Montaigne's essays. But *Appius and Virginia* does. The two lines near the beginning of the play (paralleled, as we have seen, in *The Duchess of Malfy*):

> I have seen children oft eat sweetmeats thus,
> As fearful to devour them,

were clearly suggested by this passage from Book I of the *Arcadia* (Routledge's edition, p 74):

> Zelmane's eyes were (like children before sweetmeat) eager, but fearful of their ill-pleasing governors.

It is again in the first scene of *Appius and Virginia* that Appius is represented as saying:

> I have heard of cunning footmen that have worn
> Shoes made of lead some ten days 'fore a race,
> To give them nimble and more active feet.

The 'I have heard of' is characteristic of Webster's manner of introducing scraps of information picked up in the course of his reading. The device here referred to was one that Montaigne (*Essays*, Book II, ch. ii) tells us his father adopted:

> 'I have seene some hollow staves of his filled with lead, which hee wont to use and exercise his armes withall . . . and shooes with leaden soles, which he wore to ensure himselfe to leape, to vault, and to run.'

Once more, in the advocate's speech at the beginning of the fifth act:

> I have learnt with the wise hedgehog,
> To stop my cave that way the tempest drives.

we find the author of *Appius* making use of the tale told by Montaigne of 'A certain citizen of Cyzicum', who gained a reputation for his skill in foretelling storms and the direction from which the wind would blow

> 'because he had learnt the quality of the Hedge-hogge, whose property it is to build his hole or denne open diverse waies, and toward severall winds, and foreseeing rising stormes, he presently stoppeth the holes that way.'
> *Essays*, Bk. II, ch. xii.

Turning again to the vocabulary of *Appius and Virginia* there are several words, besides those mentioned by Brooke, pointing to Webster's authorship. There is, for instance, his peculiar adverbial use of the word 'right'[1] of which this play affords two examples:

> You . . . play the modest courtier *right*.
> *A. & V.*, I. i (iii. 130).
> 'Tis the world *right*. *A. & V.*, V. iii. (iii. 218).

Compare:

> . . . o' th' captain's humour *right*.
> *W. D.*, II. i (ii. 45).
> *Right* the fashion of the world.
> *D. M.*, III. v (ii. 225).
> The gallant's fashion *right*.
> *D. L C..*, III. iii (iii. 65).

Amongst the words for which Webster shows a marked partiality the following may be mentioned: *noble, strange,*

[1] One or two instances of this uncommon use are, however, to be found in Heywood.

distraction, eminent. The two first are scattered throughout all his plays in the most remarkable profusion,[1] often associated with the most unlikely subjects. *Noble* occurs no fewer than sixty-six times in this play and *strange* twelve times. I have mentioned 'distraction' as another typical word. This occurs twice in this play in conjunction with 'strange':

> See, gentlemen, what *strange distraction*
> Your falling off from duty hath begot
> In this most noble soldier. II. ii (iii. 154).
> Virginius, in a *strange shape of distraction,*
> Enters the camp. IV. ii (iii. 204).

as several times elsewhere in his plays:

> He 's fallen into a *strange distraction.*
> *W. D.*, v. i (ii. 114).
> What accident hath brought unto the prince
> This *strange distraction*? *D. M.*, v. ii (ii. 259).
> your departure hence
> Will breed a *strange distraction* in your friends.
> *C. C.*, I. ii (iv. 23).

Brooke remarks that the word 'foul' was characteristically a common one with Webster, as it undoubtedly was. But its absence from *Appius and Virginia* is no justification for doubting his authorship. The vocabulary of almost every writer varies at different periods, and all Webster's plays possess peculiarities of their own in this respect. As an illustration of this may be instanced his use of the word *eminent.* In *The Duchess of Malfy* alone of his earlier plays is it at all conspicuous, and here it occurs only five times. But when, in 1624, he came to write *Monuments of Honour* it seems to have been always at the end of his pen. The pageant with the accompanying explanatory matter occupies only five pages of Dyce's edition of his *Works*, and eight times does 'eminent' appear. Eight

[1] 'Noble' appears 17 times in *The White Devil*, 24 times in *The Duchess of Malfy*, 27 times in *The Devil's Law Case*, 20 times in *A Cure for a Cuckold*; 'strange' 16 times in *The White Devil*, 7 times in *The Duchess of Malfy*, 25 times in *The Devil's Law Case*, 16 times in *A Cure for a Cuckold.*

times also do we find it in *Appius and Virginia*, and four times in the first eighty lines of the play.

As to Brooke's observation that the *Appius and Virginia* parallels are so few that they are of no account, even if they were as few as he has assumed, I venture to assert that it would be impossible, by internal evidence alone, to establish Webster's claim to any one of his plays if it were requisite, as he suggests, that they should be 'ten or fifteen times as numerous'.

'The metre of *Appius and Virginia*', says Brooke, is 'not Webster's.' It is certainly unlike that of his earlier plays. But so also is the metre of *A Cure for a Cuckold*, which, as Brooke notes, resembles it in its lack of 'equivalences', of the 'thinking more in lines and less in feet', characteristic of these earlier plays, and resembles it also in its comparatively low percentage of run-on lines and of lines with superfluous syllables and feminine endings.[1] There are undoubtedly other features that differentiate *Appius and Virginia* from these plays—the abundance of rimed couplets, for instance, and its comparative freedom from extrinsic poetical images, although these are already noticeably less frequent in *A Cure for a Cuckold*. There are no differences, so far as I can see, that cannot be accounted for by the circumstance that Webster is here attempting an entirely fresh *genre*.

Brooke finds the style of *Appius and Virginia* exactly like that of Heywood when he is writing solemnly. The resemblance does not strike me as close. On the contrary, the play contains many passages that it is absolutely inconceivable that Heywood should have written. Take this passage for instance:

> Come, you birds of death,
> And fill your greedy crops with human flesh;
> Then to the city fly, disgorge it there
> Before the Senate, and from thence arise
> A plague to choke all Rome! II. ii.

Is there anything resembling *that* in the whole range of

[1] See the metrical table on p. 190 of Dr. Stoll's *John Webster*.

Heywood's dramas? His language, as Symonds observes, is 'never high-flown or bombastic, rarely rising to the height of poetical diction'.[1] There is only one of the Elizabethan dramatists, and that the greatest of them, to whom this heightened utterance is natural. The author has here caught exactly the voice and accent of Shakespeare. Brooke, again, asserts that the 'numerous *slight imitations* of Shakespeare are rather more a mark of Heywood than of Webster', and refers us to *The Cambridge History of English Literature*, as if it supported this view. What does Sir A. W. Ward say there? He says—what is undoubtedly true—that when Heywood imitated Shakespeare he did it 'more or less unconsciously'.[2] Anything less unconscious or more deliberate than the imitations of Shakespeare in *Appius and Virginia* could scarcely be imagined. Here are some of them:

> The high Colossus that bestrides us all. III. i.
>
> but yesterday his breath
> Aw'd Rome. V. iii.
>
> *Minutius*. You wrong one of the honorablest commanders!
> *Omnes*. Honourable commanders! II. ii.

And the cries of the Roman soldiery, roused to fury by the pathetic speech in which Virginius explains how he has been driven to slay his own daughter to save her from dishonour:

> *1st Soldier*. O, villain Appius!
> *2nd Soldier*. O, noble Virginius!
> *1st Soldier*. Appius is the parricide!
> *2nd Soldier*. Virginius guiltless of his daughter's death.
>
> . . . .
>
> *1st Soldier*. Appius shall die for't!
> *2nd Soldier*. Let's make Virginius general.
> *Omnes*. A general! a general! let's make Virginius general! IV. ii.

Here are the voices of the mob listening to Antony's speech in *Julius Caesar*. And it is not only in occasional speeches

[1] Thomas Heywood's Plays, Mermaid edition, Introd., p. xxi. But it is not quite true that Heywood is *never* bombastic.

[2] *Op. cit.*, vol. vi, p. 106.

that Shakespeare's influence can be seen: it permeates the whole play. Heywood never imitated Shakespeare in this way. Who did? Who but Webster—Webster who aped Marston in his 'revenge' plays and Fletcher in his tragi-comedies, and who transferred to his pages scores of passages borrowed from dramatists and prose-writers alike?

One other point should be noted. A marked feature of Webster's work is the prevalence of apophthegms, of detached utterances of a sententious character. In *Appius and Virginia* they are not quite so abundant as usual, but there are nevertheless a large number of them scattered throughout the play, and it will be found that they are almost always introduced in rimed couplets, as occasionally in the earlier plays. It is evident that in this play rime has deliberately been chosen as a vehicle for these aphoristic utterances, and it is this that accounts for its comparatively large percentage of rime. There is also a large proportion of rime in many of Heywood's plays, but here the resemblance ends. Heywood does not use rime, as the author of *Appius and Virginia* does, mainly for the purpose of giving prominence to the wisdom or value of a sentiment. It was not his custom to garnish his plays with apophthegms, in fact he scarcely ever indulges in anything of the kind. This alone should be sufficient to dispose of the theory that he wrote *Appius and Virginia*, or had any substantial share in its composition. And, apart altogether from the Shakespearean imitations, the heightened rhetoric and pregnant reflections with which the play abounds, the whole treatment of Livy's story is altogether unlike Heywood's treatment of the story of Lucretia, or any other theme. There is here an evident self-restraint, a conscious aiming at a classical severity of form quite in keeping with the painstaking deliberate method of Webster and not at all with that of the fluent, facile Heywood.

Doubtless the peculiar features of *Appius and Virginia* that inspired Brooke's scepticism as to Webster's authorship were the occurrence of words elsewhere peculiar to Heywood and the introduction amongst its *dramatis personae* of a clown of the Heywoodian type; both these features obviously suggesting the explanation that Heywood himself had a hand in the composition of the play. This explanation had also occurred to me, although the play bore what seemed to me so many and such decisive indications of Webster's hand that it never occurred to me to doubt that it was substantially his. The explanation that suggested itself to my mind was that Heywood might have worked upon a (possibly unfinished) play of Webster's and completed and adapted it for representation upon the stage, writing up the Clown's part and slightly revising Webster's work, the words belonging to Heywood's vocabulary being indications of this revision. The subsequent discovery of Heywoodian words in *A Cure for a Cuckold* showed me that the peculiarities in the vocabulary of *Appius and Virginia* could not, of themselves, justify the belief that Heywood had collaborated in the play. The Clown, however, still remains to be accounted for. Is Corbulo of Webster's creation, or is he the work of a collaborator, whether Heywood or another? It would be pleasant if we could feel certain that he was not Webster's, for he is certainly one of the least mirthful and most consistently obscene clowns to be found in the Elizabethan drama. Webster's plays, with this exception, are comparatively free from indecency, and his humour elsewhere, though far from subtle, is not of the easy, shallow description exhibited by the Clown in this play. That the Clown in *Appius and Virginia* is of the same type as Heywood's clowns cannot be denied, and it is not unlikely that the Clown of *The Rape of Lucrece* was his progenitor. But the appearance of a clown in a Roman play was not an innovation of so startling a kind as Dr. Stoll [1] and Rupert Brooke suggest. There are clowns in *Titus Andronicus*, in Lodge's *Wounds of Civil War*, and Shakespeare's *Antony and Cleopatra*, though it is true that the parts they play are merely episodic. But at any rate Heywood was creating no precedent in introducing a clown into a Roman

[1] *John Webster*, p. 198.

play, and it is doubtful whether in Elizabethan or Jacobean times the anachronism involved would cause the slightest uneasiness to any of the dramatists, Jonson possibly excepted. And though the Clown is of the same type as Heywood's, he is not of a type peculiar to Heywood. Rowley has precisely the same sort of clown in *A New Wonder, A Woman Never Vext*, quite as much like Corbulo as any of his fellows in Heywood's plays.[1] Rupert Brooke says that the Heywood Clown is of an early type; Dr. Stoll also remarks that by the time *Appius and Virginia* was written he had become old-fashioned. It is true that the type is an old one—at least as old as Lyly—but it had not become old-fashioned in the sense of obsolete, or out of fashion. That the same type of clown maintained its popularity for at least twenty years after *Lucrece* was written, such plays as *A Maydenhead Well Lost* and *A Woman Never Vext*, both printed, and probably written, after 1630, bear witness. The Clown of *Lucrece* betrays his early date by his extravagant buffoonery and wildly inappropriate songs and jigs. The clowns in these later plays—one of them Heywood's, the other Rowley's—are those that on the whole most resemble the *Appius and Virginia* Clown. All three of them are, like the *Lucrece* Clown, servants to a woman, all are full of puns and quibbles, and the language of all is peculiarly gross, though in this respect the Clown of *Appius and Virginia* achieves an unenviable eminence. If this clown is not Webster's there is no more reason for supposing him to be Heywood's than Rowley's. There would, indeed, be better reason for suspecting Rowley, who had recently been working in collaboration with Webster. It is also noticeable

[1] Corbulo, it may be observed, does not, as Dr. Stoll suggests, joke in Latin because he is a Roman, but because he is a clown. It was one of the curious conventions of the time that the Clown should introduce scraps of Latin into his patter. The clowns in Heywood's *Fair Maid of the Exchange, The Royal King and Loyal Subject, Love's Mistress, A Challenge for Beauty, A Maidenhead Well Lost*, in Heywood and Rowley's *Fortune by Land and Sea*, and Rowley's *A Woman Never Vext*, all do this, and Corbulo is therefore in this respect merely following a well-worn tradition.

that two of the most objectionable of Corbulo's quibbles—and these not of the stock type—are to be found in a slightly varied form in *A Woman Never Vext.* This, however, is perhaps rather a reason for attributing him to Webster. The *Appius and Virginia* Clown has also, as Dr. Stoll notes, a greater variety of euphuism than any of Heywood's clowns—or, for that matter, any of Rowley's—and his jokes are, if possible, even more primitive than theirs. Added to this there is the fact that it is the Clown who is responsible for the 'matchless eye' jest, which appears also in *The White Devil.* And it can hardly be suggested that Webster, who in *The White Devil* and *The Duchess of Malfy* so closely imitated Marston's peculiarly savage type of humour, would have much difficulty in turning out a clown of the stock Heywood pattern. On the whole, therefore, there does not seem to be sufficient justification for suggesting another hand even in the prose scenes in which the Clown appears.

That the rest of the play is Webster's there can, I think, be no reasonable doubt, nor that the published text is of a date not earlier than 1630 or thereabouts. The text may, as Brooke suggests, have undergone some alteration and revision between the date of the original composition of the play and its appearance in print in 1654, but there is not an atom of evidence to support the conjecture that we have here a revised version of a play older than *The Duchess of Malfy*, and the resemblances to *The Devil's Law Case* and *A Cure for a Cuckold* seem to contradict such a theory. That it shows traces of Heywood's influence is undeniable, though this influence is by no means so marked as Shakespeare's, but there is no evidence whatever, either in the style or vocabulary of the play, to warrant the assumption that Heywood had even a finger in its composition—much less 'an entire hand' as Brooke would have us believe.

1914.

VI

A WEBSTER–MASSINGER PLAY: 'THE FAIR MAID OF THE INN'

IT has hitherto been assumed that Webster's extant dramatic work is limited to ten plays, four of which (*The White Devil, The Duchess of Malfy, The Devil's Law Case,* and *Appius and Virginia*) he wrote alone, three (*Sir Thomas Wyat, Westward Hoe,* and *Northward Hoe*) in collaboration with Dekker, and one (*A Cure for a Cuckold*) in collaboration with Rowley. This list is exclusive of the Induction to Marston's *Malcontent,* which is also his, and *The Thracian Wonder,* of which (though attributed by its first publisher to Webster and Rowley) his part-authorship is generally denied. It has never been suspected that Webster collaborated with Massinger. But such is the fact. *The Fair Maid of the Inn,* licensed on 22nd of January 1626 and first printed in the Beaumont and Fletcher folio of 1647, is undoubtedly a Webster-Massinger play.

Boyle[1] ascribes to Massinger Act I, Act III, sc. ii, and Act V, sc. iii. This is correct, except that there are traces of Webster's collaboration in III. ii, and in V. iii, the prose at the end of the last scene (after the entry of the Host, Forobosco, and the Clown) being substantially his. Act II, Act III, sc. i, Act IV, sc. ii, and Act V, sc. i and ii, are wholly Webster's. The evidence of Webster's authorship of these scenes is absolutely conclusive. They exhibit many of his peculiarities of vocabulary and phraseology, and not only reveal on examination a number of connexions with his acknowledged works, but, like them, borrow freely from Sidney's *Arcadia* and Overbury's *Characters.* The only scene about which there can be any doubt is Act IV, sc. i.

The following indications of Webster's authorship are noted in the order in which they occur in the play:[2]

[1] *New Shakspere Society's Transactions,* 1880–6, pp. 610, 611.

[2] The references within parentheses are to volume and page of Hazlitt's edition of Webster (Reeves and Turner, 1897).

Act II, Scene i

Cesario has been wounded by Mentivole in a duel, and whilst Cesario's father Alberto is in conference with the physician and surgeon in attendance upon his son, Clarissa (Cesario's sister) enters with her mother Mariana and loudly bewails the condition of the wounded man. Alberto chides his daughter for disturbing her brother's slumbers, and (addressing his wife) exclaims:

> . . . go, go, take caroch
> And, as you love me, you and the girl retire.

This habit of repeating the word 'go' is characteristic of Webster. There are three instances of it in *The White Devil*, three in *The Duchess of Malfy*, and one in *The Devil's Law Case*. For the purposes of illustration, I quote an instance from each play:

> go, go, complain to the great duke.
> *The White Devil*, II. i (Hazlitt, ii. 38).
> Go, go, give your foster-daughters good counsel.
> *Duchess of Malfy*, II. ii (ii. 187).
> Go, go presently
> And reveal it to the Capuchin.
> *The Devil's Law Case*, V. iii (iii. 109).

A few lines after, Alberto, urging the physician and surgeon to 'tend their patient with the best observance', adds:

> And think what payment his recovery
> Shall show'r upon you,
> Of all men breathing.

The expression 'of all men living' occurs several times in *A Cure for a Cuckold*, and once in the same play we have 'of all men breathing'.

> *Woodroff*. Why, then, of all men living, do you address
> This report to me, that ought *of all men breathing*
> To have been the last o' th' roll . . .
> That should have heard of't?
> Act V, sc. i (Hazlitt, iv. 87).

There is no reason to believe that it was any commoner in Webster's time than it is now.

At this point Mentivole appears on the scene. Alberto expresses surprise at his visit, which he suggests is due merely to a desire to exult over his adversary. This accusation Mentivole denies :

> . . . do not misconstrue
> In your distaste of me, the true intent
> Of my coming hither.

That here again the language is the language of Webster may be seen on comparison with a passage in *The Devil's Law Case*, II. iii (iii. 45–6) :

> [Ariosto to Romelio] . . . my intent of coming hither
> Was to persuade you to patience.

Over and over again in this scene we find echoes of passages in Webster's independent plays. Some of these are faint, but now and then they become very distinct. For instance, after Alberto has remarked to Mentivole, who has just announced that he is ' not sorry ' for the injury he has inflicted upon Cesario, ' You are arm'd methinks with wondrous confidence ', we come upon this passage :

> *Mentivole.* O, with the best, sir ;
> For I bring penitence and satisfaction.
> *Alberto.* Satisfaction ! Why I heard you say but now,
> You were not sorry for his wounds.
> *Mentivole.* Nor am I ; the satisfaction I bring, Sir, is to you, &c.

which is curiously similar to one that occurs in the dialogue between Leonora and Crispiano during the hearing of *The Devil's Law Case* (Act IV, sc. ii) :

> *Leonora.* . . . but, you know, repentance
> Is nothing without satisfaction.
> *Crispiano.* Satisfaction ! why, your husband 's dead ;
> What satisfaction can you make him ?
> *Leonora.* The greatest satisfaction in the world, my lord,
> To restore the land to th' right heir, &c.

In all Webster's plays from *The Duchess of Malfy* onwards will be found borrowings from Sidney's *Arcadia*. *The Duchess of Malfy* and *The Devil's Law Case* in particular are full of them. One phrase made a great impression upon the dramatist. It is in Book III of the *Arcadia*:

'Dorus wandered ... in the woods, crying for pardon of her who could not hear him, but indeed was grieved for his absence, *having given the wound to him through her own heart.*' Routledge's edition, p. 305.

He introduces it in *The Devil's Law Case*, III. iii (iii. 68):

Leonora. You have given him the wound you speak of
Quite through your mother's heart,

and in *A Cure for a Cuckold*, IV. ii (iv. 69):

Clare. O, you have struck him dead through my heart!

Not content with this he returns to it in this play:

Mentivole (*to Alberto*). I have run my sword quite through your heart
And slightly hurt your son;

and within a space of little more than fifty lines we find another echo of it in the speech in which Cesario begs Alberto not to allow the order he has given to his servants—to cut off Mentivole's right hand—to be carried into execution:

. . . if you do proceed thus cruelly
There is no question in the wound you give him,
I shall bleed to death for't.

In Alberto's reply to Mentivole's long harangue from which the earlier of these two last passages is quoted, he describes himself as:

. . . grown as deaf to all compassion
As *the cruellest sea-fight or most horrid tempest;*

using almost exactly the same words as those addressed by Brachiano to Isabella in *The White Devil*, II. i (ii. 38):

. . . let thy brother rage
Beyond a horrid tempest, or sea-fight.

The comparison must have been a favourite one with Webster, for we meet with it yet again in *The Devil's Law Case*, V. iv (iii. 113):

I do know you have a storm within you
More terrible than a sea-fight.

Act II, Scene ii

This, a prose scene introducing us to the 'Host' of the Inn and the Clown, servant to the mountebank Forobosco, is also Webster's. In the course of the dialogue between these two persons, the Host asks the Clown whether it is not a fact that in England the ladies 'take physic for fashion'. 'Yes, Sir,' says the Clown, 'and many times die to keep fashion.'

> *Host.* How? die to keep fashion?
> *Clown.* Yes, I have known a lady sick of the small-pox, only to keep her face from pit-holes, take cold, strike them in again, kick up the heels, and vanish.

This speech is quite in Webster's style, and there is in the dialogue between Bosola and the 'Old Lady' of *The Duchess of Malfy* an anecdote of much the same sort:

> There was a lady in France, that having had the small-pox,
> Flay'd the skin off her face, to make it more level.
> *Duchess of Malfy*, II. i (ii. 180).

The Hostess now enters with Biancha, her supposed daughter, 'The Fair Maid of the Inn', and the following dialogue ensues:

> *Host.* Here comes my wife and daughter.
> *Clown.* You have a pretty commodity of this night-worm?
> *Host.* Why, man?
> *Clown.* She is a pretty lure to draw custom to your ordinary.
> *Host.* Dost think I keep her to that purpose?
> *Clown. When a dove-house is empty, there is cummin-seed used to purloin from the rest of the neighbours.*

In *The Duchess of Malfy* and *The Devil's Law Case* Webster borrows from Overbury's *Characters* almost as frequently as he does from the *Arcadia*. There is good reason to believe that he himself was the author of some at least of the additional 'characters' (*New and Choise Characters of Severall Authors*) published in 1615, for not only are they just as deeply indebted to Sidney's *Arcadia* and Florio's *Montaigne* as are Webster's plays, but they borrow identical passages and occasionally vary their phrasing in a similar way. In this instance, however, Webster has had recourse to one of the first set of characters published in 1614. Of 'An Host' the character-writer observes:

> His wife is the cummin-seed of his dove-house, and to be a good guest is a warrant for her liberty.
> Overbury's *Characters*, ed. Rimbault, 1890, p. 71.

Soon afterwards Biancha, speaking of Mentivole, says to the Host:

> Sir, the gentleman
> Is every way so noble.

with which we may compare:

> . . . a man so every way
> Deserving. *Cure for a Cuckold*, IV. ii (iv. 74–5).
> You are a creature every way complete.
> *Ibid.*, V. i (iv. 82).
> . . . as you
> Are every way well-parted. *Ibid.*, V. i. (iv. 84).

Biancha goes on to say that though she is, of necessity, familiar to every guest, yet she will be a stranger to their vices, a remark which calls from the Hostess the approving exclamation:

> Right my daughter:
> She has the right strain of her mother.

This unusual adverbial use of 'right' is several times to be met with in Webster's acknowledged plays, e. g.:

> Right the fashion of the world!
> *Duchess of Malfy*, III. v (ii. 225).
> The gallant's fashion right.
> *Devil's Law Case*, III. iii (iii. 65).
> 'Tis the world right.
> *Appius and Virginia*, V. iii (iii. 218).

Act II, Scene iii

A short scene, in verse, describing an interview between Mentivole and Baptista.

The verse has the unmistakable impress of Webster, and we may note a characteristic exclamation of Baptista's:

> O my fury!

With which we may compare Cornelia's cry in *The White Devil* on witnessing the murder of Marcello (Act IV, sc. v):

O my horror!

and also a few lines later in the same scene:

O my perpetual sorrow! (Hazlitt, ii. 108.)

and Jolenta in *The Devil's Law Case*, III. iii:

O my fantastical sorrow! (Hazlitt, iii. 66.)

Such exclamations, although not peculiar to Webster, are rarely met with outside his plays.

Act II, Scene iv

In the last of Clarissa's speeches preceding the entry of Mariana with a Sailor, we have

. . . the sad
And unexpected quarrel, which divided
So noble and so excellent a friendship,
Which, *as I ne'er had magic to foresee*
So I could not prevent.

In *The White Devil*:

Man may his fate foresee, but not prevent.
v. ii (ii. 137).

and in *The Duchess of Malfy*:

O most imperfect light of human reason,
That mak'st us so unhappy to foresee
What we can least prevent! III. ii (ii. 208).

All three passages were inspired by, and the last is almost a literal rendering of, a sentence occurring in Gynecia's speech at the beginning of Book II of the *Arcadia*:

'O imperfect proportion of reason which can make too much foresee and too little prevent!'

The Sailor who accompanies Mariana brings Cesario the news that his father has met his death by drowning. This news is received by Cesario with a remark which, with slight variations, is constantly on the lips of Webster's characters:

I pray thee leave us.

Mariana then observes:

I have a sorrow of a nature equal to the former;

and Cesario replies:

> And most commonly they come together.

The reflexion that misfortunes never come singly is, of course, proverbial. But it is none the less noteworthy that it is to be found twice in *The Devil's Law Case*:

> One mischief never comes alone. II. i (iii. 40).
>
> I do look now for some great misfortunes
> To follow; for indeed mischiefs . . .
> . . . never come to prey upon us single.
> III. iii (iii. 67).

Act III, Scene i

With this scene we return to the Host, Hostess, and Biancha. All the first part of the scene (with the exception of a single speech from Biancha) is in prose and is clearly Webster's. With the entry of Forobosco and the Clown the prose changes to verse, and here the quarrel between these two is strongly reminiscent of the scene in *The Duchess of Malfy* immediately following the murder of the Duchess, where Duke Ferdinand quarrels with Bosola:

> *Forobosco.* . . . I discharge thee
> From my service; *see me no more henceforth.*
> *Clown.* Discharge me! Is that my year's wages?
> I'll not be so answer'd.
> *Foro.* Not, Camel? Sirrah, *I am liberal to thee.*
> Thou hast thy life, be gone.

Compare *The Duchess of Malfy*, IV. ii:

> *Bosola.* I challenge
> The reward due to my service.
> *Ferd.* I'll tell thee
> What I'll give thee.
> *Bosola.* Do.
> *Ferd.* I'll give thee a pardon
> For this murder.
> *Bosola.* Ha!
> *Ferd.* Yes, and 'tis
> *The largest bounty I can study to do thee.*
> . . . .
> *Never look upon me more.* (ii. 249).

After a dance in which a tailor, a dancer, a mule-driver, a schoolmaster, and a clerk—all suitors for the hand of Biancha—take part, Cesario enters and Forobosco and the dancers depart. Then follows an interview—in verse—between Cesario and Biancha. Here we may note:

> *Cesario.* Canst thou love?
> *Biancha.* Love! Is there such a word in any language
> That carries honest sense?

With which we may compare Ferdinand's speech in *The Duchess of Malfy*, III. ii (which is, by the way, almost a literal transcript of another passage from Gynecia's speech at the beginning of Book II of the *Arcadia*):

> Virtue, where art thou hid? what hideous thing
> Is it that doth eclipse thee?
> Or is it true thou art but a bare name
> And no essential thing? (Hazlitt, ii. 208.)

Act III, Scene ii

That this is substantially Massinger's is clear not only from the style of the verse but from the presence of several of Massinger's characteristic self-repetitions. Mr. Boyle attributes it entirely to Massinger, but there are one or two slight, but significant, suggestions of Webster's hand.

The first of these is in the words used by Mariana when asked by the Duke to 'deliver her aggrievances':

> Though divided
> I stand between the laws of Truth and Modesty
> Yet let my grief have vent. . . .
> . . . the burthen
> Of my charg'd soul must be laid down before you;
> Wherein, if strict opinion cancel shame,
> My frailty is my plea.

There can be little doubt that 'if strict opinion *counsel* shame', Deighton's conjectural emendation, is the correct reading here. Deighton (who did not, of course, suspect Webster's hand in this play) supports his conjecture by comparing Leonora's words in *The Devil's Law Case*, IV. ii (iii. 90), 'where precisely the same incident occurs', and

Leonora, when asked why she so late reveals the truth, answers:

> Because, my lord, I loath'd that such a sin
> Should lie smother'd with me in my grave, my penitence,
> Though to my shame, prefers the revealing of it
> 'Bove worldly reputation.

Note again, at the conclusion of the speech in which Mariana unfolds her story of Cesario's base origin:

> *Duke.* Produce your witness.
> *Mariana.* The faulconer's wife his mother
> And such women as waited then upon me.

And compare, in the corresponding situation during the hearing of Leonora's suit in *The Devil's Law Case*, IV. ii (iii. 93):

> *Crispiano.* . . . what proof is there,
> More than the affirmation of the mother,
> Of this corporal dealing?
> *Contilupo.* The deposition of a waiting-woman
> That serv'd her the same time;

where the terse, direct reply to the Judge's question seems to point to identity of authorship.

There is yet another trace of Webster in the closing words of the scene:

> *Mariana.* If all fail I will learn thee to conquer
> Adversity with sufferance.
> *Mentivole.* You resolve nobly.

These sententious remarks, with the accompanying admiring comment of the person to whom they are addressed, are a conspicuous feature of Webster's dialogue. One is conscious of the author's pride in the expression of a fine sentiment and his desire to impress it upon his audience. Compare, for instance:

> *Ferdinand.* . . . what do you think of good horsemanship?
> *Antonio.* Nobly, my lord: as out of the Grecian horse issued
> Many famous princes, so out of brave horsemanship
> Arise the first sparks of growing resolution, that raise
> The mind to noble action.
> *Ferdinand.* You have bespoke it worthily.
>
> *Duchess of Malfy*, I. ii (ii. 163).

Ercole. I will leave you to the freedom of your own soul:
May it move whither heaven and you please!
Jolenta. Now you express yourself most nobly.
The Devil's Law Case, I. ii (iii. 20).

Ercole. I do look on my action with a thought of terror;
To do ill and dwell in't is unmanly.
Capuchin. You are divinely inform'd, sir.
Ibid., II. iv (iii. 50).

Act IV, Scene i

This is the only scene as to the authorship of which I feel any doubt. It is certainly neither unalloyed Massinger nor unalloyed Webster, and I can find no positive indications of either. It is worthy of note that though Boyle attributes the play to Massinger and Fletcher 'with some mixed scenes added by Rowley', it is the only scene in which he professes himself able to trace Fletcher's hand. It is probably a mixed Massinger and Webster scene. As all the other scenes in which Biancha (here a prominent figure) appears are Webster's, it seems justifiable to assume that it is chiefly his.[1]

Act IV, Scene ii

The Host is enlarging upon Forobosco's skill in magic before a motley assemblage of his would-be clients, amongst whom figures a 'Dancer'. The dancer expresses surprise that Forobosco has 'no more resort of ladies to him'. The Host replies:

He 's scarce known to be in town yet,
Ere long we shall have 'em come
Hurrying hither in feather-beds.
Dancer. How, bedridden?
Forobosco. No, sir, in feather-beds that move upon four wheels in Spanish caroches.

which recalls the speech of one of the madmen in Act IV, sc. ii, of *The Duchess of Malfy*:

Woe to the caroch that brought home my wife from the mask . . . it had a large feather-bed in it.
(Hazlitt, ii. 240.)

[1] I leave this as written in 1915. But I now (1924) believe this scene to be Ford's, and that there are traces of his hand elsewhere in the play. My conversion to this opinion I owe to my friend Mr. William Wells, who has an intimate knowledge both of 'Beaumont and Fletcher' and of Ford's plays.

Forobosco now appears and one after another the assembled clients seek his advice. After the dancer has preferred his suit, there comes a coxcomb. He intends to set up a press in Italy 'to write all the corantoes for Christendom', and desires Forobosco to furnish him with a familiar spirit from whom to gain his intelligence. He must be quiet, as the coxcomb 'can by no means indure a terrible one'. Forobosco reassures him on this head:

> *Forobosco.* . . . I'll qualify him
> He shall not fright you,
> It shall be the ghost of some lying stationer,
> A spirit shall look as if butter would not melt in his mouth.
> A new *Mercurius Gallo-belgicus.*
> *Coxcomb.* O, there was a captain was rare at it!
> *Forobosco.* Ne'er think of him,
> Though that captain writ a full hand gallop
> And wasted indeed more harmless paper than
> Ever did laxative physic,
> Yet will I make you to out-scribble him.

That Webster is here aiming a shaft at one of his contemporaries is evident, though who this 'captain' was it is not possible to say. The passage is quoted here because the contemptuous observation applied by Forobosco to this unknown 'captain' is taken from a passage that appears only in the sixth (1615) edition of Overbury's *Characters.* The 'Character' in which it occurs is that of 'An Excellent Actor'. Its author turns from the merits of the subject of his sketch to castigate the 'imitating characterist' (i. e. Stephens, the writer of *Satyrical Essays, Characters, and others,* 1615), who, in his 'character' of 'A Common Player', had described actors as rogues:

> '. . . I would let his malicious ignorance understand that rogues are not to be imploide as maine ornaments to his Majesty's Revels; but this itch of bestriding the presse . . . hath defil'd more innocent paper than ever did laxative physic.'

In the subsequent editions of Overbury's *Characters* this passage was suppressed.

The next person to apply to Forobosco is a 'Pedant'

who wishes to confer with him 'about erecting four new sects of religion at Amsterdam'. Forobosco observes:

> This is somewhat difficult
> And will ask some conference with the devil.

Compare *A Cure for a Cuckold*, I. i (iv. 13):

> . . . 'tis a strange difficulty
> And it will ask much counsel.

When Forobosco has dealt with the requests of all his clients, the Clown enters with the Hostess and Biancha. There is in one of the Clown's speeches a curious expression applied to Forobosco's gullible customers:

> . . . you whose purses are ready to cast the calf,

which is to be found again in 'An Improvident Young Gallant', one of the 1615 *Characters.*

> Thus, when his purse has cast her calf, he goes down to the country.

Shortly afterwards the Clown says of Forobosco that

> for his conjuring, the witches of Lapland are the devil's charwomen to him, for they will sell a man wind to some purpose; he sells wind, and tells you forty lies over and over;

while in *A Cure for a Cuckold* Lessingham observes:

> Trust a woman!
> Never, henceforward I will rather trust
> The winds which Lapland witches sell to men.
>
> IV. ii (iv. 71).

The Clown continuing his abuse of Forobosco, thus sums up his career:

> in brief, he is a rogue of six reprieves, four pardons of course, thrice pilloried, *twice sung Lacrymae to the virginals of a cart's tail*, &c.

The last expression, or one that closely resembles it, is to be found in *The Devil's Law Case.* The Waiting Woman whose perjury in the 'law case' has been discovered, apprehensively inquires of Sanitonella, the lawyer's clerk, what will become of her, and Sanitonella replies:

> You'll be made dance *Lacrymae* I fear, at a cart's tail.
>
> IV. ii (iii. 99).

The Clown throws scorn upon his late master's claims

to the possession of magical powers—'use all thy art, all thy roguery', he says to Forobosco, 'and make me do any thing before all this company I have not a mind to, I'll . . . give thee leave to claim me for thy bond slave'. Forobosco who accepts the challenge, replies:

> *Forobosco.* I will first send thee to Green-land for a haunch of venison, just of the thickness of thine own tallow.
> *Clown.* Ha, ha, ha, I'll not stir an inch for thee!
> *Forobosco.* Thence to Amboyna i' th' East Indies, for pepper to bake it.
> *Clown.* To Amboyna? So I might be pepper'd.

This reference to Amboyna affords decisive proof that *The Fair Maid of the Inn* was written after May 1624, when the news of the massacre first reached England. Now in *The Devil's Law Case* there is a passage in which Dyce recognized another allusion to this same massacre of Amboyna:

> *Contarino.* Is 't possible Romelio 's persuaded
> You are gone to the East Indies?
> *First Surgeon.* Most confidently.
> *Contarino.* But do you mean to go?
> *Second Surgeon.* How! go to the East Indies! and so many Hollanders gone to fetch sauce for their pickled herrings! some have been pepper'd there too lately.
> IV. ii (iv. 80).

Such an allusion is, however, out of the question, seeing that *The Devil's Law Case* was published in the year preceding the massacre. Possibly the reference is, as Dr. Stoll has suggested, to an affray with the Dutch in the East Indies which took place in 1619, the Dutch attacking some English vessels engaged in lading pepper at Sumatra. The important thing for the present purpose, bearing in mind the fact that Webster so frequently repeats himself, is the occurrence of the same witticism in both plays.

It will perhaps be thought that such a word as 'instantly' can be of little use as an indication of a writer's individuality. Yet it may be remarked that it is peculiarly conspicuous in Webster's vocabulary, and in this connexion it is perhaps not trivial to compare Cesario's:

> We will instantly to bed, and there be married

with

> (*Contarino*) To avoid which, we will instantly be married.
> (*Waiting Woman*) To avoid which, get you instantly to bed

in *The Devil's Law Case*, I. ii (iii. 27); and

> I will marry you,
> Instantly marry you

in *A Cure for a Cuckold*, IV. ii (iv. 70).

At the end of this scene a sailor enters, for no apparent purpose except to serve as a mouthpiece for an indifferent jest. He tells Cesario that he has news for him but will only divulge it on condition that Cesario will drink with him:

> We are like our sea provision, once out of pickle,
> We require abundance of drink,

an adaptation of an observation found in the character of 'A Sailor' (Overbury's *Characters*, 1614):

> He is part of his own provision, for he lives ever pickled.

Act V, Scene i

Apart from minor indications of Webster's phraseology, note (in Cesario's first speech):

> . . . I humbly beg,
> Since 'tis not in your power to preserve me
> Any longer in a noble course of life,
> Give me a worthy death.

The sentiment is derived from the *Arcadia*, Book III,

> for then will be the time to die nobly, when you cannot live nobly. (Routledge, p. 419).

already utilized by Webster in *The Devil's Law Case*, I. ii:

> There is a time left for me to die nobly,
> When I cannot live so. (Hazlitt, iii. 25.)

Alberto's advice to his son to 'bear his wrongs'

> With noble patience, the afflicted's friend
> Which ever in all actions crowns the end,

recalls the closing couplet of *The Duchess of Malfy*:

> Integrity of life is fame's best friend,
> Which nobly, beyond death, shall crown the end.
> (Hazlitt, ii. 282.)

Cesario replies:

I will not lose
My former virtue, my integrity
Shall not yet forsake me; but as the wild ivy
Spreads and thrives better in some piteous ruin
Of tower, or defac'd temple, than it does
Planted by a new building; so shall I
Make my adversity my instrument
To wind me up into a full content.

There is a comparison of much the same sort in *The White Devil*:

Antonio (*to Lodovico*). Have a full man within you:
We see that trees bear no such pleasant fruit
There where they grew first, as where they are new set
. . . and so affliction
Expresseth virtue fully. I. i (ii. 13).

But here, Lodovico being under sentence of banishment, it is the fruit-tree, which is said to thrive better by being transplanted, that is chosen for the purpose of illustration.

Alberto greets Cesario's noble sentiment with:

'Tis worthily resolved,

an expression of approval which I have already noted (see Act III, sc. ii, above) as typical of Webster.

Act V, Scene ii

A prose scene, occupied entirely by dialogue between Forobosco and the Clown.

Almost at the beginning we have:

Forobosco. . . . We must remove.
Clown. Whither?
Forobosco. Any whither.

Compare:

Jolenta. Let thou and I, wench, get as far as we can from the noise of it (i. e. the combat between Ercole and Romelio).
Angiolella. Whither?
Jolenta No matter, any whither.
The Devil's Law Case, V. i (iii. 105).

Forobosco proposes that they shall break into one of the rooms of the inn and steal the gold and jewels of one of the guests during his absence. This, he says, 'might be a means to make us live honest hereafter'. ''Tis but an ill-road to 't', observes the Clown, 'that lies through the highway of thieving', an observation which recalls a passage in the soliloquy of Rochfield 'the honest thief' of *A Cure for a Cuckold*:

> To beg is out of my way
> And borrowing is out of date. The old road,
> The old highway (i. e. thieving) 't must be, and I am in't.
> II. i (iv. 25).

Act V, Scene iii

Though this last scene (with the exception of the brief passage of prose with which it concludes) is undoubtedly in the main Massinger's, there are, I think, occasional traces of Webster. The very first line of Mariana's opening speech:

> This well may be a day of joy long wish'd for

recalls the opening of *A Cure for a Cuckold*:

> This is a place of feasting and of joy
> . . . .
> A day of mirth and solemn jubilee.

Again, in one of Alberto's speeches the phrase 'slave-born Muscovite':

> I tamely bear
> Wrongs which a slave-born Muscovite would check at.

is taken from a passage in Sidney's *Astrophel and Stella*:

> And now, like slave-born Muscovite,
> I call it praise to suffer tyranny,

already utilized by Webster in *The Duchess of Malfy*, III. v (ii. 227):

> Must I, like to a slave-born Russian,
> Account it praise to suffer tyranny?

More significant than this is Clarissa's reference to the heavens as a 'star-chamber':

> Mentivole,
> My husband, registered in that bright star-chamber,

which occurs in Webster's *Appius and Virginia*, I. iv (iv. 139):

> This three months did we never house our heads,
> But in yon great star-chamber,

but elsewhere, so far as I am aware, only in Dekker's *Whore of Babylon*,[1] from which source Webster probably derived it:

> Shepherds (whose flocks are men, lambs, angels) you
> That hold the roof of yon star-chamber up.
> Dekker's *Dramatic Works*, ed Pearson, ii. 199.

However this may be, the prose at the end, like all the rest of the prose in the play, is Webster's. As a proof of this we may note what the Clown says of Forobosco:

> . . . all the skill that ever he had in the black art, was in making a sea-coal fire,

which is borrowed from the Character of 'A Quack-salver' (1615):

> He took his first being from a cunning woman, and stole this black art from her, while he made her sea-coal fire.

And again, the final benedictory speech of the Duke:

> This day that hath given birth to blessings beyond hope, admits no criminal sentence

closely resembles Ariosto's:

> . . . it does remain
> That these so comical events be blasted
> With no severity of sentence

in the concluding scene of *The Devil's Law Case* (iii. 120).

The result, then, of my examination is to show that far the larger part of the play is Webster's, including the character of the 'Fair Maid' herself and the entire underplot, of which Forobosco and his attendant Clown are the central figures.

Finally, it is to be observed that the style of the writer of the scenes here attributed to Webster is that of the Webster of *The Devil's Law Case* and *A Cure for a Cuckold*. It is unnecessary to enlarge upon the resemblance of the

[1] It is not quite so rare as this. I have since found it in the anonymous *Edward III* and once or twice elsewhere.

plot of the former play to that of the *Fair Maid of the Inn*, as this has frequently been commented upon. The resemblance is so striking that it led Swinburne to the conclusion that the plot of *The Devil's Law Case* must have been derived from *The Fair Maid.* A word may be added in reference to the unusual names—Forobosco and Prospero—given to two of the characters appearing in this play. Both these names had previously been used by Webster. There is in *The Duchess of Malfy* a mysterious Forobosco, who, though he figures on the list of *dramatis personae* and is also once referred to in the text, has no speaking part assigned to him, and there is a Prospero in *The Devil's Law Case.* For the name Forobosco Webster was probably indebted to Marston's *Antonio's Revenge.* Prospero seems to be an almost equally rare name in Elizabethan drama. The only other known to me, apart from the Prospero of *The Tempest*, is in the earlier version of *Every Man in his Humour.*

The place of *The Fair Maid* amongst Webster's works is between *The Devil's Law Case* and *A Cure for a Cuckold.* It has more connexions with the latter play than any other of Webster's productions. That it is of an earlier date can safely be pronounced on internal evidence alone. Like *The Duchess of Malfy* and *The Devil's Law Case*, as we have seen, it contains many passages derived from Sidney's *Arcadia* and Overbury's *Characters*; while in *A Cure for a Cuckold* the traces of indebtedness to these works have almost disappeared. Again the play shows no evidence of the influence of Heywood's vocabulary, for the first time distinctly perceptible in *A Cure for a Cuckold*, and afterwards to become so apparent in *Appius and Virginia.*

1915.

VII

A WEBSTER–MIDDLETON PLAY: 'ANYTHING FOR A QUIET LIFE'

THE comedy *Anything for a Quiet Life* was published by Kirkman as Middleton's in 1662, thirty-five years after that dramatist's death.

That this play is partly Middleton's there is no reason to doubt, but most of it is Webster's. Webster's is the main action of the play, which is concerned with two independent themes—Lady Cressingham's device to cure her husband's extravagance by temporarily divesting him of the ownership of his property, and the lawyer Knavesby's unsuccessful attempt to secure advancement at the cost of his wife's honour. The chief characters, Sir Francis and Lady Cressingham, Lord Beaufort, Knavesby and his wife, are his. The subsidiary action involving George Cressingham, Franklin, junior, Water-Camlet, his wife and his apprentices, and Sweetball, the barber-surgeon, is Middleton's. Until the final scene is reached the shares of the two authors are quite distinct. Webster wrote (I think) practically the whole of Act I, Act II, sc. i, Act III, sc. i, Act IV, sc. i, the dialogue between Knavesby and his wife at the beginning of Act IV, sc. ii, Act V, sc. i and ii, and collaborated with Middleton in the final scene, V. iii.

To me the evidence of Webster's authorship is conclusive. In the parts of the play that I attribute to him I find clear traces of his style and vocabulary as well as numerous passages bearing a close resemblance to passages in his acknowledged plays. And to put the matter beyond doubt, this play—like *The Duchess of Malfy*, *The Devil's Law Case*, *A Cure for a Cuckold*, and *The Fair Maid of the Inn*—contains borrowings both from Sidney's *Arcadia* and from

Overbury's *Characters*, or rather from the additions to these *Characters* published in 1615.[1]

The more palpable marks of Webster's hand are here noticed in the order in which they occur in the play. I have included connexions between this play and *The Fair Maid of the Inn*, since they are not without interest in themselves and are of some (if slight) value as corroborative evidence of Webster's authorship of both plays. References are to the pages of vol. iv of Dyce's edition of Middleton's works.

Act I, Scene i

p. 419. Lord Beaufort reproves Sir Francis Cressingham for marrying again only a month after the death of his first wife, whom he describes as:

> . . . one that, to speak the truth,
> Had all those excellencies which our books
> Have only feign'd to make a complete wife
> Most exactly in her practice.

In this vague reference to 'our books' I suspect an allusion to Sir Thomas Overbury's poem 'A Wife'. Webster borrows a line from this poem [2] both in his preface to *The Duchess of Malfy* and in *The Devil's Law Case*,[3] and many a passage in his plays reveals his familiarity with the *Characters* published with it.

p. 419. A sentiment from the *Characters* will be found in the concluding lines of this very speech. Lord Beaufort warns his friend that he is likely to regret his marriage with the new Lady Cressingham, who is only fifteen years of age and has been 'bred up i' the Court', adding:

> . . . you shall make too dear a proof of it,
> I fear, that in the election of a wife,

[1] It seems probable that some of these additional 'Characters' were written by Webster himself. On this subject see the papers by Baron Bourgeois and the present writer, *Notes and Queries*, 11 s. x. 3, 23 [1914], and 11 s. xi. 313, 335, 355, 374 [1915].

[2] 'Gentry is but a relique of time past.' Webster has slightly altered the phrasing.

[3] Act. I, sc. i (Hazlitt's *Webster*, vol. iii, p. 10).

As in a project of war, to err but once
Is to be undone for ever.

Of 'A Worthy Commander in the Warres' we read:

He understands in warre there is no meane to erre twice; the first and least fault being sufficient to ruine an army.

It is to be noted that other aphorisms from this character of 'A Worthy Commander' (one of the 1615 additions to Overbury's *Characters*) reappear in Webster's *Devil's Law Case* and *Monumental Column.*

p. 420. Speaking of Lady Cressingham, Lord Beaufort observes:

She was not made to wither and go out
By painted fires, that yield her no more heat
Than to be lodg'd in some bleak banqueting house
I' the dead of winter.

A similar allusion to 'painted fires' will be found in *The Devil's Law Case*, IV. ii (Hazlitt's *Webster*, iii. 84):

As void of true heat as are all painted fires.

p. 420. Sir Francis Cressingham's praise of his wife:

I confess she was bred at Court,
But so retiredly, that, as still the best
In some place is to be learnt there, so her life
Did rectify itself more by the court-chapel
Than by th' office of the revels:

recalls several passages in Webster's works, and particularly Icilius's description of Virginia in *Appius and Virginia*, I. ii (iii. 135), as:

. . . one whose mind
Appears more like a ceremonious chapel
Full of sweet music, than a thronging presence,
. . . her port,
Being simple virtue, beautifies the court.

p. 420. Sir F. Cressingham continues:

. . . best of all virtues
Are to be found at court; and where you meet
With writings contrary to this known truth,
They're fram'd by men that never were so happy
To be planted there to know it.

That this was Webster's opinion we may gather from a remark given to Romelio in *The Devil's Law Case*, III. iii (iii. 60):

> Indeed the court to well-composed nature
> Adds much to perfection.

p. 421. The entry of Water-Camlet brings us to a patch of prose. Water-Camlet speaks of his wife making his collection of silkworms (then no doubt somewhat of a novelty) an excuse for introducing gallants into his house:

> *Lord Beaufort.* . . . how thrives your new plantation of silk-worms? those I saw last summer at your garden.
> *W.-Cam.* They are removed, sir.
> *L. Beau.* Whither?
> *W.-Cam.* This winter my wife has removed them home to a fair chamber, where divers courtiers use to come and see them, and my wife carries them up.

This allusion will be found again in Webster's part of *The Fair Maid of the Inn*, II. i:

> . . . in England you have several adamants to draw in spurs and rapiers: *one keeps silk-worms in a gallery*; a milliner has choice of monkeys and paraquitos, &c.

p. 422. Water-Camlet twits Sir Francis Cressingham with his fantastic projects, amongst which he mentions:

> Your devising new water-mills for recovery of drowned land.

—a palpable reference to the scheme of the projector Meercraft in Jonson's play, *The Devil is an Ass*. This play evidently made a great impression upon Webster, for he twice borrows from it in *The Devil's Law Case*.[1]

p. 424. Water-Camlet has married a shrew, who keeps a strict watch over all his actions:

> She has a book, which I may truly nominate
> Her Black Book, for she remembers in it,
> In short items, all my misdemeanours.

[1] The warning addressed by Romelio to the Waiting Woman (*D. L. C.*, I. ii) relative to the conveyance of letters by bawds bringing cut-works, &c., and Ariosto's reference (*D. L. C.*, II. i) to the passing of lands from client to lawyer, are from II. i of Jonson's play.

We are here reminded of the Cardinal, Monticelso, in *The White Devil*, III. iii (ii. 76), who also keeps a 'black book':

Francisco. It is reported you possess a book
Wherein you have quoted, by intelligence,
The names of all notorious offenders
Lurking about the city.
Monticelso. Sir, I do;
And some there are which call it my black book,
Well may the title hold, &c.

p. 426. Franklin junior tells Lord Beaufort that he has been encouraged by the Duke of Florence

To do him some small service 'gainst the Turk.

In the same speech also there is a reference to the trade with the East Indies. Both these allusions are continually cropping up in Webster, especially allusions to service ''gainst the Turk'. Thus in *The White Devil*, IV. iv (ii. 99), Brachiano says to the disguised Francisco:

We have heard at full
Your honourable service 'gainst the Turk.

and in *The Devil's Law Case*, I. ii (iii. 20), Leonora says of Ercole:

. . . his intents are aim'd
For an expedition 'gainst the Turk.

Cf. also *W. D.*, IV. iv (ii. 103); *D. L. C.*, IV. ii, and V. vi (iii. 102, 121).

p. 427. When Knavesby, the lawyer, enters, George Cressingham (Sir Francis's son) asks what he is, and Franklin junior replies:

a very knave and rascal,
That goes a-hunting with the penal statutes.

Compare the description of 'A Meere Pettyfogger' (Overbury's *Characters*, 1615):

. . . in a long vacation his sport is to goe a-fishing with the penal statutes.

Knavesby, says Cressingham, is a 'scurvy informer':

. . . has more cozenage
In him than is in five travelling lotteries.

Webster again alludes to 'cozening' by means of lotteries in *A Cure for a Cuckold*, III. i (iv. 45):

> But, when it came to the proof, my gentlemen
> Appear'd to me as promising and failing
> As cozening lotteries.

and once more in *The Fair Maid of the Inn*, II. i, where the reference is specifically to travelling lotteries. Here the mountebank Forobosco, speaking to the Clown, observes that their cheating does not prosper as it used to do, and the Clown replies:

> No sure, why in England we could cozen 'em as familiarly as if we had travell'd with a Brief or a Lottery.

Franklin junior has been cast adrift by his patron Lord Beaufort and George Cressingham has fallen out with his father. Franklin asks George what is to become of them:

> *G. Cress.* Faith, I'm resolved to set up my rest
> For the Low Countries.
> *Frank. jun.* To serve there?
> *G. Cress.* Yes, certain.
> *Frank. jun.* There's thin commons;
> Besides, they've added one day more to the week
> Than was in the creation.

The Pedant who appears in Webster's part of *The Fair Maid of the Inn* (IV. ii) makes the same resolution to settle in the Low Countries, and he wishes Forobosco (a professed magician) to add yet another day to the week there:

> *Pedant.* . . . I mean
> To leave Italy and bury myself in those nether parts
> Of the Low Countries.
> *Forobosco.* What's that, sir?
> *Pedant.* Marry, I would fain make nine days to the week for the more ample benefit of the captain.

In this act there are four conspicuous instances of the omission of the relative pronoun in the nominative. Such omissions are frequent in Webster's plays.

Act II, Scene i

Knavesby tells his wife that he has had a strange dream. He dreamt that each confessed to the other the number of times they had broken their marriage vows. Mistress Knavesby exclaims:

> There was a dream, with a witness!

and Knavesby replies:

> No, no witness;
> I dreamt nobody heard it but we two.

—a wretched quibble, but no quibble was too wretched for Webster to make, or, having made, to repeat. He has this again in *The Fair Maid of the Inn*, II. i. The Clown has just told the Host a story of a woman who has caught cold in the endeavour to rid her face of the marks of the small-pox and 'kicked up her heels':

> *Host*. There was kicking up the heels with a witness!
> *Clown*. No, Sir; I confess a good face has many times been the motive to the kicking up of the heels with a witness, but this was not.

p. 435. Mistress Knavesby, urged to confess her matrimonial offences, tells her husband that when she was in Cambridge a handsome scholar of Emmanuel College fell in love with her, whereupon Knavesby exclaims:

> O, you sweet-breathed monkey!

like the Waiting-Woman in *The Devil's Law Case*, when she sees Jolenta whispering to Contarino:

> O sweet-breath'd monkey! how they grow together!

I have not met with the epithet 'sweet-breathed' elsewhere. A reference to the sweet breath of monkeys in Book III of Sidney's *Arcadia* (Philisides' song) may have suggested it to Webster.

p. 437. Knavesby remarks that he thinks more of his wife since Lord Beaufort has taken a fancy to her:

> . . . like one
> That has variety of choice meat before him,
> Yet has no stomach to 't until he hear
> Another praise it.

This is from Book I of Sidney's *Arcadia.* Artesia challenges Phalantus, who is always praising her, to proclaim her beauty through all the courts of Greece. By this means she hopes to attract the attention of Amphialus, whom she loves :

> . . . persuading herself, perhaps, that it might fall out in him as it doth in some that have delightful meat before them, and have no stomach to it, before other folks praise it (Routledge's edition, p. 77).

p. 437. Knavesby endeavours to overcome his wife's objections to his proposals that she shall enter into an adulterous intrigue with Lord Beaufort :

> . . . to confute all reason in the world which thou canst urge against it, when 'tis done, we will be married again, wife, which some say is the only *supersedeas* about Limehouse to remove cuckoldry.

This certainly seems a patent allusion to Webster and Rowley's *Cure for a Cuckold.* The remarriage of Compass (of Blackwall, near Limehouse) with his erring wife is, indeed, the ' cure ' referred to in the title of that play. Had it not been for this passage I should have been disposed to date *Anything for a Quiet Life* before Webster and Rowley's comedy, since it shows more indebtedness to Sidney's *Arcadia* and Overbury's *Characters,* thus suggesting a date nearer that of *The Devil's Law Case.* Moreover, it does not borrow from Thomas Heywood's vocabulary as *A Cure* unquestionably does—a feature which (though not to the same extent) it possesses in common with *Appius and Virginia,* apparently the latest of Webster's dramas. Perhaps the passage is an interpolation, or it may refer to some incident that suggested the sub-plot of the Webster-Rowley play.

Act III, Scene i

The disagreeable story of the Knavesbys and Lord Beaufort is here resumed, the three intervening scenes (showing no vestige of Webster's style) being concerned with a dishonest prank played upon Water-Camlet, the mercer, by Franklin junior and Sir Francis Cressingham's son. A feeble quibble occurring in the dialogue between Mistress Knavesby and Mistress George Cressingham (disguised as Lord Beaufort's page) may serve as a definite mark of Webster's hand in this scene :

p. 456.

Mistress Knavesby. I could kiss you now, spite of your teeth, if it please me.

Mistress Geo. Cressingham. But you could not, for I could bite you with the spite of my teeth, if it pleases me.

Compare, in the dialogue between Raymond and Clare in *A Cure for a Cuckold*, III. iii :

Raymond. I do love you in spite of your heart.
Clare. Believe it,
There was never a fitter time to express it,
For my heart has a great deal of spite in it.

Act IV, Scene i

There are plenty of indications of Webster's hand here.

p. 471. In order to comply with Lady Cressingham's wish that he shall sell his lands, it is necessary that Sir Francis shall obtain the concurrence of his son, who must join in the conveyance to bar his right of succession. Sir Francis, being one of Webster's puppets, cannot tell his son in plain language what it is that he wishes him to do. He must first mystify him by remarking that 'somewhat he should write will be dangerous to him'. When it afterwards appears that it is his signature to the deed which is required, George Cressingham exclaims:

Sir, I do now *ingeniously perceive* why you said lately somewhat I should write would be my undoing.

In *The Devil's Law Case* we have 'ingenuously perceive' but with the same meaning, for 'ingenious' and 'ingenuous' were at this time used indiscriminately. Here again the reference is to the perception of the significance of an obscure observation. Contarino has asked Leonora for her picture, and he credits her with superhuman intelligence, for he assumes that she has fathomed his real meaning, which is that he wishes to marry her daughter :

> She has . . . *ingenuously perceiv'd*
> That by her picture, which I begg'd of her,
> I meant the fair Jolenta.
>
> *D. L. C.*, I. i (iii. 16).

p. 472. The son begs his father not to disinherit him simply to indulge his step-mother's whim, bidding him

> think how compassionate the creatures of the field, that only live on the wild benefits of nature, are unto their young ones.

For the 'wild benefits of nature' Webster is indebted to the *Arcadia*, Book IV. Speaking of 'a rascal company of rebels' who have sought refuge in some woods, Sidney says that

> . . . as they were in the constitution of their minds little better than beasts, so were they apt to degenerate to a beastly kind of life, having now framed their gluttonish stomachs to have for food the wild benefits of nature.

Webster had previously made good use of this phrase. Applied in the same way as in this play, it comes still more effectively from the lips of the unfortunate Duchess of Malfy:

> The birds that live i' th' field
> On the wild benefit of nature, live
> Happier than we; for they may choose their mates.
>
> *D. M.*, III. v (ii. 225).

It is only one of several instances in which Webster has used a passage adapted from the *Arcadia* in more than one play. Dyce first drew attention to these parallels. Had *Anything for a Quiet Life* been wholly the work of Middleton, it would have been difficult to account for them, for this play is later than *The Duchess of Malfy*, and Middleton was not in the habit of borrowing phrases either from the *Arcadia* or from the works of his friends.

p. 472. George Cressingham warns his father against his stepmother:

> . . . you shall find her beauty as malevolent unto you as a red morning, that doth still foretell a foul day to follow.

Webster has this again in *A Cure for a Cuckold*, III. i (iv. 44):

Bonville. You look, methinks, fresh colour'd.
Lessingham. Like a red morning, friend, that still foretells
A stormy day to follow.

p. 473. George, Water-Camlet's apprentice, enters with the news that Mistress Water-Camlet is 'departed'. 'Dead!' exclaims Sir F. Cressingham, and George replies:

In a sort she is, and laid out too, for she is run away from my master.

Webster had a strange partiality for this paltry kind of equivocation. To quote one of many instances, in *A Cure for a Cuckold* (III. i) Lessingham refuses to fight a duel with Bonville on the ground that 'it would show beastly to do wrong to the dead':

. . . to me
You are dead for ever, lost on Calais sands
By the cruelty of a woman.

Act IV, Scene ii

The first part of this scene—the interview between the Knavesbys, in which the wife leads the husband to suppose that she has become Lord Beaufort's mistress—is Webster's; the prose portion (after the entry of George, the apprentice) Middleton's.

Act V, Scene i

This is wholly Webster's. We have a typical sample of the sententious, super-elegant diction affected by the gallants and well-bred personages of his later plays in the passage of verse dialogue between George Cressingham and the elder Franklin with which the scene opens. After the entry of George (the apprentice) all three speak in prose.

p. 487. George has been discharged by his master and is much excited in consequence. Franklin asks him what is the matter, and he replies:

I may turn soap-boiler, I have a loose body:
I am turn'd away from my master.

For this coarse pleasantry compare, in the speech of one of the madmen in *The Duchess of Malfy*, IV. ii:

All the college may throw their caps at me, I have made a soap-boiler costive.

Act V, Scene ii

p. 490. Saunders, steward to Sir Francis Cressingham, counsels George Cressingham to adopt a profession, suggesting the law or ' divinity ', adding :

> I have heard you talk well, and I do not think but you'd prove a singular fine churchman.

George Cressingham responds :

> I should prove a plural better, if I could attain to fine benefices.

—a laborious jest already used in *The Devil's Law Case*, III. iii (iii. 62) :

> (Jolenta to Romelio.)
> Nay, I will get some singular fine churchman,
> Or though he be a plural one, shall affirm
> He coupled us together.

p. 492. Sir Francis Cressingham is in despair at the abject dependence upon his wife to which she has reduced him :

> O my heart 's broke ! weighty are injuries
> That come from an enemy, but those are deadly
> That come from a friend,[1] for we see commonly
> Those are ta'en most to heart.

Webster harps upon this sentiment in *The Fair Maid of the Inn*. In Act II, sc. i, of this play, Cesario has been wounded in a duel with his friend Mentivole. Cesario's father greets the physician's announcement that the wound is only a trivial one, with :

> O, but from a friend,
> To receive this bloody measure from a friend,
> . . . 'tis that which multiplies
> The injury.

[1] Mr. William Wells (who, I am pleased to find, had independently come to the conclusion that *Anything for a Quiet Life* is partly Webster's) has drawn my attention to the resemblance between these lines and the following, from one of Flamineo's speeches in *The White Devil*, v. i (ii. 119–20) :

> Those are found weighty strokes which come from th' hand
> But those are killing strokes which come from th' head.

And when the wounded man's mother and sister enter, and the physician again affirms that the wound is 'but a scratch', the sister replies:

> But he received it from a friend
> And the unkindness ta'en from that may kill him.

Act V, Scene iii

The collaboration of the two authors in this final scene seems to have been of the most intimate kind, as might be expected, seeing that nearly all the characters are brought together for a general reconciliation. Every now and then Webster's hand becomes apparent, especially in the passages of verse at the beginning and end. The scene opens with a feeble pun:

> *Lord Beaufort*. Sirrah, begone! you're base.
> *Knavesby*. Base, my good Lord!
> 'Tis a ground part in music, trebles, means,
> All is but fiddling.

As this is put into the mouth of the Clown in *Appius and Virginia*, III. iv (iii. 187):

> . . . though I can sing a treble, yet I am accounted but as one of the base;

and is found in association with the word 'fiddle', used equivocally (as again in *The Devil's Law Case* and in Webster's part of *The Fair Maid*), there need be no hesitation in attributing it to Webster. And if evidence is sought of his participation in the closing lines of the play, we may with equal confidence assign to him this passage from the last speech of Franklin senior:

> My son was dead; whoe'er outlives his virtues
> Is a dead man.

Years ago the late A. H. Bullen expressed doubts of Middleton's sole authorship of this play. To him the character of Lady Cressingham seemed more in Shirley's manner than Middleton's, and he suggested that Shirley might have revised and completed the play after Middleton's death. Swinburne (though finding this suggestion 'ingenious and plausible') objected that the conception of the character in question was 'happier and more original' than could be accounted for on such a hypothesis. His high opinion of Lady Cressingham is of particular interest in view of the light here thrown upon the identity of her creator. 'The young stepmother,' he says, 'whose affectation of selfish levity and grasping craft is really designed to cure her husband of his infatuation, and to reconcile him with the son who regards her as his worst enemy, is a figure equally novel, effective, and attractive.' [1]

Dyce dated this play 1617, on very slender grounds. If the passage in II. i to which I have alluded does refer to *A Cure for a Cuckold*, it cannot have been written much before 1626, the year previous to Middleton's death, the internal evidence that the latter play followed Massinger's *Parliament of Love* being too strong to be resisted.

1916.

[1] *The Age of Shakespeare*, p. 160.

VIII

JOHN FORD'S POSTHUMOUS PLAY 'THE QUEEN'

The Queen, or The Excellency of her Sex, was first printed in 1653. Its authorship was clearly unknown to the publisher, who is content to describe it as 'An Excellent Old Play. Found out by a Person of Honour, and given to the Publisher, Alexander Goughe'.[1] In 1906 it was reprinted by Professor Bang of Louvain (*Materialien zur Kunde des älteren englischen Dramas*, vol. xiii) and ascribed to Ford. As the text is not easily accessible, I give here an account of its plot.

Alphonso, who has led an unsuccessful rebellion against the Queen of Arragon, has been condemned to death and is on the point of being executed, when the Queen makes her appearance. She questions Alphonso, and learns that his hostility is inspired not by any motive personal to herself, but by an all-embracing hatred of her sex. Notwithstanding that he shows no disposition to repent his conduct, she magnanimously pardons him and bestows her hand upon him in marriage. Immediately the wedding ceremony is over, the new King asks for and obtains the Queen's consent to a separation for a period of seven days, in order, as he explains, that he may expiate his wrongful thoughts of her sex. A month passes and still he continues to absent himself. The efforts of the Queen's counsellors to persuade him of the injustice of this treatment of her are unavailing, and when the Queen herself goes to him and beseeches him to let her know why he refuses to live with her, she is met

[1] Alexander Goughe, an actor of women's parts at the Blackfriars theatre, wrote the 'Address to the Reader' prefixed to Middleton's comedy, *The Widow* (printed 1652). Langbaine ('Account of the English Dramatic Poets') speaks of him as 'an actor, who during the suppression of the theatres helpt Mr Moseley to this (the MS. of *The Widow*) and several other dramatic manuscripts'.

with a wild tirade against her modesty, the King bidding her, if she can live chaste, to live alone as he does. The Queen, whose love of her husband remains unshaken, leaves his presence overcome with grief.

Muretto, the King's counsellor, now begins to instil into his master's mind suspicions of the Queen's behaviour with the noble Petruchi, a young lord of unimpeachable character, loyally devoted to her service. The King summons both before him and they are arrested. He refuses to credit the Queen's protestations of innocence, but tells her that if any one appears to champion her cause within a month, he is prepared to meet him in single combat, in which event the result of the duel shall decide the truth of the accusation against her: if, on the other hand, no champion is forthcoming within that time, she is to lose her head. The Queen hears Alphonso's sentence with noble fortitude. She will make no effort to save her life at the risk of her husband's, and exacts from her adherents an oath that they will not raise arms against their sovereign. The King has no sooner delivered judgement on the Queen than he begins to be perturbed by thoughts of her surpassing loveliness, and is seized by feelings of remorse which become more and more poignant as the day fixed for the combat approaches. If he could be convinced that she is 'as fair within as she is without' he would willingly resign his crown and 'live a slave to her perfections', and only a stern sense of justice compels him to fulfil the terms of his decree. The fateful day arrives. When the herald's trumpet first sounds the challenge there is no response. But the delay is only momentary. At the second blast, Velasco, the Queen's general, enters the lists. The Queen implores him not to oppose the King, and swoons when he stubbornly refuses to obey. Once more the trumpet sounds, and another champion appears in the person of Petruchi, and then, close upon his heels, Muretto himself, sword in hand, proclaiming that he is 'as ready to stand in defence of that miracle of chaste women as any man in this presence'. The King's astonishment at this behaviour on the part of the very man who has prompted his suspicions is unbounded. Muretto then explains that, realizing that Alphonso's attitude towards the Queen was due to a morbid hatred of womankind, he had set himself to cure him of his perversity. Observing that he was of a jealous disposition, he had cunningly mingled with suggestions of the Queen's unchastity praises of her beauty, thus rousing his royal master to a due appreciation of her perfections. Having satisfied himself that nothing but a conviction of the Queen's unfaithfulness could ever again estrange the King from her, he had directed suspicion towards Petruchi merely in order to demonstrate the groundlessness of any imputations against her honour. Matters thus being satisfactorily explained, the Queen forgives the King and all ends happily.

The humbler love-affairs of the widow Salassa and Velasco, the Queen's general, form the subject of the underplot, and a seasoning of not very agreeable comedy is provided by Bufo, a captain, and Pynto, an astronomer, belonging to the King's party.

Professor Bang gives many good reasons for assigning *The Queen* to Ford, and Mr. Stuart P. Sherman, who has made a special study of this dramatist's work, confirms this verdict.[1] There can be no doubt that they are right. The artificiality of the plot, the cadence of the verse, the elevated rhetoric and marked tendency to hyperbole in the serious portion of the drama, the mirthless vulgarity of the prose scenes, all point to Ford. But merely to affirm this is not to prove that the play is Ford's, and to Mr. Sherman's statement that, to those familiar with his works, 'corroborative testimony of vocabulary, parallel passages, &c., is superfluous', I would respectfully demur. If Ford wrote *The Queen* his authorship should be deducible from its vocabulary and from a comparison of its language with that which we know to be his, and I propose here to show that its authenticity can be established by this method in so conclusive a fashion that those possessing no more than an ordinary

[1] See his article ('A New Play by John Ford') in *Modern Language Notes* (Baltimore), vol. xxiii.

reader's acquaintance with Ford will be able to recognize that its claim to a place amongst his dramatic productions is unquestionable.

Though some of the evidence that follows has not escaped the attention of Professor Bang, I have thought it better to conduct my investigation independently of his, and accordingly my notes on the play owe nothing to those appended to his reprint.

A careful study of Ford's independent dramas soon satisfied me that a valuable aid to the identification of his work in those written by him in collaboration with Dekker was afforded by his predilection for certain words, the most noteworthy being 'antic' (as noun and adjective), 'bosom' (noun and verb), 'bounty' and 'bounties', 'chronicle', 'crave', 'dally', 'destiny', 'fate', 'forfeit' (noun), 'nimble', 'partake', 'penance', 'proffer' (verb and noun), 'sift' (= to subject to a searching test), 'thrive', 'thrift', and 'thrifty'. 'Bosom', 'bounty', and 'thrive' are doubtless common words. But in his seven plays Ford has 'bosom' no fewer than forty-two times, or an average of six times in each play: 'bounty' and 'bounties' thirty-three times; 'thrive', 'thrift', and 'thrifty' (together) thirty-one times. 'Fate' and 'penance' are of scarcely less frequent occurrence. The other words in this list, though they appear less often, are yet used with abnormal frequency, ranging from seventeen times in the case of 'antic' to nine times in that of 'sift'. All but two ('nimble' and 'partake') are to be found in *The Queen*—'bosom', 'bounty', 'chronicle', and 'penance' four times each; 'crave' and 'fate' five times; 'antic', 'destiny', and 'thrive' twice; 'thrift', 'dally', 'forfeit', 'proffer', and 'sift', once. Of these words 'antic' and 'sift' are perhaps the most distinctive. 'Antic' appears in this play, both as an adjective (1205):[1]

[1] For *The Queen* my references are to the numbers of the lines as in Professor Bang's reprint; other references are to page and column of Hartley Coleridge's edition of *The Dramatic Works of Massinger and Ford.*

I'll sooner dig a dungeon in a molehill,
And hide my crown there, that both fools and children
May trample o'er my royalty, than ever
Lay it beneath an *antic* woman's feet;

and as a noun (1500):

. . . spit on, revil'd, challeng'd, provok'd by fools, boys, *antics*, cowards.

'Sift' is used by the author of *The Queen* exactly in Ford's way (1418):

You dare not *sift* the honor of my faith
By any strange injunction, &c.

Compare *The Lover's Melancholy*, IV. i. 15 b:

If I have us'd a woman's skill to *sift*
The constancy of your protested love;

and *The Fancies*, III. ii. 133 b:

So shall we *sift* her love and his opinion.

Apart from words notable from the frequency of their appearance in Ford's unquestioned works, *The Queen* exhibits other marks of his vocabulary.

When Salassa is told by her friend Shaparoon that if she does not show favour to Velasco's friend Lodovico, he 'is no long lives man', she retorts (805–6):

Very well; how long have you been a factress for such merchants, Shaparoon?

'Factress' (= pandress) appears again in *The Fancies*, III. iii. 136 b (Castamela to Octavio):

I scent your cruel mercies;
Your *factress* hath been tamp'ring for my misery,
Your old temptation, your she-devil.

Twice in *The Queen* we find 'unnoble' for 'ignoble':

It were unnoble
On your part to demand a gift of bounty, &c. 1428.

Wrong not majesty
With an unnoble rigour. 2187.

as in *'Tis Pity She's a Whore*, III. v. 36 b:

'Tis an unnoble act, and not becomes
A soldier's valour.

Again 'itch of concupiscence', 'itch of letchery' (*Queen*, 1026, 3779), should be compared with 'itch of lust' (*'Tis Pity*, IV. iii. 40 b).

Although Ford does not repeat himself so frequently or so literally as some of his contemporaries, his tendency in this direction is sufficiently pronounced to enable us to determine whether his hand is actually present in a work suspected to be his. It remains to be shown that the parallel passage test is here no less decisive than the vocabulary.

When Petruchi asks Alphonso if he is prepared to ascend the scaffold, the time fixed for his execution having arrived, Alphonso replies (323–4):

Petruchi, yes. I have a debt to pay,
'Tis nature's due;

again, in the last act of the play, Velasco observes (3289–90):

Yet we must die at last, and quit the score
We owe to nature.

So in *The Broken Heart*, V. ii. 71 a (Calantha to Orgilus, condemned to death for murder):

. . . Those that are dead,
Are dead; had they not now died, of necessity
They must have paid the debt they owed to nature
One time or other;

and in *Love's Sacrifice*, I. i. 76 a (Fiormonda to the Duke of Pavia):

. . . should your grace now pay,
Which heaven forbid! the debt you owe to nature,
I dare presume, she'd not so soon forget
A prince that thus advanced her.

The entry of the Queen, just as the axe is about to fall on his neck, is greeted by Alphonso (343–9) with:

What newer tyranny, what doom, what torments,
Are borrowed from the conclave of that hell,
Where legions of *worse devils than are in hell*
Keep revels, a proud woman's heart?

Alphonso's opinion of the whole sex is no more favourable than the Duke's opinion of the faithless Bianca, in *Love's Sacrifice*:

. . . I had thought
I match'd a woman, but I find she is
A devil, worser than the worst in hell.
v. i. 94 b.

The Queen endeavours to extract from Alphonso an admission of his sorrow for his late misdeeds, but he truculently exclaims (388–93):

Had I a term of life could last for ever,
And you could grant it, yes, and would, yet all
Or more should never reconcile my heart
To any she alive.

Compare *The Lady's Trial*, IV. iii. 158 a:

Had *any he alive* then ventur'd there
With foul construction, I had stampt the justice
Of my unguilty truth upon his heart.

In Act II (755–8) Mopas, Velasco's man, observes:

She 's a rank jade that being past the breeder, cannot kick up her heels, wince, and cry wee-hee.[1]

This we get again in *The Fancies*, III. iii. 135 b:

Wince and cry wee-hee! like a colt unbroken.

Collumello, one of the Queen's counsellors, expostulates with the King for his cold treatment of their royal mistress:

The commons murmur, and the streets are fill'd
With busy whispers. 1111–13.

In *The Lover's Melancholy*, II. i. 6 a, Sophronos complains of the injury to the commonwealth caused by the lethargy of the prince:

The commons murmur, and the nobles grieve;
The court is now turn'd antic and grows wild, &c.

[1] A variant of a proverbial saying, see *The Partial Law*, III. i. (Dobell's edition, 1908, p. 65): ‘They say he 's an errant jade that can neither wihye nor wagge his taile’ and Dekker's *The Wonder of a Kingdom*, I. i (Pearson, iv. 223): ‘*Nicoletto*. What think you then of me, sweet lady? *Alphonsina*. Troth, my lord, as of a horse, vilely, if he can neither wihy nor wagge taile.’

The violent speech in which Alphonso rejects the modest advances of the Queen (1181–94)—a typical sample of the exaggerated diction of Ford's characters in moments of passion—I quote in full:

Hence
Monstrous enchantress, *by the death I owe*
To Nature, thou appear'st to me in this
More impudent than impudence, the tide
Of thy luxurious blood is at the full;
And 'cause thy raging *plurisy of lust*
Cannot be sated by our royal warmth,
Thou try'st all cunning petulant charms to raise
A wanton devil up in our chaste breast.
But we are cannon-proof against the shot
Of all thy arts.

Here we have three characteristic marks of Ford's phraseology. 'The death I owe to nature' needs no further illustration. 'Plurisy of lust' occurs again in *'Tis Pity*, IV. iii. 40 b:

(Soranzo to Annabella)

Must your hot itch and plurisy of lust,
The hey-day of your luxury, be fed
Up to a surfeit, &c.,

and with 'raise a wanton devil up in our chaste breast', we may compare

if the nimble devil
That wantoned in your blood,

in the first scene of *The Witch of Edmonton.*

Later on in this second act Velasco indulges in such extravagant protestations of his devotion to Salassa, that she suspects his sincerity. 'Phew,[1] my Lord', she exclaims, 'It is not nobly done to mock me thus'. Velasco replies (1391–4):

Mock you? Most fair Salassa, if e'er truth
Dwelt in a tongue, my words and thoughts are twins.

[1] This interjection occurs three times elsewhere in this play, at line 1617 ('Phew, that 's thy nobleness') and twice in Act. I (lines 469, 701). It is a favourite exclamation of Ford's.

The same periphrastic mode of expression is used by Nearchus in *The Broken Heart*, III. iv. 61 b:

> My tongue and heart are twins,

whilst the final couplet of Act II:

> There is no act of folly but is common
> In use and practice to a scornful woman,

recalls that with which Soranzo concludes his interview with Annabella in *'Tis Pity*, IV. iii:

> My reason tells me now, that ''tis as common
> To err in frailty as to be a woman'.

So much for the first two acts of this play. Even those most sceptical of 'purely internal evidence' will surely agree that here alone there is sufficient to convict Ford. All that it seems worth while to add is that nowhere does the text suggest the presence of another hand, and that Ford has put his final stamp on the play in Velasco's penultimate speech a few lines before its close (3853–5):

> To strive against the ordinance of fate
> I find is all in vain.

The impossibility of escaping one's 'fate' or 'destiny' was the cardinal article of Ford's creed, and there are few of his dramas in which it does not find explicit utterance. See for instance *Love's Sacrifice* (end of IV. ii):

> No toil can shun the violence of fate.

The Lover's Melancholy (III. ii):

> . . . in vain we strive to cross
> The destiny that guides us.

and *Perkin Warbeck* (end of V. i):

> being driven
> By fate, it were in vain to strive with heaven.

Though it contains a number of fine declamatory speeches, *The Queen* falls far below the level of Ford's dramatic work at its best, exhibiting scarcely a trace of the tragic power and psychological insight manifested in *'Tis Pity*, *The Broken Heart*, or *Perkin Warbeck*. The Queen of Arragon, who out-Grissils Griselda in patience and wifely obedience, is but little better than a lay figure, a colourless image of perfections incapable of rousing more than a tepid interest in her sorrows, while the King is equally remote from the semblance of humanity—a morose monomaniac whose base ingratitude towards the Queen and readiness to put the worst construction on her actions, not all Ford's lofty eloquence can render tolerable or plausible.

1917.

IX

JOHN FORD THE AUTHOR OF 'THE SPANISH GIPSY'

Although, so far as I can find, no critic has heretofore questioned the ascription to Middleton and Rowley of *The Spanish Gipsy*, I have long doubted whether Middleton had any hand in this play, finding it utterly dissimilar in style from his other dramatic work, whether assigned to him alone or to Middleton and Rowley. Recently a prolonged study of Middleton's plays converted my doubts into a feeling of absolute certainty that he was in no way concerned in *The Spanish Gipsy* either as original author or reviser. At first I was inclined to suspect that Webster wrote the tragic and romantic parts usually assumed to be Middleton's. These are certainly more in Webster's manner than Middleton's, and I was the more disposed to suspect Webster because I had previously found palpable traces of his collaboration with Middleton in *Anything for a Quiet Life*, published under Middleton's name alone in 1662.[1] However, a closer examination of the text of *The Spanish Gipsy* convinced me that I was on the wrong track, its resemblances to Webster's acknowledged dramas being too slight and of too vague a kind to afford any sound basis for my suspicion. Accordingly, having other work on hand at the time, I put the play aside. I did not return to it until some months afterwards, and then, aided by the notes made on my previous examination, almost immediately found the clues which led me (as I believe) to the discovery of the real author. It is, I am convinced, substantially, if not wholly, from the pen of John Ford. That the main part of the play is his I feel no doubt whatever, and as clear traces of his hand are also to be found in the Sancho and Soto and gipsy scenes (usually attributed to Rowley) I am strongly disposed to believe that Ford wrote the whole play. These scenes

[1] See pp. 159–72.

are, however, more pleasing than is usual with Ford, whose efforts at frivolity are seldom successful and usually disgusting. For this reason one must admit the possibility that these gipsy scenes have been revised or rewritten by some other dramatist. But, if this be the case, I see no reason for supposing that this dramatist was Rowley. I can find no satisfactory internal evidence for Rowley in any part of the play, and if the external evidence can be shown to be false as regards Middleton, it is clearly equally worthless evidence for Rowley. The internal evidence is at least sufficient to show that *The Spanish Gipsy* is substantially Ford's play, that henceforth it should be included among his dramatic works and excluded from Middleton's.

Before I deal with this internal evidence, it is necessary that I should say a few words regarding the attribution to Middleton and Rowley. The play was first printed twenty-six years after Middleton's death, the title-page running as follows:

> 'THE SPANISH GIPSIE. As it was Acted (with great Applause) at the Privat House in Drury-Lane, and Salisbury Court. Written by Thomas Middleton and William Rowley, Gent. Never Printed before. London, Printed by J.G. for Richard Marriot in St. Dunstan's Church-yard Fleetstreet, 1653.'

Assuming Marriot to have been wrong in attributing *The Spanish Gipsy* to Middleton and Rowley, there would—apart from any reason to suspect his good faith—be no need to suppose that he knew the attribution to be incorrect. It is, of course, possible that he acted innocently. On the other hand it is not only possible, but probable, that he did not. That he was capable of assigning a play to a well-known dramatist knowing the attribution to be false is shown by his conduct with regard to a play published by him in the following year. In 1654 he published *Revenge for Honour* as 'A Tragedie by George Chapman'. Internal evidence shows that this was written not by George Chapman but by Henry Glapthorne.[1] And Marriot *knew* that it was

[1] See *Notes and Queries*, 12th Series, i [1916], pp. 401–4.

Glapthorne's, having entered it as his in the Stationers' Register only the year before. In this case, then, we find Marriot entering a play in the Register under the name of its real author, a little-known playwright, and immediately afterwards publishing it as the work of another dramatist of established reputation. That is all that need be said about Marriot's attribution of the play to Middleton and Rowley.

The first feature of the text that brought Ford to my mind was the double-rimed couplet at the end of I. iii—the scene immediately following the rape of Clara by Roderigo. As he leaves his victim, Roderigo exclaims:

> My shame may live without me,
> But in my soul I bear my guilt about me.

I could not recollect the use of such a couplet anywhere in Middleton's plays. And this particular kind of double rime is specially characteristic of, if not peculiar to, Ford. In *Love's Sacrifice* (v. ii) he has:

> No counsel from our cruel wills can win us
> But, ills once done, we *bear our guilt within us.*

and in *The Broken Heart*, I. i, is a couplet even more closely resembling that in *The Spanish Gipsy*:

> Souls sunk in sorrows never are without them,
> They change fresh airs, but *bear their griefs about them.*

The next point I noted struck me as still more significant. About fifty lines further on—in Roderigo's fourth speech in I. v—we meet with the expression 'the float of those desires'. Speaking of Clara, Roderigo says to Lewis—

> I found, even in that beauty that invited me,
> Such a commanding majesty of chaste
> And humbly glorious virtue, that it did not
> More check my rash attempt, than *draw to ebb*
> *The float of those desires*, which in an instant
> Were cool'd in their own streams of shame and folly.

—'float' here meaning 'flood', as contrasted with 'ebb'. Nowhere else, outside Ford's dramatic works, have I found 'float' in this sense. Ford has it at least three or four times. 'The float of the unruly faction in my blood' is in *Love's Sacrifice* (I. ii), 'float of spleen' in *The Sun's Darling* (Act I) and, again in *Love's Sacrifice* (II. ii), we have 'the float of infinite desires'. Here, when Bianca rejects his advances, Fernando exclaims:

> . . . though *the float*
> *Of infinite desires swell to a tide*
> *Too high too soon to ebb*, yet, by this hand,
> . . . .
> I swear henceforth I never will . . . presume
> To make a repetition of my griefs.

The occurrence in this speech of Roderigo's of one of the most distinctive words in Ford's vocabulary is not its only suggestion of his hand. Ford, like most dramatists of the time, occasionally echoes himself, and in *The Lady's Trial* he echoes this very speech. In IV. ii Adurni tells his friend Auria that when he attempted to undermine the virtue of Spinella, Auria's wife,

> . . . so much majesty
> Of humbleness and scorn appear'd at once
> In fair, in chaste, in wise Spinella's eyes
> That I grew dull in utterance, and one frown
> From her cool'd every flame of sensual appetite.

These two features, then—the double-rimed couplets (there is another at the end of I. v) and the use of the word 'float'—were what caused me to suspect that *The Spanish Gipsy* was written by Ford, and led me to compare it with his unquestioned work. The results of this comparison I shall now give.

To take the vocabulary first, the play contains, as we have seen, one very uncommon word used by Ford—the only really rare word to be found in it. It contains also almost all the more characteristic words of Ford's vocabulary. Many of these are quite common words which nevertheless gradually obtrude themselves on the notice of a reader in the course of repeated perusals of Ford's plays owing to the unusual frequency with which he uses them. *Antic, bosom, chronicle, crave, creature, dally, fate, forfeit* (as noun), *mad* (as verb), *partake-r*, *penance*, and *thrive*, all of them favourite words of Ford's, are all found in *The Spanish Gipsy*. Three or four may be selected for special notice.

Bosom. A common word enough. But it is one which Ford uses with extraordinary frequency. He has it (on an average) about six times in a play. In *The Spanish Gipsy* it occurs five times.

Creature. A favourite expression of Ford's, as applied to a woman. It is here used eight times, e. g. 'a young creature' (I. i), 'that fair creature' (I. v), 'a handsome creature' (III. ii), 'a sweet creature' (IV. iii), 'lost creature' (V. i), 'talking creature' (V. iii). I have noted 'young creature' in *The Fancies, Chaste and Noble* (II. ii), 'sweet creature' in *'Tis Pity She's a Whore* (IV. i), 'lost creature' in *Perkin Warbeck* (IV. iii).

Forfeit (n.). Ford usually has this two or three times in a play. It occurs three times in *The Spanish Gipsy*.

> . . . on the forfeit
> Of thine own life or mine, seal up thy lips.
>
> I. ii.
>
> How are so many harmless virgins wrought
> . . . to yield
> Too easy forfeits of their shames and liberty.
>
> I. iii.
>
> The forfeit of her shame shall be her pawn.
>
> V. i.

We may compare:

> Wishing the laws of England could remit
> The forfeit of your life.
>
> *Perkin Warbeck*, II. ii.
>
> My wretched wife . . . hath paid too soon
> The forfeit of her modesty and life.
>
> *'Tis Pity*, IV. ii.
>
> Penthea's, poor Penthea's, name is strumpeted,
> But since her blood was season'd by the forfeit
> Of noble shame . . .
>
> *The Broken Heart*, IV. ii.

Partake, partaker. There is scarcely a play of Ford's in which one or other of these words is not used at least once. Both are in *The Spanish Gipsy*:

My honourable lord, *partake* my blessings. v. iii.
No friend but thee alone . . . shall be *partaker* of my griefs. I. v.

There is one favourite word of Ford's not used in *The Spanish Gipsy*—the word *bounty* (or *bounties*, in the plural). I mention this as showing that one cannot rely upon this vocabulary test (the testing of the vocabulary of a suspected work for the presence of an author's pet words) to yield satisfactory results in every instance. As Ford has *bounty* on an average six or seven times in a play, I naturally expected to find it here. But on reference to my notes I found that in one of his plays (*'Tis Pity*) the word occurs only once, so that its absence from *The Spanish Gipsy* need cause no surprise.

A habit particularly characteristic of Ford is the use of the abbreviated forms 'd'ee' and 't'ee' for 'do you' and 'to you'. Until I came to study *The Spanish Gipsy*, using an edition reproducing the spelling of the early quartos, I was under the impression that 'd'ye' and 't'ye' were the forms habitual with Ford. But these are the modern substitutes for Ford's 'd'ee' and 't'ee' adopted (in my opinion unwarrantably) by his nineteenth-century editors, as I discovered on referring to the original editions of his plays in the British Museum. In *The Spanish Gipsy* we find, 'My lord, d'ee know this crucifix?' (III. ii), 'Why d'ee mock my sorrows?' (v. i), 'I come for justice t'ee' (v. i), 'What d'ee mean', 'But why d'ee use me thus?' and 'I may be bold To make a suit t'ee' (v. iii). This of itself is almost sufficient to prove Ford's presence, for no other dramatist of the time habitually adopts these abbreviations. Certainly Middleton does not. They will be found in Ford *passim*. To take a play at random, 'When d'ee intend to visit my noble-spirited sister', 'Las, why d'ee use me thus' (the same phrase as in *The Spanish Gipsy*), 'Take your jewel t'ee', 'Good time of day t'ee', are to be found in *The Lover's Melancholy*, and it may be added that three times Ford uses the phrase 'I have a suit t'ee' (*Love's Sacrifice*, I. ii, *The Fancies*, III. iii, *The Witch of Edmonton*,

I. i).[1] A most valuable piece of evidence this, which, through using modern editions of Ford's plays, I came near to missing.

I now take the play scene by scene in order that the reader may see how clear and how abundant are the traces of Ford's hand in its imagery and phrasing.

Act I

Scenes i and ii. There is not much to suggest Ford in the two very brief scenes with which the play opens. But, at the end of the first scene, 'traitors to all goodness'—

> I will raise Madrill to find
> These traitors to all goodness.

—is likely to be his ('traitor to honour and shame' is in *The Lover's Melancholy*, I. iii, 'traitor to friendship' in *Love's Sacrifice*, I. ii), and in the second (third speech of Lewis) we have Ford's favourite word 'forfeit',

> . . . on the forfeit
> Of thine own life or mine, seal up thy lips.

Scene iii. The marks of Ford are here unmistakable. Clara's opening speech:

> Though the black veil of night hath overclouded
> The world in darkness, yet, ere many hours,
> The sun will rise again, and then this act
> Of my dishonour will appear before you
> More black than is the canopy that shrouds it

—plainly speaks of the hand that wrote Livio's speech in V. i of *The Fancies*:

> . . . she was once an innocent,
> As free from spot as the blue face of heaven
> Without a cloud in 't; she is now as sullied
> As is that canopy when mists and vapours
> Divide it from our sight.

'Forfeits of their shames and liberty' is in Clara's fourth speech, and Roderigo's exclamation 'Phew!' at the end of the speech is a common interjection with Ford, but comparatively rare in the plays of other writers of the time.

[1] So also in *The Queen*: 'I will make an earnest suit t'ee', 'How d'ee, sir?', 'How d'ee like it?', 'D'ee hear, sir? what d'ee dream on?' &c.

Next, in Clara's second speech after 'Re-enter Roderigo', we have 'to write an epitaph' used metaphorically:

> . . . if you mean to write upon my grave
> An epitaph of peace, forbear to question.

as in *The Lady's Trial*, I. i:

> A woman's virtue in her lifetime writes
> The epitaph all covet on their tombs.

A few lines later on in this speech:

> . . . for my part
> I have *wash'd off the leprosy* that cleaves
> To my just shame *in true and honest tears.*

we have a passage that recalls the language of the Friar's exhortation to Giovanni in the first scene of *'Tis Pity*:

> *Wash every word thou utter'st*
> *In tears* (and if 't be possible) of blood.
> Beg Heaven to *cleanse the leprosy* of lust
> That rots thy soul.

The scene ends with the double-rimed couplet already referred to:

> My shame may live without me
> But in my soul I bear my guilt about me.

Scene iv. This is another very short scene; but, short as it is, there need be no doubt that it is Ford's. Compare these lines from Don John's speech at the end of the scene:

> She is not noble, true. Wise nature meant
> Affection should ennoble her descent,

with these words of Giovanni in *'Tis Pity*, I. i:

> . . . to which intent
> Wise nature first in your creation meant
> To make you mine.

The early quartos read 'enable' for 'ennoble' in the passage quoted from *The Spanish Gipsy*, and Professor E. C. Morris, in his edition of the play for the 'Belles Lettres' series, retains and defends this reading. But it is plain from the context that 'ennoble' is the right word. Ford uses this ('sweetness of disposition ennobles a freedom of birth') in his dedication of *'Tis Pity* to the Earl of Peterborough.

Scene v. I have already quoted the passage in Roderigo's speech beginning:

I found, even in that beauty that invited me,
Such a commanding majesty of chaste
And humbly glorious virtue, &c.,

with its parallel in *The Lady's Trial* and its use of the phrase 'the float of those desires', so clearly pointing to Ford. Some twenty lines further on, when he says to Lewis:

. . . here I unclasp
The secrets of my heart.

his language again reminds one of Giovanni's during his talk with the Friar in the opening scene of *'Tis Pity*:

To you I have unclasped my burdened soul,
Emptied the storehouse of my thoughts and heart,
Made myself poor of secrets.

and, immediately after this, his commendation of Clara as 'a creature that deserves a temple' is also characteristic of Ford, whose heroines are frequently spoken of by their worshippers as 'temples' or 'shrines'. Roderigo next informs his friend that, to avoid temptation, he has determined to leave Madrid for Salamanca:

Speed me
For Salamanca, court my studies now
For physic 'gainst *infection of the mind*;

and here we may compare the reply of Crotolon to Orgilus in *The Broken Heart*, III. iv, when Orgilus explains that he has hurried back from Athens on account of the 'general infection' prevailing in that city—

I fear
Thou hast brought back a worse infection with thee,
Infection of thy mind.

In his next speech Roderigo impresses upon Lewis that the cause of his departure is to be kept secret from every one but himself, adding:

No friend but thou alone, for whose sake only
I undertake this voluntary exile,
Shall be partaker of my griefs.

The second line is repeated in *The Broken Heart*, I. i, where

Orgilus (who is leaving Sparta for Athens) exclaims to his father, Crotolon:

> Hence, from hence,
> I undertake a voluntary exile.

His motive for undertaking this voluntary exile is, it may be noted, similar to Roderigo's—the desire to escape from the dangerous proximity of that 'shrine of beauty', the fair Penthea. Ford repeats the phrase again in *The Lover's Melancholy*, I. i, where Amethus tells his sister Thamasta that Menaphon has long and truly loved her, and that, 'to witness his obedience to her scorn'—

> Twelve months, wronged gentleman, he undertook
> A voluntary exile.

This scene also ends with a double-rimed couplet in Ford's manner:

> Pleasure and youth like smiling evils woo us
> To taste new follies; tasted, they undo us.

Act II

Scene i. This, the first of the gipsy scenes, is almost wholly in prose. Unless a writer has some marked peculiarity of style, or tendency to repeat himself (which Ford has not), it is always much more difficult to assign prose passages than verse. But 'pastime'—a word he frequently uses—and the adjective 'roguy' (though not peculiar to him) slightly suggest Ford, and there is a stronger suggestion in the remark made by Soto when he sees Constanza, disguised as a gipsy,

> Is this the little ape does the fine tricks?

since Spadone, in *The Fancies*, IV. i, speaks in like fashion of his master's page Nitido, as he urges the barber Secco to thrash him—

> Lash him soundly; *let the little ape show his tricks.*

A more peculiar expression used by Spadone occurs a little later in this scene. Soto says to Eugenia:

> Grave Mother Bumby, *the mark's out a your mouth.*

In *The Fancies*, II. i, Secco asks Spadone if the letter that Spadone has brought for him is from ‘the glory of beauty, Morosa, the fairest fair’, and Spadone comments, aside:

> Fairest fair, quotha! so is an old rotten coddled mongrel, parcel bawd, parcel midwife; *all the marks are quite out of her mouth.*

Scene ii. All the verse part of this scene has the ring of Ford's verse. In particular, we may compare Lewis's protestation to Clara:

> If ever I embrace another choice,
> Until I know you elsewhere match'd, may all
> The chief of my desires find scorn and ruin!

with a passage in the first scene (Ford's) of *The Witch of Edmonton* (Frank to Winnifred),

> . . . Whenever
> The wanton heat of youth, by subtle baits
> Of beauty, or what woman's art can practise,
> Draw me from only loving thee, let Heaven
> Inflict upon my life some fearful ruin!

In the prose at the end (after ‘Enter Sancho and Soto’, about one-third of the scene) I find no definite suggestion of Ford's hand.

Act III

Scene i. This also is mostly prose, presenting no tangible evidence of Ford's hand. But when (in the short passage of verse at the beginning) we find Roderigo referring to Clara as a ‘temple’ that he has ‘profaned’—

> . . . should this temple,
> By me profaned, lie in the ruins here,
> The pieces would scarce shew her me,

—we may be fairly confident that his speech is Ford's. It is in the same fashion that Fernando speaks of Bianca in *Love's Sacrifice*, II. i:

> Heaven forbid that I
> Should by a wanton appetite profane
> This sacred temple.

and Bassanes of Penthea in *The Broken Heart*, IV. ii :

> I, who was made a monarch
> Of what a heart could wish for, a chaste wife,
> Endeavour'd, what in me lay, to pull down
> That temple built for adoration only
> And level 't in the dust of causeless scandal.

Scene ii. A long scene, largely occupied with gipsy dialogue and songs. There are a few words and phrases that point to Ford. In the two first lines :

> Lewis de Castro, since you circled are
> In such a golden ring of worthy friends,

we have some reason for inferring his authorship, for 'circled with friends' appears again in *The Lover's Melancholy*, V. i :

> Thus princes should be circled, with a guard
> Of truly noble friends ;

and there is a stronger hint of it in the dialogue between Alvarez and Lewis later in the scene, where the former is professing to tell the latter's fortune from an examination of his hand :

> *Alvarez.* That great ship was De Castro call'd, your father.
> *Lewis.* And I must hew the rock that split him ;

since in *The Broken Heart*, IV. i, we find Orgilus using the same metaphor and applying it in the same way :

> Thou barren rock,
> By thee we have been split in ken of harbour.

Here Orgilus himself is the ship and Bassanes the rock that has split him.

Scene iii. Ford's imagery and phrasing are clearly apparent in this scene. Note Clara's 'D'ee know this crucifix ?' and (in Fernando's speech immediately after his re-entry)

> What 's beauty but a *perfect white and red* ?
> Both here well mixt *limn* truth,

with which we may compare:

> He who . . . will merely wed
> A face because 'tis round, or *limn'd* by nature
> In *purest red and white* . . .
> *The Lover's Melancholy*, III. ii.

Act IV

Scene i. Though there is little to connect Ford with this scene (again concerned chiefly with the gipsies), I see no reason why it should not be his. It contains several songs, of which one (Sancho's first song) is much after the style of Folly's songs (which I believe to be Ford's) in Act I of *The Sun's Darling*. One cannot, of course, attach much weight to this. But, in the later portion, the allusion by Don John to Cardochia's 'better stars'—

> 'Las, pretty soul,
> Better stars guide you!

points more clearly to Ford. The same expression occurs in one of Euphranea's speeches in Act I, sc. iii, of *The Broken Heart*:

> . . . it had been
> A fault of judgment in me . . . not to . . . thank
> My better stars that offered me the grace
> Of so much blissfulness.

Scene ii. A short scene, in which the gipsies again appear. I note only one slight indication of Ford. In the Sancho and Soto part the allusion to ciphers making up numbers—

> *Fernando.* What 's your number?
> *San.* The figure of nine casts us all up, my lord.
> *Fer.* Nine, let me see—you are ten, sure.
> *Soto.* That 's our poet, he stands for a cipher.
> *Fer.* Ciphers make numbers.—

occurs again in *'Tis Pity*, I. ii:

> . . . look, sweetheart, look what thing comes now!
> Here 's another of your ciphers to fill up the number.

Scene iii. This is the scene containing the play performed by the gipsies, and as, on the assumption that our play is by Middleton and Rowley, this inset play has been assigned to Rowley, it is of particular interest to note that there are passages in the dialogue strongly pointing to Ford. For instance, when Soto says to Alvarez:

> Hold his nose to the grindstone, my lord,

he uses an expression that also occurs in the dialogue between Poggio and Bergetto in III. i of *'Tis Pity*: [1]

> Hold him to the grindstone, and give not a jot of ground.

When Sancho speaks of 'slicing' Soto 'into collops' he talks as Bassanes does to Grausis in *The Broken Heart*, II. i:

> I'll spit thee on a stake
> Or chop thee into collops.

and when he exclaims:

> We'll fight dog, fight bear,

he talks like Spadone in *The Fancies* (IV. i) as he watches the fight between Morosa and Secco:

> Well played dog; well played bear.

Act V

Scene i. In the interview between Fernando and his son Roderigo with which this opens we find in Fernando's utterances the same impressive solemnity of tone as in the Friar's admonishments of Giovanni in *'Tis Pity.* These speeches of Fernando have the full flavour of Ford. Nothing more typical of him could be quoted than this:

> Peace! thou wilt blaze a sin beyond all precedent:
> Young man, thou should'st have married her; the devil
> Of lust that riots in thy eye should there
> Have let fall love and pity, not on this stranger
> Whom thou hast doted on.

This is exactly in the vein of the Friar's speech at the beginning of II. v of *'Tis Pity*:

> Peace! thou hast told a tale, whose every word
> Threatens eternal slaughter to the soul, &c.

[1] I have since found that it is also used by Middleton—in *Blurt, Master-Constable*, III. iii.

Moreover, in 'the devil of lust that riots in thy eye' we have an image characteristic of Ford, who has analogous expressions in *Perkin Warbeck*, V. iii ('the devil that ranges in your tongue'), and in *The Witch of Edmonton*, I. i ('the nimble devil that wantoned in your blood'). The marks of his hand are abundant throughout the scene, amongst them Pretiosa's peculiar exclamation 'deed, la!'

> I am honest,
> Deed, la! I am;

which recurs in *The Fancies*, II. ii:

> No, no, deed, la!
> A very grave, stale bachelor

and Lewis's allusion to his 'better genius'—

> Oh fate! Now tell me where,
> And be my *better genius*;

also found in *Perkin Warbeck*, III. iv, where the Earl of Crawford's remark that the King is 'deep in his meditations' brings from Dalyell the pious ejaculation:

> Lift them up
> To Heaven, his *better genius*!

No Ford play would be complete without a fatalistic utterance of some kind, and this we get in the concluding couplet:

> The miserable and the fortunate
> Are alike in this, they cannot change their fate.

Scene ii. This short scene also plainly bears Ford's impress. When Alvarez says to Lewis:

> Tremble not, young man, trust me, I have wept
> Religiously to wash off from my conscience
> The stain of my offence,

we again seem to hear the voice of the Friar in *'Tis Pity*. And the idea of guilt as a stain (or 'leprosy') to be 'washed off' with tears, already noted in that play and in I. iii of the present play, appears again in *Love's Sacrifice*, V. i:

> such a guilt
> As, were the sluices of thine eyes let up,
> Tears cannot wash it off.

Scene iii. In this final scene I have already drawn attention to the 'd'ee' and 't'ee' abbreviations as characteristic of Ford. There is little else to which I can point. But I note the hour-glass metaphor:

> The glass of misery
> Is, after many a change of desperate fortune,
> At length run out;

because, though not peculiar to Ford, it reappears in a passage of *The Witch of Edmonton* (v. i) clearly attributable to him:

> . . . the glass of thy sins is full, and it must run out at gallows;

in the last act of *The Sun's Darling*, which is also his:

> Thy sands are number'd, and thy glass of frailty
> Here runs out to the last;

and in *The Broken Heart*, III. v:

> My glass of life, sweet princess, hath few minutes
> Remaining to run down; the sands are spent.

As Professor E. C. Morris says in his edition of the play to which I have already referred, 'The attitude of most critics towards the composition of *The Spanish Gipsy* has been one of caution'—an attitude, one may add, amply justified, since they were confronted with the task of dividing between two authors a play wrongly assigned to them. Some have professed to find Rowley's hand in the second act, others would allot to him the gipsy scenes. Fleay, who was not easily baffled by such problems, has not attempted a division, merely expressing his belief that the whole play was written by Middleton and afterwards 'touched up' by Rowley. Professor Morris is alone in a courageous attempt to split the text up between the two authors by scene and line. Yet after an elaborate discussion and comparison of the style and versification of the two authors, he has been unable to arrive at any more satisfactory conclusion than that certain parts of the play (about two-thirds of the text) are 'by Middleton with here and there a slight touch of Rowley' and the rest 'revised by

Rowley, though showing here and there the original lines of Middleton'. His division is based merely on general impressions, and one looks in vain for specific evidence of either author's hand. His and Fleay's failure to arrive at any definite assignment of the shares of the two supposititious authors tends to confirm my own opinion that it is from one hand. As I have shown above, traces of Ford's style and phrasing are to be found in every scene, and not only in 'the tragic or the romantic part of the play' which according to the rash assertion of Swinburne 'bears the stamp of Middleton's genius alike in the sentiment and the style' but in the less 'high-toned' passages that he would assign to Rowley. It is the stamp of Ford's genius that is apparent in the sentiment and style of the serious scenes of *The Spanish Gipsy*, a genius so unlike Middleton's that no thought of the latter's authorship could have entered the head of any critic had not Middleton's name appeared on the title-page. That Ford's style is less clearly traceable in the prose comedy scenes is true, but it would be equally difficult to find internal evidence to establish his authorship of the prose parts of his signed plays.

That the text of *The Spanish Gipsy* may have undergone some revision during the course of the thirty years that elapsed between the first recorded performance of the play (by the Cockpit company in 1623) and its publication is, of course, not at all unlikely; all that I claim to have proved is that Ford wrote the play and that his hand can be traced in every scene. A new edition of his collected works is long overdue, none having been issued since Dyce's edition of 1869. When it does appear, it is to be hoped that it will include both *The Spanish Gipsy* and *The Queen, or the Excellency of her Sex* printed (though by a more honest publisher) in the same year, and reclaimed for Ford by Professor Bang of Louvain.

1923.

X

NATHANIEL FIELD'S WORK IN THE 'BEAUMONT AND FLETCHER' PLAYS

THOUGH it has with good cause been suspected that Nathaniel Field had a hand in some of the plays printed in the Beaumont and Fletcher folios, and portions of certain plays have (more or less tentatively) been assigned to him by different critics, there is no general agreement either as to the identity of the plays in which he collaborated, or the extent of his contributions to them. It is not strange that this should be so, since Field is not a writer whose work can easily be recognized. He does not, like Massinger, constantly repeat himself, nor has he, like Fletcher, strongly marked metrical peculiarities. The most distinctive characteristic of Field's verse—a characteristic exhibited in both his acknowledged plays (*A Woman is a Weathercock* and *Amends for Ladies*), in the parts of *The Fatal Dowry* written by him, and in all the work here assigned to him on other internal evidence—is the free use of rimed couplets, not only at the ends of scenes as commonly in the dramatic work of the period, but interspersed with the blank verse. This feature makes it easy to distinguish him from Massinger or Fletcher, both of whom are sparing in the use of rime, but is useless as a means of distinguishing between Field and Beaumont, since Beaumont also introduces rimed couplets in his blank verse. Field's style has indeed much in common with that of Beaumont, and it is therefore not surprising to find that Beaumont has been credited with work written by Field. This mistake has been made both by Boyle and by Fleay. Speaking of what he called Boyle's 'absurd theory' that Beaumont contributed certain scenes to *The Knight of Malta*, Fleay (*Biog. Chron. Eng. Drama*, i. 205) observes that Boyle 'is, as I have frequently pointed out, incapable of distinguishing Field's work from Beaumont's'. But Boyle's error is a venial one compared with that of Fleay, who has actually made use of a work of Field's to establish the canon for Beaumont's verse. Of the *Four Plays in One* (*op. cit.*, i. 179) he remarks: 'The shares of Beaumont and Fletcher are singularly independent, and the marked difference of their metrical forms afforded me the starting-point for the separation of all these [Beaumont and Fletcher] plays in 1874, which was till then regarded universally as an insoluble problem.' The two first 'Triumphs' of the *Four Plays in One*, assumed by Fleay to be by Beaumont, are Field's, as I hope shortly to prove. Fortunately for Fleay, however, the metrical styles of these two authors are so similar that the value of his conclusions has not seriously been affected by his choice of these 'Triumphs' as the standard for Beaumont's verse.

The other plays of the Beaumont and Fletcher folio in which Field collaborated are *The Queen of Corinth*, Acts III and IV of which are his, and *The Knight of Malta*, of which he wrote Acts I and V.

There is no evidence to connect Field with the authorship of any of these plays[1] but such as can be obtained by comparing them with his acknowledged works *A Woman is a Weathercock* and *Amends for Ladies* and his share of *The Fatal Dowry*, written in collaboration with Massinger. Field's share of *The Fatal Dowry* is Act II, Act III, sc. i, after the second entry of Novall Junior, and Act IV, sc. i. As the assignment of these parts of the play to him has hitherto rested chiefly upon evidence of a negative kind, having been arrived at by subtracting the scenes that clearly show the more easily recognizable hand of Massinger, it is desirable that I should give some positive evidence of his authorship of the parts of this play referred to before I proceed to assign to him plays, or portions of plays, of which external proof of his authorship is lacking. First, then, at the beginning of Act II, sc. i, we have the word 'practic':

> . . . a man but young
> Yet old in judgment; theoric and *practic*
> In all humanity.

[1] It is, however, known that he acted in *The Queen of Corinth* and *The Knight of Malta*.

This is a word that, to the best of my knowledge, Massinger never uses in his independent plays. Field has it in the first scene of *Amends for Ladies*:

> Indeed, my knowledge is but speculative
> Not *practic*; I have it by relation, &c.

In the same scene we have the verb 'to exhaust' used in its primary sense of 'draw out':

> your thankless cruelty
> And savage manners of unkind Dijon,
> *Exhaust* these floods;

an uncommon use of the word—not to be met with in Massinger—which will be found again in *A Woman is a Weathercock*, I. i:

> Were you my father flowing in these waves,
> Or a dear son *exhausted* out of them.

Three times in *The Fatal Dowry* we have allusions by gallants to the disarranging or crumpling of their 'bands'. Two of these occur in the second scene of Act II. Here Liladam says to Novall junior

> Ud's light, my lord, one of the purls of your band is, without all discipline, fallen out of his rank,

and a little later on when Malotin says to Pontalier

> Dare these men ever fight on any cause?

Pontalier replies:

> Oh, no! 'twould spoil their clothes and put their bands out of order.

The third is in IV. i, where Aymer, who has been roughly handled by Romont, exclaims:

> Plague on him, how he has crumpled our bands!

These allusions point clearly to Field, in whose *Amends for Ladies* there are two more allusions of the same kind—one in III. iii, where Lady Bright says of Master Pert:

> I have seen him sit discontented a whole play, because one of the purls of his band was fallen out of his reach to order again;

and the other in IV. iii, where Ingen, during the course of his duel with Lord Proudly, observes that he 'had like to have spoiled' his lordship's 'cutwork band'.

In II. ii Novall junior addresses Bellapert in this strain:

> No autumn nor no age ever approach
> This heavenly piece; which Nature having wrought,
> She lost her needle, and did then despair
> Ever to work so lively and so fair;

while in IV. i Aymer begs Novall junior to put his looking-glass aside lest, 'Narcissus-like', he should dote upon himself and die

> . . . and rob the world
> Of Nature's copy, that she works form by.

No doubt hyperbolical speeches not much differing from these may be found in Massinger, but they are particularly characteristic of Field, who has two references to Nature's fashioning of men in each of his independent plays. With the above passages we may compare Pendant's adulatory speech addressed to Count Frederick in *A Woman is a Weathercock*, I. ii:

> Nature herself, having made you, fell sick,
> In love with her own work, and can no more
> Make man so lovely, being diseased with love.

Count Frederick mildly protests:

> Pendant, thou'lt make me dote upon myself

and Pendant replies:

> Narcissus, by this hand, had far less cause.

Both in *The Fatal Dowry* and *A Woman is a Weathercock* there is much talk of clothes and tailors. Pontalier in *The Fatal Dowry* (II. ii) says of Liladam and Aymer:

> If my lord deny, they deny; if he affirm, they affirm; they *skip into my lord's cast skins some* twice a year, &c.

and in *A Woman is a Weathercock* (II. i) Pendant, when asked by Mistress Wagtail how he came by his good clothes, replies:

> By undoing tailors; and then *my lord* (*like a snake*) *casts a suit every quarter, which I slip into.*

Again in IV. i Aymer says of Novall junior

> . . . his vestaments sit as if they grew upon him, or art had *wrought them on the same loom as Nature framed his lordship.*

Compare Lady Bright's comment on Pert in *Amends for Ladies*, III. iii :

> I do not think but he lies in a case o' nights. He walks as if he were made of gins—*as if Nature had wrought him in a frame.*

Almost at the end of IV. i there is an allusion to fairy's treasure, which vanishes if its possessor reveals it:

> But not a word of it :—'tis fairies' treasure,
> Which, but revealed, brings on the blabber's ruin.

This is found again in *A Woman is a Weathercock*, I. i :

> I see you labour with some serious thing,
> And think (like fairy's treasure) to reveal it
> Will cause it vanish.

These are, so far as I have noticed, the only explicit allusions to this belief in the Elizabethan drama, though Shakespeare glances at it in *The Winter's Tale*, III. iii, 'This is fairy gold, boy', says the Shepherd to the Clown, when he discovers the gold left by the sea-shore, 'and 'twill prove so; up with 't, keep it close. . . . We are lucky, boy; and to be so still requires nothing but secrecy'.

This brief examination of *The Fatal Dowry* will, I hope, satisfy the reader that it is possible to detect Field's hand in his anonymous work, or work of his that has been assigned to others, from its connexions with his acknowledged writings.

Before I attempt to do this, it will be well to add a few words as to Field's vocabulary as displayed in the three plays to which his name is attached. It is not very distinctive. It is true that he has a few uncommon Latinisms, but they are of little use to us in this investigation since scarcely any of them are used more than once. 'Pish' and 'hum' (or 'humh' as the Folio usually prints it) are characteristic exclamations of his. Other noticeable words are 'continent' or 'continence' (four times in the three plays), 'importune' (three times), 'innocency' (four times), and 'integrity' (four times). I draw attention to these words merely because they are characteristic words that one may expect to find in Field, and do not suggest that some, perhaps most, of them are not occasionally used by one or other of the other authors of the Beaumont and Fletcher plays. 'Continent', 'importune', and 'innocency' are the more valuable. I may note also 'transgress' (used once in *Amends for Ladies*) because it is of comparatively infrequent occurrence in these plays, and therefore affords slight corroborative evidence of Field's authorship where there are other suggestions of his hand. Generally with regard to the weight to be attached to words such as these—words that are characteristic but not uncommon—while one or two in a play are obviously of little or no value, the presence of several much increases their importance, though in all cases they need the support of other evidence.

I come now to the three plays of the Beaumont and Fletcher folios.

I. *The Triumph of Honour* and *The Triumph of Love* ('Four Plays in One')

It was not until after I had completed my own investigation of these 'Triumphs', that I found that Beaumont's claim to them had already been challenged by Mr. E. H. C. Oliphant and Professor Gayley. Mr. Oliphant (*Englische Studien*, xv (1891), pp. 348–9) accepts Beaumont's authorship of *The Triumph of Love*, but gives the Induction and *The Triumph of Honour* to Field. Professor Gayley (*Francis Beaumont*, p. 303) further assigns to Field three scenes (i, ii, and vi) of *The Triumph of Love*. I go further still, claiming for Field the whole of both 'Triumphs' as well as the Induction. If the two authors collaborated in the same piece, I should have little faith in the ability of any critic to distinguish them by the characteristics of their verse, and as I find in every scene of *The Triumph of Love* suggestions of Field's vocabulary and imagery, I see no reason for assuming that Beaumont had any share at all in the *Four Plays in One*. Moreover, there is, as will be seen, strong presumptive evidence that they belong to a considerably later date than is usually assigned to them, and it is more than probable that they were not written until after Beaumont's death.

If a critic with a knowledge of Beaumont's characteristics as intimate as Professor Gayley's cannot find Beaumont's hand in the Induction or *The Triumph of Honour*, one may rest satisfied that there are substantial grounds for rejecting his authorship. But the reason given by Professor Gayley (*op. cit.*, p. 302) for attributing them to Field can hardly be called satisfactory. After remarking that they are full of polysyllabic Latinisms such as Field uses, he adds: 'Beaumont never uses: "to participate affairs", "torturous engine", &c., and they are marked by simpler Fieldian expressions, "wale", "gyv'd", "blown man", "miskill", "vane", "lubbers", "urned", and a score of others not found in Beaumont's undoubted writings.'

It is true that not one of these words or expressions is used by Beaumont. But the first two, though they occur in Field's *A Woman is a Weathercock* do *not* occur in either of the two 'Triumphs', while the other words (with the sole exception of 'vane', which *is* significant) occur in the 'Triumphs' but not in any of Field's undoubted writings, and to call them 'Fieldian expressions' is merely to beg the question. On the other hand 'basilisk', noted by Professor Gayley as one of the few words slightly suggestive of Beaumont, is equally characteristic of Field, who has it twice in *A Woman is a Weathercock* and once in *Amends for Ladies*.

What led me to the conclusion that *The Triumph of Honour* and *The Triumph of Love* had been wrongly attributed to Beaumont was the discovery that they were written by the author of Acts III and IV of *The Queen of Corinth*, in which Beaumont's collaboration has never been alleged and is, indeed, all but impossible, since Act III contains an allusion to Coryat's *Greeting*, not published until 1616, the year of Beaumont's death. The two 'Triumphs' are so closely related to these two acts of *The Queen of Corinth* that I propose first to show that they are by the same hand, and afterwards to identify that hand as Field's.

In Scene ii of *The Triumph of Honour*, Martius, the Roman general, makes advances to Dorigen, the chaste wife of the Duke of Athens, and she reproaches him for his violation of 'friendship, hospitality, and all the bonds of sacred piety' in an eloquent speech that contains these lines:

> When men shall read the records of thy valour,
> Thy hitherto-brave virtue, and approach
> (Highly content yet) to this foul assault
> Included in this leaf, this ominous leaf,
> They shall throw down the book, and read no more
> Though the best deeds ensue.

In Act IV, sc. iii of *The Queen of Corinth* Euphanes, the Queen's favourite, says to the Corinthian general Leonidas:

> . . . when posterity
> Shall read your volumes fill'd with virtuous acts,
> And shall arrive at this black bloody leaf,
> . . . what follows this
> Deciphering any noble deed of yours
> Shall be quite lost, for men will read no more.

There are only two possible explanations of the resemblance between these passages; either both were written by the same man, or one is a deliberate imitation of the other. Any doubt as to the correct inference to be drawn will soon be dispelled if the two 'Triumphs' and the acts of *The Queen of Corinth* referred to are compared more closely.

To begin with the Induction, the Queen of Portugal in her first speech thus addresses the King:

> Majestic ocean, that with plenty feeds
> Me, thy poor tributary rivulet;
> . . . .
> Curs'd be my birth-hour, and my ending day
> When back your love-floods I forget to pay.

In Act III, sc. ii, of *The Queen of Corinth*, Euphanes says to his mistress:

> I came to tender you the man you have made,
> And, like a thankful stream, to retribute
> All you, my ocean, have enrich'd me with.

In *The Triumph of Honour* note first that the alliteration 'arts and arms' in scene i (third speech of Martius):

> This Athens nurseth arts as well as arms

is found again in *The Queen of Corinth*, III. i:

> Five fair descents I can decline myself
> From fathers worthy both in arts and arms;

and with the couplet that concludes one of Cornelius's speeches in the latter half of the scene:

> Yet when dogs bark, or when the asses bray
> The lion laughs; not roars, but goes his way.

Compare the observation of Crates in *The Queen of Corinth*, III. i:

> . . . the lion should not
> Tremble to hear the bellowing of the bull.

In scene ii there is the speech of Dorigen containing the striking parallel with that of Euphanes in IV. ii of *The Queen of Corinth* already noted.

In scene iii Dorigen uses the word 'antedate' in the sense of 'anticipate':

> Yet why kneel I
> For pardon, having been but over-diligent,
> Like an obedient servant, *antedating*
> My lord's command?

so also Euphanes in *The Queen of Corinth*, III. i:

> You need not thank me, Conon, in your love
> You *antedated* what I can do for you.

The word is not used by Beaumont.

In *The Triumph of Love*, just before Gerrard's entry in scene ii, Benvoglio says to Ferdinand:

> Thy person and thy virtues in one scale
> Shall poise hers, with her beauty and her wealth.

Compare, in IV. iii of *The Queen of Corinth*,

> . . . when in the scales
> Nature and fond affection weigh together,
> One poises like a feather.

A little later in scene ii we have the rare adjective 'antipathous':

> . . . doth thy friendship play
> In this *antipathous* extreme with mine,
> Lest gladness suffocate me?

which appears again in *The Queen of Corinth,* III. ii:

> She extends her hand
> As if she saw something *antipathous*
> Unto her virtuous life

and in the last scene there is the almost equally uncommon adverb 'jocundly':

> Oh Violanta!
> Might my life only satisfy the law,
> How *jocundly* my soul would enter Heaven!

also found in *The Queen of Corinth,* III. ii:

> . . . cast ope the casements wide
> That we may *jocundly* behold the sun.

Here is enough evidence to prove that these two 'Triumphs' and Acts III and IV of *The Queen of Corinth* are from the same hand. And it is clear also that they must have been composed much about the same time—probably in the same year. Apart from the parallels I have noted, they are so exactly alike in style and metre, and so much more intimately connected with one another than with any play to which Field's name is attached, that it is impossible to arrive at any other conclusion than that they were written practically contemporaneously. If *The Queen of Corinth* cannot be dated before 1617, it is to that year, or one very close to it, that the *Four Plays in One* belong.

The direct clues to Field in *The Triumph of Honour* and *The Triumph of Love,* if not quite so plain as those connecting these plays with *The Queen of Corinth,* are yet clear enough.

To take first the vocabulary test, of the words noted as characteristic of Field we find the exclamations 'pish' and 'hum' and the word 'transgress' in the Induction; 'pish' occurs again in the second 'Triumph' and 'hum' twice in the first and once in the second. Either 'continent' or 'continence' appears in all three of Field's acknowledged plays. The latter is to be met with in scene ii of *The Triumph of Love*:

. . . you have over-charg'd my breast
With grace beyond my continence; I shall burst;

in a context which suggests a passage in *A Woman is a Weathercock* (I. i):

. . . to conceal it [a secret]
Will burst your breast; 'tis so delicious,
And so much greater than the continent.

'Innocency' (Field shows a marked preference for the quadrisyllabic form of the word) appears twice in *The Triumph of Love* (scenes iv and v), 'integrity' once in each play, and 'transgress' twice in *The Triumph of Honour* and once in *The Triumph of Love.* In scene ii of *The Triumph of Honour* appears the 'vane' metaphor. See the second speech of Martius:

. . . the wild rage of my blood
Doth ocean-like o'erflow the shallow shore
Of my weak virtue; my desire 's a vane,
That the least breath from her turns every way.

It is not used by Beaumont, Fletcher, or Massinger. One would expect it from the author of *A Woman is a Weathercock,* who has it in *The Fatal Dowry,* II. ii:

Virtue strengthen me!
Thy presence blows round my affection's vane:
You will undo me, if you speak again.

In the same scene of *The Triumph of Honour* Martius says to Dorigen:

thy *words*
Do fall like rods upon me; but they have
Such silken lines, and silver *hooks, that I*
Am faster snar'd.

Compare these lines from the song ('A Dialogue between a Man and a Woman') in *The Fatal Dowry,* II. ii:

Set, Phoebus, set; a fairer sun doth rise
From the bright radiance of my mistress' eyes
Than ever thou begat'st: I dare not look;
Each hair a golden line, *each word a hook,*
The more I strive, the more still I am took.

In his last speech in scene iii of *The Triumph of Honour* Sophocles thus apostrophizes the deity:

Thou that did'st order this congested heap
When it was *chaos*, 'twixt thy spacious palms
Forming it to this vast rotundity,
Dissolve it now; *shuffle the elements*,
That no one proper by itself may stand!

In III. i of *The Fatal Dowry* Charalois says to Romont:

Had I just cause,
Thou know'st I durst pursue such injury
Through fire, air, water, earth, nay were they all
Shuffled again to chaos.

In scene v of *The Triumph of Love*, for the curious application of the adjective 'female' in the expression 'female tears' (Benvoglio's last speech)

Come, turn thy female tears into revenge.

compare 'female hate' in *Amends for Ladies*, III. ii, where Lord Proudly, who suspects that his sister is in Ingen's custody, exclaims:

. . . be she lost,
The female hate shall spring betwixt our names
Shall never die.

Finally, in the last scene of *The Triumph of Love* Gerrard observes that:

. . . the law
Is but the great man's mule, he rides on it,
And tramples poorer men under his feet.

Which is much the same as what Strange says of the law in *A Woman is a Weathercock*, II. i, except that he compares it not to a mule, but to an ass:

. . . some say some men on the back of law
May ride and rule it like a patient ass.

II. *The Queen of Corinth* (Acts III and IV)

This play is by three authors, Massinger, Fletcher, and Field, Massinger's part being Acts I and V, Fletcher's Act II, and Field's Acts III and IV. All the critics who have discussed its authorship recognize that it contains work that cannot be either Massinger's or Fletcher's. Macaulay (*Camb. Hist. Eng. Lit.*, vol. vi) and Boyle (*New Shaks. Soc. Trans.*, 1880–6, p. 609) attribute it to Massinger, Fletcher, and a third author whom they do not identify, though Boyle, who gives III and IV to the unknown author, suggests Field as a possible candidate. Fleay at one time favoured Middleton's claim, but later, in his *Biographical Chronicle of the English Drama*, he correctly assigned these acts to Field.

Though it will involve some repetition, I propose to include with the other indications of Field's hand in this play references to its connexions with the first two of the *Four Plays in One* already noted, in order to show that the marks of Field are sufficiently numerous throughout Acts III and IV to justify the assumption that they are entirely his.

Act III. In scene i we have:

(i) . . . the lion should not
Tremble to hear the bellowing of the bull,

paralleled in *The Triumph of Honour.*

(ii) Theanor, the vicious son of the Queen of Corinth, says of Euphanes, whom the Queen favours and protects,

. . . like a young pine,
He grows up planted under a fair oak.

Compare II. i of *The Fatal Dowry*, where Charalois, distributing his father's effects among those who have done him service, commends Romont, to whom he gives a medal of the dead marshal, as one

. . . that, like
A hearty oak, grew'st close to this tall pine.

(iii) With these lines from the last speech of Euphanes immediately preceding the Queen's entry:

Virtue 's a solid rock, whereat being aim'd
The keenest darts of envy, yet unhurt
Her marble heroes stand, built on such bases,
Whilst they recoil, and wound the shooters' faces.

compare these from Seldom's speech at the end of II. i of *Amends for Ladies*:

> . . . even as dirt, thrown hard against a wall,
> Rebounds and sparkles in the thrower's eyes,
> So ill words, uttered to a virtuous dame,
> Turn and defile the speaker with red shame.

In addition to these three passages, note in the portion of the scene between the entry of Euphanes and that of the Queen, the exclamations ‘ pish ! ’ and ‘ hum ! ’ ‘ antedate ’, ‘ transgress ’, and the alliteration ‘ arts and arms ’.

In scene ii there is the figure used by Euphanes :

> I came . . . like a thankful stream, to retribute
> All you, my ocean, have enrich'd me with.

which occurs again in the Induction to *The Triumph of Honour,* also the exclamation ‘ pish ’, the adverb ‘ jocundly ’, and the adjective ‘ antipathous ’.

Act IV. In the first scene I find no noteworthy parallels either with the two ‘ Triumphs ’ or Field's acknowledged plays ; but ‘ hum ’, ‘ importune ’, and ‘ innocency ’ may serve to suggest his hand here. There are no parallels either for the short second scene, but in scene iii (where the word ‘ innocency ’ again appears) besides the lines :

> . . . when in the scales
> Nature and fond affection weigh together,
> One poises like a feather,

recalling a passage in *The Triumph of Love,* and the lines in Euphanes' speech beginning :

> . . . when posterity
> Shall read your volumes fill'd with virtuous acts

so closely paralleled in scene ii of *The Triumph of Honour,* we have Conon's description of the Queen's erratic behaviour :

> She chafes like storms in groves, now sighs, now weeps,
> And both sometimes, like rain and wind commixt.

resembling Ferdinand's words in scene iii of *The Triumph of Love* :

> I weep sometimes, and instantly can laugh :
> Nay, I do dance and sing, and suddenly
> *Roar like a storm.*

In the fourth and final scene we have the exclamation

'pish' and (in the two last lines) the image of two streams flowing together:

> Nature's divided streams the highest shelf
> Will over-run at last, and flow to itself,

appears again in *The Fatal Dowry*, II. ii:

> . . . let these tears, an emblem of our loves,
> Like crystal rivers individually
> Flow into one another, make one source,
> Which never man distinguish, less divide!

III. *The Knight of Malta* (Acts I and V)

We find Field again collaborating with Massinger and Fletcher in *The Knight of Malta*, this time contributing the first and last acts. Boyle assigns these to Beaumont, Fleay 'has little doubt' that they are Field's, while Macaulay observes that the style of their author, though somewhat like that of Field, is better than his usual work. There can, however, be no doubt that it was he who wrote them, and the best evidence of this is to be found in what is undoubtedly the finest scene in the play—Act V, sc. i—the scene in which Oriana by her eloquence transforms the earthly passion of the young knight Miranda to a pure, spiritual love. It is of this scene that Sir A. W. Ward (*Hist. Eng. Dram. Lit.*, ii. 689) observes that he can recall 'no nobler vindication of the authority of the moral law in the whole range of the Elizabethan drama'. It seems strange that no one has remarked its extraordinarily close resemblance to scene ii of *The Triumph of Honour*, where Dorigen, in precisely similar circumstances, makes her lofty appeal to the higher nature of the infatuated Martius, and makes that appeal in language that can leave no shadow of a doubt that the two scenes are from the same hand. I have already had occasion to quote from the speech in which Dorigen refers to the deeds of Martius as being entered in a volume and urges him not to commit an unworthy act that will cause the reader, on reaching the leaf that records it, to cast the book away, for it was this that gave me the first clue to the common authorship of *The Triumph of Honour* and the fourth act of *The Queen of Corinth.* The parallel in *The Knight of Malta* is even more striking, since, the situations being identical, it is more complete.

Dorigen thus addresses Martius:

> Oh Martius, Martius! wouldst thou in one minute
> Blast all thy laurels, which so many years
> Thou hast been purchasing with blood and sweat?
> Hath Dorigen never been written, read,
> Without the epithet of *chaste,*—chaste Dorigen,
> And wouldst thou fall upon her chastity,
> Like a black drop of ink, to blot it out?

Oriana says to Miranda:

> Miranda's deeds
> Have been as white as Oriana's fame,
> From the beginning to this point of time,
> And shall we now begin to stain both thus?

Dorigen continues:

> When men shall read the records of thy valour,
> Thy hitherto-brave virtue, and approach
> (Highly content yet) to this foul assault
> Included in this leaf, this ominous leaf,
> They shall throw down the book, and read no more:

and Oriana:

> Think on the legend which we two shall breed
> Continuing as we are, for chastest dames
> And boldest soldiers to peruse and read,
> Ay, and read thorough, free from any act
> To cause the modest cast the book away,
> And the most honour'd captain fold it up.

Martius is so overcome by Dorigen's eloquence that he exclaims:

> Oh, thou confut'st divinely, and thy words
> Do fall like rods upon me! but they have
> Such silken lines and silver hooks, that I
> Am faster snared.

Her words produce upon him the same effect as Oriana's on Miranda:

> Oh, what a tongue is here! whilst she doth teach
> My heart to hate my fond, unlawful love,

She talks me more in love, with love to her;
My fire she quencheth with her arguments,
But as she breathes 'em they blow fresher fires.

As it is not questioned that Acts I and V are by the same hand, I need add little by way of corroborative evidence of Field's authorship. In the first act we have 'pish!' and 'hum' (each of them only once), also 'continence', 'importune', and 'integrity'; in the fifth 'continence' and 'transgress'. With the words addressed by Mountferrat to his servant Rocca (almost at the beginning of the first scene of Act I):

. . . thy pleas'd eyes send forth
Beams brighter than the star that ushers day.

we may compare the two last lines of the song in *Amends for Ladies*, IV. i:

All want day, till thy beauty rise,
For the grey morn breaks from thine eyes,

and the first lines of that in Act II of *The Fatal Dowry* in which Phoebus is urged to set, because:

. . . a fairer sun doth rise
From the bright radiance of my mistress' eyes.

The expression 'to stupify sense' used by Mountferrat in the same scene:

. . . to report her [Oriana's] soft acceptance now
Will *stupify sense* in me, if not kill,

occurs again in *The Triumph of Honour*, sc. iii (first speech of Sophocles):

These wonders
Do *stupify my senses.*

In Act V, in addition to the marks already noted, we have Oriana's reference to herself (scene i) as 'a garment worn':

How much you undervalue your own price,
To give your unbought self for a poor woman,
That has been once sold, us'd, and lost her show!
I am a garment worn, &c.

which recalls Lady Bright's remark in *Amends for Ladies*, I. i:

A wife is like a garment us'd and torn:
A maid like one made up, but never worn;

and Lady Honour's reply:

> A widow is a garment worn threadbare,
> Selling at second-hand, like broker's ware.

At the beginning of the second scene, the allusion to Time's running hand 'beating back' the world to 'undistinguish'd chaos' connects it with passages already noted in *The Fatal Dowry* and *The Triumph of Honour.* We find also that Miranda, in the same scene, uses the expression 'to indue (=put on) a robe', also used by Benvoglio in scene iv of *The Triumph of Love.* Finally, there is a characteristically Fieldian speech from Miranda, as he restores Oriana to her husband's arms:

> . . . busy Nature,
> If thou wilt still make women, but remember
> To work 'em by this sampler.

Of the other plays in the Beaumont and Fletcher folios containing work that is clearly neither Beaumont's nor Fletcher's nor Massinger's, there are three in which Field's collaboration has been suspected or asserted by one or other of the critics—*The Honest Man's Fortune, Thierry and Theodoret*, and *The Bloody Brother.* I have closely examined all three plays and am satisfied that Field had nothing to do with any of them except the first, of which one act seems to be his. I add a few words on each play.

The Honest Man's Fortune. Fleay and Macaulay both assign parts of this to Field; Fleay giving him Acts III and IV, Macaulay Act IV alone. I find nothing whatever to suggest Field in Act III. This (as well as Act II) I believe to be partly Webster's. In Lamira's sixth speech:

> . , . my sleeps are enquired after,
> My risings up saluted with respect,

is a borrowing from Sidney's *Arcadia* [1] which also appears in *Thierry and Theodoret* (II. i), another play in which it is clear to me that Webster collaborated. Field seems to have been concerned in Act IV. In Montague's first speech

[1] Book III, Routledge's edition, p. 307: 'my sleeps were enquired after, and my wakings up never unsaluted' (Cecropia to her son Amphialus).

'manacle' appears as a verb, as again in *The Triumph of Love*, and (in scene ii) the Duke of Orleans's exclamation, 'Art thou there, basilisk?' is also used by Dorigen in the second scene of *The Triumph of Honour*. Moreover, as Oliphant has noted, in IV. i Veramour's

> . . . thus we'll breed a story
> To make every hearer weep,
> When they discourse our fortunes and our loves

seems clearly to speak of the hand that wrote Oriana's speech ('Think of the legend which we two shall breed', &c.) in Act V, sc. i of *The Knight of Malta*. It should be noted that the allusion to 'Roman deaths' in Act IV, sc. i, recurs in *The Maid of Honour* (end of IV. iii), but although Massinger undoubtedly had a hand in Act III, I see no trace of his style in this fourth act.

Thierry and Theodoret. Fleay attributes Acts III and V, sc. i to Field, and Macaulay gives them to a third author (not Massinger or Fletcher). They are clearly from the same hand—Webster's in my opinion. Nowhere is there any suggestion of Field's versification or vocabulary.

The Bloody Brother. Macaulay assigns to Field Act IV, sc. iii, and part of Act III, sc. i. I can find no justification for this attribution. The authorship of this play presents perhaps the most difficult problem of all the plays in the Beaumont and Fletcher folios. At least four hands seem to have been engaged upon it.

To complete the list of the plays in which it has been conjectured that Field was concerned, either as collaborator or reviser, three yet remain to be mentioned. Of these, two (*Cupid's Revenge* and *Bonduca*) were published either in one or both of the Beaumont and Fletcher folios, while the third (*The Faithful Friends*) appears in neither, but was entered in the Register as by Beaumont and Fletcher in 1660. Though most of the critics (including Gayley and Macaulay) regard *Cupid's Revenge* as pure Beaumont and Fletcher, Boyle and Fleay both find a third hand in it, and Oliphant a third and fourth, adding Massinger as well as Field to Beaumont and Fletcher. Boyle does not identify the third author 'whose verse has not the Beaumont ring'. Fleay affirms that the play has been revised by Field, who has condensed or altered almost every scene, but I can find no trace of him in any part of the play. *Bonduca* is usually assigned to Fletcher. Fleay and Macaulay, however, suggest that Field may have been concerned in Act II, sc. i, and Act IV, sc. iv. In both these scenes there are rimed couplets suggestive of a hand other than Fletcher's, but apart from these, I see no reason to suspect Field. As for *The Faithful Friends*, which Fleay (*Englische Studien*, xiii (1889), 32) attributes to Field and Daborne, and Oliphant (*ibid.*, xvi (1892), 198) believes to be an early play by Beaumont and Fletcher revised by Massinger and Field, although no doubt it contains phrases and passages faintly suggestive, sometimes of one, sometimes of another, of these authors, the most reasonable conclusion would seem to be that it is by none of them. It is written in a florid, forcible-feeble style quite unlike that of Field, and is throughout full of peculiar words and trite mythological allusions as little characteristic of him as they are of Beaumont or Fletcher.

1919.

APPENDIX

In this Appendix I give my views concerning the authorship of a number of Elizabethan and Jacobean plays other than those dealt with in *Sidelights on Shakespeare* and the present volume. It is, of course, impossible in this place to indicate the grounds upon which my conclusions are based. Some of the plays I have discussed at length elsewhere, and in these cases have added references to the papers (mostly published in *Notes and Queries*) in which the reasons for my attributions are stated. Except in a few instances I have omitted any reference to the opinions of other critics.

ANONYMOUS PLAYS

Barnavelt, The Tragedy of Sir John Van Olden, Massinger and Fletcher. Massinger: I. 1, 2, II. 1, III. 2, 5, IV. 5. Fletcher: I. 3, II. 2–6, III. 1–4, IV. 1–3, V. 2, 3. The scenes presenting difficulty are III. 3, 6, IV. 4, and V. 1. III. 3 and 6 seem to me chiefly by Fletcher, IV. 4 and V. 1 mainly, if not wholly, by Massinger. There is an excellent discussion in Miss W. P. Frijlinck's edition of the play (H. G. Van Dorssen, Amsterdam; Humphrey Milford, Oxford University Press, 1922), with a table giving the opinions of the principal critics.

Captives, The, or The Lost Recovered. By Heywood, to whom it was first ascribed by A. H. Bullen.

Charlemagne (*The Distracted Emperor*). Chapman. See the edition by Prof. F. L. Schoell (Princeton, University Press; London, H. Milford, 1920).

Edward IV (*Parts I and II*). Undoubtedly by Heywood.

Fair Em. Correctly ascribed by Fleay to R. Wilson.

Fair Maid of the Exchange. Heywood. See *N. & Q.* 12 S. iv (1918), pp. 261, 292.

Grim the Collier of Croydon, or The Devil and his Dame. (Ascribed on the title-page of 1662 to I. T.) Haughton. See *Mod. Lang. Review*, vol. xiv (1919), pp. 245–53.

How a Man may choose a Good Wife from a Bad. Heywood.

Jack Straw, The Life and Death of. Peele.

Knack to Know a Knave, A. Mainly by Peele, but with alterations and interpolations by another hand. See *N. & Q.* cxlvi (1924), pp. 389, 410.

Lady Mother, The. Undoubtedly by Glapthorne, to whom it was ascribed by Bullen. See *N. & Q.* 13 S. i (1923), p. 503.

Look About You. Mainly by Chettle. His hand is clearly present in seventeen at least of the thirty-three scenes in which the play is divided in Hazlitt-Dodsley, vol. viii. But I suspect that he had a collaborator (? Munday). See *N. & Q.* 12 S. xii (1923), pp. 324–7.

Nobody and Somebody. Mainly Heywood's, but with suggestions of another hand.

Revenger's Tragedy, The. Tourneur. Notwithstanding the difference between the versification of this play and *The Atheist's Tragedy* (the only extant play printed as Tourneur's), I believe the ascription to him (by Kirkman and Archer) to be correct. See *N. & Q.* 12 S. v (1919), pp. 225–9.

Second Maiden's Tragedy, The. Tourneur. See *N. & Q.* as above.

Trial of Chivalry, The. Heywood certainly had a hand in this, but it cannot be entirely his.

Weakest Goeth to the Wall, The. By Dekker and another. Dekker: I. 2, 3, II. 3, III. 4, 5, IV. 3, V. 2. Miss M. L. Hunt (*Thomas Dekker*, Columbia University Press, 1911) first assigned to Dekker a share in this play. His work is almost entirely confined to the Barnaby Bunch scenes. I cannot identify the principal author—certainly it was not Chettle (as Miss Hunt suggests) nor Munday.

OTHER PLAYS

[Title-page ascriptions enclosed within brackets.]

Blind Beggar of Bednall Green. [Day.] Day and Chettle. Day: I. 3, II. 5, III. i, IV. i. Chettle: II. 3, IV. 2. The rest: I. 1, 2, II. 1, 2, 4, III. 2, 3, IV. 3, and V. apparently of composite authorship. The quarrel between Cardinal Beaufort and Gloster in I. 2, and the forced betrothal of Sir R. Westford's daughter to Young Playnsey in II. 1, are substantially Chettle's, the fifth act is mainly Day's, but with touches of Chettle towards the close. See *N. & Q.* 12 S. xii (1923), pp. 386–8.

Cure for a Cuckold, A. [Webster and Rowley.] Webster and Rowley. Webster: I. 1, 2, II. 1, 2, III. 1, 3, IV. 1, 2 (to entry of Compass). Rowley: II. 3, III. 2, V. 2 (after Compass's entry): II. 1, IV. 1, and IV. 3, of mixed authorship. See *N. & Q.* 11 S. IX (1914), pp. 382, 404, 443, 463.

Death of Robert Earl of Huntingdon, The. Munday and Chettle. Chettle: II. 1, III. 4, 5, V. 1, 2. Munday: III. 2, 3, IV. 1. The rest (I. 1–3, II. 2, III. 1, IV. 2, 3) of mixed authorship. I. 1 contains Skelton rhymes, and if those in *The Downfall* (see below) are Chettle's, presumably these are also his. I. 2 is Munday's as far as exit of Friar Tuck (Hazlitt-Dodsley, viii. 224); immediately after the exit of Robin Hood, Chettle's hand becomes evident. The assassination of Warman is his, and the scene continues to show traces of his hand up to the entry of King and Queen, i. e. the point marked 'Scene IV' in the early quarto; from this point onward it is Munday's. After the entry of the dying Robin Hood in I. 3 (p. 238), Chettle's style is unmistakable. His work here does not end with Robin Hood's death but continues to be recognizable in Friar Tuck's speeches introducing the fresh play—'Matilda's Tragedy'. See *N. & Q.* 12 S. xii (1923), pp. 303–6.

Downfall of Robert Earl of Huntingdon. Munday and Chettle. Usually attributed to Munday alone, in spite of the entry (18 November 1598) in Henslowe's Diary of a payment to Chettle 'upon the mendynge of the first part of Robarte Hoode'. Adopting the arrangement in Hazlitt's Dodsley (vol. viii) all the scenes are of composite authorship, containing Munday's work substantially revised and occasionally added to by Chettle, except I. 3, which is Chettle's. Munday is almost wholly responsible for the characters of Little John, Scarlet, Scathlock, Jenny, Friar Tuck, Much, Bishop of Ely; in the speeches of King Richard, Prince John, Fitzwater, Warman, Leicester, and Queen Elinor, Chettle's hand preponderates. Robin Hood's and Marian's speeches have been much revised, and sometimes entirely rewritten, by Chettle. Internal evidence of his authorship of the Skelton rhymes is lacking, but the structure of the play seems to indicate that these form part of his revision. The most important scenes, III. 2, IV. I, and V. I, I divide as follows:

III. 2. To the departure of Scathlock, Scarlet, and Little John (Hazlitt-Dodsley, p. 154) this is Munday's. Robin Hood's poetical speech to Marian following their departure is Chettle's, the Jenny and Tuck dialogue (156–8) Munday's. The scene in which Robin Hood is discovered sleeping on a bank, with Marian strewing flowers upon him, is Chettle's.

IV. I. Substantially Munday's to entry of Leicester (p. 170). His and Richmond's speeches, if not written by Chettle, have been substantially revised by him, Richmond's description of Richard's combat with the lion (pp. 178–9) being unquestionably Chettle's.

V. I. Warman's speeches at the beginning, with the scene of his attempted suicide (189–91), are Chettle's. From entry of Friar Tuck to that of Marian (194–8) there is no trace of his hand. From this point onward the scene is wholly Chettle's. See *N. & Q.* 12 S. xii (1923), pp. 283–6.

Honest Man's Fortune. [Beaumont and Fletcher.] Webster, Massinger, Field, and Fletcher. At least four authors were concerned in this. Act I, of doubtful authorship, perhaps Webster's (not by Tourneur, as surmised by Boyle and Macaulay). Act II, Webster. Act III, Massinger and Webster. Act IV, Field? Act V, Fletcher.

Law Tricks, or Who Would Have Thought It? [Day.] Day and Wilkins. Day: III. I, 2, IV. 2, V. I. Wilkins: I. 2, II., IV. I: I. I, and V. 2, of mixed authorship. Boyle first assigned a share in the composition of this play to Wilkins. (*New Shakspere Society's Transactions*, 1880–6, pp. 329–31.)

Laws of Candy, The. [Beaumont and Fletcher.] Massinger and another. Massinger wrote I., IV. 2, and V. III. 1, 2, by the second author alone. II., III. 3, and IV. 1, by both authors. I cannot identify the second hand in this play (not Beaumont, Fletcher, Field, or Webster). See *N. & Q.* 12 S. vi (1920), pp. 101, 122.

Love's Cure. [Beaumont and Fletcher.] Massinger, Webster, and Dekker. Act I, Massinger; Act II, Webster and Dekker; III. 1–4, Webster, III. 5, Dekker; IV and V. 1, 2, Massinger and Webster; V. 3, Webster.

Northward Hoe. [Dekker and Webster.] Dekker and Webster. Dekker clearly the predominant author; I find only one scene without conclusive marks of his hand. Several of the collaborated scenes are, however, substantially Webster's. Dekker: I. 2, 3, II. 1, IV. 1–4. Webster: II. 2. Webster and Dekker: I. 1, III. 1, 2, V. 1.

Patient Grissil. [Chettle, Dekker, and Haughton.] Chettle, Dekker, and Haughton. The Grissil story proper is Chettle's, the Babulo and Welsh scenes Dekker's. Haughton's share is small: the scenes in which Julio and Onophrio figure are his, and he is also chiefly responsible for those in which the coxcomb Emulo appears, though here there are occasional slight traces of Dekker. The co-operation of the partners was clearly of the most intimate kind, there being only two scenes (both Chettle's) assignable to a single author. I. 1, Chettle and Dekker; II. 1, Haughton and Dekker; II. 2, Chettle; III. 1, Dekker and Chettle; III. 2, Haughton and Dekker; IV. 1, Chettle; IV. 2, Dekker and Chettle, IV. 3, Dekker, Haughton and Chettle; V. 1, Dekker and Chettle; V. 2, Chettle and Dekker. I believe that all the songs are by Chettle (not Dekker, as usually supposed). See *N. & Q.* 12 S. xii (1923), pp. 345–7, 365–6.

Revenge for Honour. [Chapman.] Henry Glapthorne. See *N. & Q.* 12 S. i (1916), pp. 401–4.

Roaring Girl, The. [Middleton and Dekker.] Middleton and Dekker. The co-operation of the two authors very close, many scenes containing marks of both. Act I and II. 1, Middleton and Dekker; II. 2, Middleton; III. 1, 2, 3, Middleton and Dekker; IV. 1, Middleton; IV. 2 and V. 1, Dekker; V. 2, Middleton and Dekker.

Sea Voyage, The. [Beaumont and Fletcher.] Massinger and Fletcher (Fletcher the original author, Massinger the reviser). Far the larger part is Massinger's. Act I, Fletcher; Act II, Massinger; Act III the work of both authors (Fletcher to entry of Rosellia and others, Massinger from this point to end of act); Act IV, Fletcher; Act V, Massinger. But there are slight traces of Massinger's revision of Act I and IV. 2, 3, and traces of Fletcher in V. 2. My division corresponds very closely with Boyle's and Oliphant's. See *N. & Q.* 12 S. xi (1922), pp. 443–6, 484–6.

Sun's Darling, The. [Ford and Dekker.] Ford and Dekker. Act I, Ford, with perhaps a substratum of Dekker in the prose; Act II, Dekker, slightly revised by Ford; III. 1, Dekker; III. 2, Ford; III. 3, Dekker; IV, substantially Ford's, but with occasional faint indications of Dekker; V, Ford. Most of the songs in this masque I believe to be Ford's, certainly those in the first and fifth Acts. But the cuckoo song in Act II and the country song in III. 3 are no less certainly Dekker's.

Thierry and Theodoret. [Beaumont and Fletcher.] Fletcher, Webster, and Massinger. Fletcher: I. 1, II. 2, 3, IV. 1, V. 2. Massinger: I. 2, II. 1, IV. 2. Webster: III. 2, 3, V. 1. Webster and Massinger: II. 4, III. 1.

Travels of the Three English Brothers, The. [Wilkins, Day, and Rowley.] Wilkins, Day, and Rowley. Prologue by Day, Epilogue by Day and Wilkins. Far the greater part of this play is by Wilkins. Adopting Boyle's thirteen scene-divisions (*New Shakspere Society's Transactions*, 1880–6, p. 326), scenes 2, 4, 5, 6, 8, 10, 12, and part of 13 (to 'Enter Countess')—pp. 14–27, 34–46, 50–3, 64–75, and 78–88 of Bullen's edition—are by Wilkins. Scene 3 is by Day and scenes 1, 7, 9, 11, and end of 13, by Day or Rowley.

Virgin Martyr, The. [Massinger and Dekker.] Massinger and Dekker. Massinger: I. 1, III. 1, 2, IV. 3, V. 2. Dekker: II. 1, III. 3, IV. 2. The presence of both authors can be detected in II. 2, 3, IV. 1, and V. 1. See *N. & Q.* 12 S. x (1922), pp. 61–5, 83–8.

Westward Hoe. [Dekker and Webster.] Dekker and Webster. Chiefly Dekker's; there is only one short scene that does not show traces of his hand. The first and last scenes are those in which Webster's collaboration is most apparent, but even here his work is closely intermixed with his partner's. Act I, Webster and Dekker; II, Dekker; III. 1, Dekker; III. 2, 3, Webster and Dekker; III. 4, Webster; IV and V. 1, 2, Dekker; V. 3, Webster and Dekker. The extent of Webster's share in the composition of this play may well be greater than any examination of its phraseology can disclose. The character of Justiniano is probably chiefly of his creation. But it can be confidently asserted that all his work has been revised or touched up by the older and more experienced dramatist.

Witch of Edmonton, The. [Ford, Dekker, Rowley, &c.] Ford, Dekker, and Rowley. I. 1, Ford; I. 2, Dekker and Ford; II. 1, Dekker and Rowley; II. 2, Dekker and Ford; III. 1, Rowley with slight traces of Dekker; III. 2, Ford; III. 3, Dekker with some traces of Ford; III. 4, Rowley and Ford; IV. 1, Dekker; IV. 2, Ford and Dekker; V. 1, Rowley and Ford; V. 2, Ford. The greater part is certainly Ford's. Dekker's hand is chiefly apparent in the Witch scenes and the character of Susan. His share in the prose, though considerable, is less than it is usually assumed to be, there being only one scene entirely attributable to him. Rowley's share was clearly small, apparently confined to the Cuddy Banks scenes, as these alone are noticeably free from traces of the style or vocabulary either of Ford or Dekker.

INDEX

For Product Safety Concerns and Information please contact our EU representative GPSR@taylorandfrancis.com
Taylor & Francis Verlag GmbH, Kaufingerstraße 24, 80331 München, Germany

www.ingramcontent.com/pod-product-compliance
Lightning Source LLC
Chambersburg PA
CBHW071522110726
47908CB00003B/917